Praise for *Competing in Tough Times*

"If you're in retail, this is a must-read! I'm buying copies for all of my managers and executives. And since I'm in retail, I'm also going to try for a discount!"

—**Stew Leonard, Jr.**, CEO, Stew Leonard's

"The economic downturn and excessive overstoring has changed the definition of what it takes to be a successful retailer, and this book translates the new requirements into understandable terms. *Competing in Tough Times* should be required reading for anyone interested in what it takes to be a successful retailer in the 'new normal' marketplace. Few authors have the range to successfully integrate strategy with practical tactics. Barry Berman is one of those unique talents."

—**Bill Bishop**, Chairman, Willard Bishop

"The ten diverse retailers highlighted in Barry Berman's fascinating book, *Competing in Tough Times*, offer students and practitioners of retailing a unique insight into a myriad of successful strategies that will encourage the reader's own creative ideas flowing. Berman's theory-based, yet practical analysis of successful strategies used by top retailers today may be the needed tool in putting the brakes on the downward spiral facing many retailers in today's economic uncertainty. This timely, practical book should be required reading. Its key takeaway points, thorough reference, endnotes, table summaries, and up-to-the-minute data make this book invaluable as a guide for those developing strategic plans in these tough times."

—**Susan S. Fiorito**, Ph.D., Professor of Retail Merchandising and Product Development, Florida State University

"Tough times are no excuse for complacency. To gain a competitive advantage in today's 'new normal' economy requires retailers to have a clear vision of their cost structure, their strategic differentiation, and the varied hues of value. In *Competing in Tough Times*, Barry Berman shows how retailers like Amazon.com, Costco, Publix, Trader Joe's, and others have become market leaders by adapting their strategies, challenging long-standing assumptions, and being hyper-vigilant about building and maintaining customer loyalty. Filled with meaty revelations and compelling insights and data, this book is a building block in the quest for retail success."

—**Susan Reda**, Editor, *STORES*

Competing in Tough Times

Competing in Tough Times

Business Lessons from L.L.Bean, Trader Joe's, Costco, and Other World-Class Retailers

BARRY BERMAN

Vice President, Publisher: Tim Moore
Associate Publisher and Director of Marketing: Amy Neidlinger
Executive Editor: Jeanne Glasser
Editorial Assistant: Pamela Boland
Development Editor: Russ Hall
Operations Manager: Gina Kanouse
Senior Marketing Manager: Julie Phifer
Publicity Manager: Laura Czaja
Assistant Marketing Manager: Megan Colvin
Cover Designer: Alan Clements
Managing Editor: Kristy Hart
Project Editor: Betsy Harris
Copy Editor: Water Crest Publishing, Inc.
Proofreader: Apostrophe Editing Services
Indexer: Lisa Stumpf
Compositor: Nonie Ratcliff
Manufacturing Buyer: Dan Uhrig

FT Press offers excellent discounts on this book when ordered in quantity for bulk purchases or special sales. For more information, please contact U.S. Corporate and Government Sales, 1-800-382-3419, corpsales@pearsontechgroup.com. For sales outside the U.S., please contact International Sales at international@pearson.com.

Company and product names mentioned herein are the trademarks or registered trademarks of their respective owners.

Printed in the United States of America

First Printing December 2010

ISBN-10: 0-13-245919-1
ISBN-13: 978-0-13-245919-8

Pearson Education LTD.
Pearson Education Australia PTY, Limited.
Pearson Education Singapore, Pte. Ltd.
Pearson Education Asia, Ltd.
Pearson Education Canada, Ltd.
Pearson Educación de Mexico, S.A. de C.V.
Pearson Education—Japan
Pearson Education Malaysia, Pte. Ltd.

Library of Congress Cataloging-in-Publication Data
Berman, Barry.
    Competing in tough times : business lessons from L.L. Bean, Trader Joe's, Costco, and other world-class retailers / Barry Berman.
        p. cm.
    ISBN-13: 978-0-13-245919-8 (hardback : alk. paper)
    ISBN-10: 0-13-245919-1
    1. Retail trade—Management. 2. Strategic planning. I. Title.
    HF5429.B449 2011
    658.8'7—dc22
                                            2010031430

To my loving family—my wife, Linda; and our children and grandchildren, Glenna, Paul, Danielle, Sophie, and Joshua; and Lisa, Ben, Philip, and Emily.

Contents

Acknowledgments

Although all books have authors, in reality the preparation and completion of any project involves a team effort. I have been fortunate to have led a dedicated team of people who are true professionals.

A number of people have been very helpful to me on this project. Jeanne Glasser, the executive editor at Financial Times Press, provided me with constructive comments, guidance, and super-fast turnaround on my correspondence. Diane Schoenberg, my editorial associate, copy edited the several iterations of the manuscript with her characteristic accuracy and speed. Kunal Swani, my graduate assistant, was diligent in searching secondary sources, in verifying my calculations, and in assuming other book-related responsibilities.

I have asked key personnel at each of the 10 benchmark retailers to verify and update a draft version of this manuscript. Special thanks to Michael How at Aldi, Carolyn Beem at L.L.Bean, James Sinegal at Costco, Tara Darrow and Shelby Koontz at Nordstrom, Meghan Bell at Stew Leonard's, and Valerie Fox at Wegmans for reviewing the manuscript relating to their company for accuracy and currency.

About the Author

Dr. Barry Berman is the Walter 'Bud' Miller Distinguished Professor of Business and Director of the Executive M.B.A. program at Hofstra University. He earned his Ph.D. degree in marketing management from the Graduate School and University Center of the City University of New York (CUNY).

Barry Berman is co-author of *Retail Management: A Strategic Approach* (Prentice Hall). This is the best-selling retail management college textbook in the world. Currently in its 11th edition, this book has been published in Canadian, Chinese, Indian, Philippine, and Russian editions. Dr. Berman has also published articles that have appeared in *Business Horizons*, *California Management Review*, *The International Journal of Retailing and Distribution Management*, and other journals.

Dr. Berman is Vice-President of the American Collegiate Retailing Association. He was also co-founder of the American Marketing Association's Special Interest Group in Retail Management.

Barry Berman has consulted for Duane-Reade, Fortunoff's, Kohl's, Simon Properties, NCR, Lord & Taylor, Tesco-Ireland, and other retailers.

Preface

Competing in Tough Times: Business Lessons from L.L.Bean, Trader Joe's, Costco, and Other World-Class Retailers is the result of a two-year-long project. Through my experience as a professor with a special interest and expertise in retailing, as well as a marketing consultant, I carefully examined the overall strategies of 10 world-class retailers, looking for common principles that can be universally applied to other retail firms.

I started this project without any preconceived notions of what firms would comprise my list of world-class retailers, as well as what common principles these firms shared. I eventually identified 10 retailers based upon examining such key indicators of performance as sales per square foot, sales growth, return on equity, increase in stock market value membership retention rates for warehouse clubs, and conversion rates for web-based retailers. I also looked at retailer ratings in *Fortune's* "World's Most Admired Companies," *Fortune's* "100 Best Companies to Work For," and customer service rankings by the American Consumer Satisfaction Index, *Consumer Reports*, and *Business Week*. In evaluating retailers for inclusion in my top 10 listing, I looked for retailers that were consistent performers on these measures. Each retailer's rankings on selective indices are contained in the Appendix, "Individual and Composite Financial Performance, Customer Service, and Worker Satisfaction Metrics of the Best-Practice Retailers."

The 10 benchmark retailers are diverse in terms of retail format: supermarket (Publix, Stew Leonard's, Wegmans, and Whole Foods), extreme discount food operation (Aldi), specialty food operation (Trader Joe's), warehouse club (Costco), web-based (Amazon.com), and multichannel apparel and accessories (Nordstrom and L.L.Bean). They also vary greatly in size (from $400 million in annual revenues for Stew Leonard's to over $70 billion for Costco) and ownership organization. (Stew Leonard's, Wegmans, Trader Joe's, and Aldi are privately held, and Publix is an ESOP.)

As with the selection of the firms for inclusion as benchmark retailers, I did not start out with any perceived conclusions of common retail strategies. Instead, I began to research each company's strategies using data from annual reports (where available, as four firms are privately held), industry analyses, and articles in financial and business publications.

Despite the disparity in industry, size, and ownership format, these 10 benchmark retailers shared common strategies relating to operating at low cost (see Chapter 2, "Low-Cost Strategies I: Key Elements of a Low-Cost Provider Strategy"), providing consumers with a carefully edited selection of products (as examined in Chapter 3, "Low-Cost Strategies II: Delivering Low Costs Through Minimizing Product Proliferation"), stressing the importance of human resource management (see Chapter 4, "Differentiation Strategies I: Effective Human Resource Strategies"), focusing on consumers' service experience (see Chapter 5, "Differentiation Strategies II: Enhancing the Service Experience"), and having an aggressive private label strategy (as discussed in Chapter 6, "Differentiation Strategies III: Developing and Maintaining a Strong Private Label Program").

The strategies discussed in this book mirror Porter's low-cost differentiation model that argues that a retailer's competitively defensible position needs to be based on either of these extremes. A value orientation combines elements of each of these strategies. Chapters 2 and 3 focus on low-cost strategies, and Chapters 4, 5, and 6 describe differentiation strategies. Another integrating model that explains the success of many of these retailers is the value profit chain model. This model suggests that employee satisfaction and loyalty translates into high levels of customer service and customer loyalty, and ultimately to high profits.

I have written this book with a managerial orientation. It is in an easy-to-read decision-making format. When academic studies are often cited, they are used to document my discussion. With my academic orientation, I have heavily footnoted this book. I have also taken great care in updating all data to the most current available, as of the date of publication. To verify the accuracy of my comments, I gave executives at each of the 10 firms the opportunity to review applicable portions of the manuscript. I received responses from six firms; these comments were incorporated into the final manuscript.

Chapter 7, "Implementing Cost-, Differentiation-, and Value-Based Retail Strategies," focuses on implementing cost-, differentiation-, and value-based strategies, as the title suggests. This chapter contains a number of figures designed to help retail managers and owners more effectively utilize the principles discussed in earlier chapters.

Who Can Benefit from Reading *Competing in Tough Times: Business Lessons from L.L.Bean, Trader Joe's, Costco, and Other World-Class Retailers?*

I have aimed this book at a wide audience that includes middle to top managers at a wide variety of retailers, owners of independent retail establishments (including chains), supply chain partners who need to have a better understanding of retail practices, industry consultants, and undergraduate and graduate students with a special interest in retailing.

Introduction

The overall focus of this book deals with competitive strategies that retailers can undertake that are based on cost, differentiation, and value. In the current low-growth economic environment, any retail business store that conducts "business as usual," using the same strategies and tactics that have worked in the past, will not prosper or perhaps even survive. One way that business consultants improve a firm's performance is to study the "best practices" in the industry. It should come as little surprise to most industry observers that the "best-practice retail leaders" chosen by the author are Aldi, Amazon.com, Costco, L.L.Bean, Nordstrom, Publix, Stew Leonard's, Trader Joe's, Wegmans, and Whole Foods. In each chapter, the strategies used by these best-practice retailers are examined.

According to Michael Porter, the Harvard Business School strategy guru, there are two major competitive strategies that firms can pursue. A *low-cost strategy* argues that the retailer with the lowest cost structure benefits by charging prices that are so low, its competitors cannot match them and still earn a profit. This low-cost strategy is especially critical in this time period when a much larger than usual proportion of the market is concerned with low prices. To achieve low costs, retailers need to reduce their operating cost structure through a variety of strategies (such as self-service, more efficient use of labor, use of less-costly locations, and supply chain management initiatives), including reducing inventory carrying costs through lessening product proliferation.

The second broad strategy alternative is based on a retailer's differentiating its goods and services from competing retailers. Differentiation can be based on the quality of customer interaction and customer service, as well as through offering truly distinctive products, including private brands. The *differentiation strategy* appeals to a market segment more concerned with service quality or a product's uniqueness than its price. Retailers can also reduce direct price competition by the extent to which their products or services are differentiated from the offerings of direct and indirect competitors.

An intermediate strategy, based on value, combines elements of cost and differentiation. Value is not necessarily based on providing either the lowest costs or the highest degree of differentiation. It involves providing trade-offs of price and differentiation that are desired by the retailer's target market. *Value* is provided through offering only those services that customers either (1) absolutely require as a condition of purchasing your goods or (2) are willing to pay extra for because they view these services as meaningful. One conceptualization of value is based on four measures: results, process quality, price, and customer access costs:[1]

$$\text{Value} = \frac{\text{Results} + \text{Process Quality}}{\text{Price} + \text{Customer Access Costs}}$$

Let's briefly look at each of the four components of value. *Results* include a product's overall quality (including warranties), product convenience (precut fruits and vegetables, prehemmed slacks, easy-to-set-up computer network routers), product health (low salt, low fat, low cholesterol, product safety), and durability. The concept of results extends beyond the product concept to focus on solutions, as opposed to the basic product.

Process quality includes positive customer experiences, such as high levels of customer support, high quality of salesperson interactions, successful service recovery efforts (what the retailer will do when things go wrong), ease of finding items, short waiting lines, high in-stock positions for advertised specials, a "fun" in-store experience, and adequate parking. To an electronics store, process quality includes rewriting the manufacturer's directions to installing a wireless router, special access to the store's technical service department hotline, and bundling HDMI cables with a high-definition television router (that generally needs to be purchased separately).

Price is the final purchase cost including delivery charges and credit terms. This is the primary competitive advantage in a low-cost strategy.

In contrast to process quality that focuses on positive customer experiences, *customer access costs* include negative customer experiences. Large stores that require extensive in-store browsing, discount operations that are located in inconvenient locations, and downtown stores with insufficient parking all have high access costs. Warehouse clubs have direct dollar outlay access costs in terms of membership fees. Access costs can be measured in terms of membership fees and wasted time, as well as consumer frustration.

Value in this model can be viewed as benefits divided by costs. Benefits include results (functional aspects of a product), as well as process quality (customer service). Costs include a product's price, as well as access costs (negative customer experiences).

The Organization of This Book

Chapter 1, "The Questionable Future Facing Global Retailers," looks at the questionable future facing the retailing industry and the long-term changes in buyer behavior that have carried over from the recent recession. It also examines retail competitive strategies that focus on low cost and differentiation.

Chapters 2 and 3 focus on how retailers can effectively reduce costs to compete against Wal-Mart, limited assortment stores, warehouse stores, factory outlet stores, dollar stores, and web-based retailers that appeal to a market that is increasingly price conscious.

Chapter 2, "Low-Cost Strategies I: Key Elements of a Low-Cost Provider Strategy," concentrates on strategies that can be implemented to reduce a retailer's operating costs, whereas Chapter 3, "Low-Cost Strategies II: Delivering Low Costs Through Minimizing Product Proliferation," specifically examines cost reductions that can be accomplished through reducing product proliferation. The Appendix, "Individual and Composite Financial Performance, Customer Service, and Worker Satisfaction Metrics of the Best-Practice Retailers," at the end of this book discusses the rationale for choosing the best-practice leaders based on three criteria: financial performance, customer service, and employee satisfaction.

In contrast to these earlier chapters, Chapters 4, 5, and 6 focus on differentiation strategies utilizing human resources, customer service, and private branding. Chapter 4, "Differentiation Strategies I: Effective Human Resource Strategies," looks at the elements and benefits of an effective human resources strategy. Chapter 5, "Differentiation Strategies II: Enhancing the Service Experience," and Chapter 6, "Differentiation Strategies III: Developing and Maintaining a Strong Private Label Program," examine how a retailer can achieve differentiation through the in-store service experience and branding strategies, respectively. Chapter 7, "Implementing Cost-, Differentiation-, and Value-Based Retail Strategies," covers value-based retail strategies that combine elements of low-cost and differentiation strategies.

Endnotes

1. James L. Heskett, W. Earl Sasser, Jr., and Leonard A. Schlesinger, *The Value Profit Chain* (New York: The Free Press, 2003), p. 26.

1

The Questionable Future Facing Global Retailers

There are a number of financial ratios and other benchmarks that can be used to document the questionable future of retailing after the formal recession has ended: comparable or same-store sales data, sales per square foot, net profit as a percent of sales, increases in bankruptcies, store closings, the proportion of retailer-based credit accounts that are delinquent beyond 90 days, and so on.

The most troubling barometer of the poor health of the retail industry is data showing stagnant or declining same-store sales of many retailers. Slow or negative same or comparable sales growth directly affects a retailer's profits, stock market valuation, and capability to purchase new goods, pay current operating expenses, and raise capital. Indirectly, slow sales growth also results in increased competition as retailers seek to expand their offerings into unrelated merchandise to offset their recent sales declines. This form of increased competition is commonly referred to as *format blurring*.[1]

To illustrate the effect of low growth across a broad spectrum of retailers, *Retailer Daily* compiled comparable store data from the Securities and Exchange Commission for 26 major retailers in 2009. Comparable store sales were negative for 12 of these retailers: Target, Sears, Supervalu, Best Buy, Home Depot, Lowe's, Staples, Macy's, J.C. Penney, Kohl's, Gap, and Arby's.[2] Even more troubling, many of these retailers have faced declining same or comparable store sales for several consecutive periods. Both a decline in consumer spending, as well as a new frugality among consumers, have contributed to this slow growth.

Consumer spending is considered to be vital to the economic recovery because it accounts for about two-thirds of total economic activity. Although the U.S. economy has been growing since the middle of 2009 (after going into a recession in December 2007), the March 2010 income growth was the slowest since July 2009. According to Scott Hoyt, senior director of consumer economics for Moody's Economy.com, "The near-term outlook is still problematic. Wage income is rising only modestly. With unemployment near 10 percent, the labor market power is clearly in employers' hands, so there is little prospect for much more acceleration in wage income."[3] This unemployment rate does not include an additional 7 percent as of June 2010 that is either underemployed, that is so discouraged that they are no longer seeking employment, or that has accepted early retirement as an alternative to being laid off. What is clear to the author is that job losses associated with the recession will not be quickly restored in certain key industries, such as banking, finance, and automotive (as well as firms that service these industries). There has also been a shift in consumer mentality as to the role of savings versus spending. According to a strategist for Janney Montgomery Scott, "the broader issue here is that the credit crisis taught the consumer that borrowing is bad, savings is good."[4]

The high level of real estate foreclosures and more strict overall lending standards by banks and financial institutions has reduced consumer spending. In the first quarter of 2010, the seasonally adjusted mortgage delinquency rate was 10.06 percent on all outstanding loans. The delinquency rate includes loans that are at least one payment overdue but not in the process of foreclosure.[5] The situation is particularly poor in Nevada (with 1 of every 17 homes receiving a foreclosure filing), Arizona (with 1 in every 30 homes in foreclosure), and in Florida (with 1 in every 32 homes in foreclosure). The high number of foreclosures and underwater loans serves as a threat to the overall stability of the housing market.[6]

Much of the temporary economic recovery of the past recession has been due to the federal government's purchasing billions of dollars of mortgage-backed securities, offering tax incentives for first-time home buyers, a "cash for clunkers" auto rebate program, and other programs that have reduced foreclosures. Many of these programs are now expiring. It is questionable as to whether consumer spending activity will increase without these government incentives.[7]

A second major factor impeding growth in retail sales is the continuation of consumer caution that was originally associated with the most recent recessionary period. The authors of a *Harvard Business Review* article argued that unlike in previous recessions when consumers "greeted the return of financial stability with a buying spree," after this recession is over, "they'll continue to buy simpler offerings with the greatest value."[8] Similarly, the president of Retail Metrics, a research firm, stated that "It's [Wal-Mart] going to be a primary destination for a lot of people who may not have gone there in recent years, but who will elect to go there for the price and the value."[9]

A survey of 2,000 U.S. consumers conducted by Booz & Company suggests that only 9 percent of consumers intend to spend at pre-recession levels on household products, 10 percent on cellular phone service, 11 percent on health and beauty products, and 18 percent on apparel, clothing, and shoes as of 2011. Close to two-third of consumers (64 percent) stated that they'll shop at a different store with lower prices even if the store is less convenient.[10]

Finally, a Kantar Retail/PricewaterhouseCoopers report states that post-recession shopping will become more purposeful in nature. Rather than limiting purchases, the post-recession shopper will become more prone to seeking deals, being more open to comparison shopping, buying fewer items, shopping less often, and purchasing more private labels.[11] This report states that retailers that rely on Baby Boomers will be particularly hard hit due to their loss in wealth and the need to fund retirement.

Overall, these studies suggest that many of the competitive inroads made by web-based merchants and discounters, such as off-price chains, warehouse clubs, and dollar stores, will continue even after the recession ends. Even firms with a loyal base of customers and a clear market positioning as a "fun place to shop" like Whole Foods have had to adjust pricing strategies to deal with an increasingly value-conscious consumer base.[12]

Increased Competition Across Retail Formats

The current retail environment is characterized by increased competition across retail formats (called *format blurring*), as well as a significant increase in retail bankruptcies. This new competitive environment will be discussed separately for food and nonfood retailers.

According to two academic researchers, the sales of similar categories of merchandise across different types of retailers has resulted in format blurring.[13] Although retailers have always looked for opportunities to increase sales through selling goods and services not normally part of their line of merchandise, the pressure to pursue format blurring is much greater when retailers need to quickly increase sales levels.

Format blurring is self-perpetuating, as it generates a vicious cycle of action and reaction. A retailer that has recently lost sales to another retail format needs to quickly and aggressively seek out opportunities to offset its lost sales and profits. As an example, pharmacies need to sell greeting cards, chocolates, and cosmetics to make up for lost sales from Wal-Mart and Target that now have in-store pharmacies. Supermarkets now increasingly sell seasonal merchandise (such as barbecue grills, lawn furniture, and snow blowers) to make up for lost sales of paper towels, toilet tissues, and frozen foods to warehouse clubs. And similarly, traditional appliance retailers increasingly sell mattresses and other furniture-related items to make up for lost sales in major appliances due to increased competition from Home Depot and Lowe's.

As a result of format blurring, the broad competitive environment for grocery stores now includes supercenters, drug stores, warehouse clubs, convenience stores, dollar stores, and limited assortment stores, as well as fast-food and traditional restaurants. As Stew Leonard, Sr. aptly stated, "Anybody who sells food and has their lights on is a competitor."[14] Bill Bishop, president of Barrington-based Willard Bishop Consulting, has commented, "There is almost a game of musical chairs being played as the market share of the general purpose supermarket is reduced by all sorts of players that are taking a fraction of that business.... You can buy an awful lot of groceries at places other than grocery stores."[15]

Similarly, the competition for consumers' clothing dollars comes from a variety of retail formats, including specialty stores, department stores, mass merchants, warehouse outlets, factory outlet stores, and off-price merchants (that operate store and web-based formats). Another example of format blurring is Target's book club, which the retailer calls "Bookmarked Breakout." Unlike traditional booksellers such as Barnes & Noble that stock 200,000 titles per location, Target sells about 2,500 titles. Although Target stocks best-sellers, it also resembles independent bookstores by offering a collection of "hand-picked titles from emerging authors."[16] In another example of format blurring, Best Buy is experimenting with selling patio furniture and electric scooters. According to Barry Judge, the chain's chief marketing executive, Best Buy could "eventually end up [selling] electric cars."[17]

Competition Across Retail Formats—Food-Related Products

Progressive Grocer magazine, in its *72nd Annual Report of the Grocery Industry*, stated: "...we find it difficult to argue against the overwhelming amount of data we've collected that shows the demise of the supermarket, as a format, over the past decade."[18] Support of this statement comes from several key statistics relating to supermarket market share data, as well as the increased competitive environment. The Food Marketing Institute recently reported that traditional supermarket chains (those for which food generates at least 65 percent of total sales) have lost 30 percent of the grocery market (down from 89 percent in 1988). Another forecast by TNS Retail Forward estimates that supermarkets will have zero real growth from 2008 to 2013. The 3.3 percent forecast growth during this time period will be totally offset by a 3.3 percent inflation rate.[19]

Traditional grocery stores now receive only a portion of a consumer's total purchases of foods and other items (like health and beauty aids) that in the past were purchased there in much greater quantities. An example of this trend is a family's purchase of bulk-package sizes of paper towels, toilet paper, and freezer bags at warehouse clubs; milk and eggs at a local drug store; prepared soups, breads, and coffees at specialty grocers; ready-to-serve "heat and eat" prepared fish dinners at a local fish market; and light bulbs and batteries at dollar stores. Many of these alternate channels for food and related products have established strong competitive positions in these product categories due to a combination of very low prices, unique merchandise, and one-stop shopping appeals.

A major potential threat to the traditional supermarket industry is that its overall market share will be continually eroded by price-oriented merchants at one end (such as dollar stores, warehouse stores, extreme value stores like Aldi, and Wal-Mart), by convenience-oriented merchants (such as convenience stores, supercenters, and combination stores), and by quality-oriented merchants (such as specialty independently owned food stores and chains like Whole Foods) at the other end of the spectrum.

Firms as disparate as Wal-Mart, Costco, Target, and Dollar General are now formidable competitors to traditional grocery stores. In its 2009 fiscal year, grocery items (meat, produce, deli, bakery, frozen foods, floral, dry groceries, and consumables—health and beauty aids, household chemicals, paper goods, and pet supplies) made up 51 percent of Wal-Mart's total sales.[20] Similarly, 54 percent of Costco's 2009 sales consisted of sundries (such as candy, snack foods, and tobacco), packaged foods, and fresh foods (meat, bakery, deli, and produce).[21] In its listing of the top food retailers for 2009, *Supermarket News* reported Wal-Mart as the largest food retailer; Costco was third largest.[22] Wal-Mart has been the largest U.S. food retailer since 2003, largely through growth in its supercenter format.[23]

Target is also using food as a means of improving shopping frequency and shopper convenience. Each of its SuperTarget stores has an in-store bakery, as well as a full-service deli. SuperTarget has also been a U.S. Department of Agriculture-certified produce retailer of fruits and vegetables since 2006.[24] In its 2009 fiscal year, household essentials (including pharmacy, beauty care, personal care, baby care, cleaning, and paper products) and food and pet supplies made up 39 percent of Target's sales, up from 32 percent in 2006.[25]

Dollar stores continue to expand their offerings, particularly in the perishables area. They have added coolers and freezers in many locations as a means of increasing shopper frequency, average sales per transaction, and same-store sales. Dollar General has instituted its cooler program in a majority of its 8,877 stores. Family Dollar has installed coolers in 5,600 of its 6,500-store chain as of the end of fiscal year 2008. In 2009, 70.8 percent of Dollar General's net sales consisted of packaged foods, candy, snacks and refrigerated products, health and beauty aids, home cleaning supplies, and pet supplies (up from 65.7 percent in 2006).[26] Consumables (household chemicals, paper products, candy, snacks, health and beauty aids, hardware and auto supplies, and pet foods) accounted for 64.4 percent of Family Dollar's net sales in 2009, up from 58.8 percent in 2007.[27] These are the same product categories that are sold by supermarkets.

Competition Across Retail Formats—Nonfood-Related Products

The high degree of competition among retail formats exists in virtually all sectors of retailing. Pharmacies currently face competition from in-store pharmacies at supermarkets, warehouse clubs, and mass merchants (in addition to mail-order pharmacies). Wal-Mart, Kohl's, Costco, and Target have extensive selections of housewares, clothing, electronics, jewelry, and so forth. One can purchase eyeglasses at Costco, Sears, BJ's, and J.C. Penney, as well as in chain and independent optical stores. Costco's ancillary businesses—which are made up of gas stations, pharmacies, food courts, optical, one-hour photo, hearing aids, and travel—accounted for 15 percent of Costco's total revenues in 2009.[28] In addition, 19 percent of Costco's revenues in 2009 came from *hardlines* (items such as major appliances, garden, sporting goods, patio, and furniture) and 10 percent came from *softlines* (apparel, jewelry, cameras, and small appliances). Home improvement centers like Lowe's and Home Depot now feature major appliances and carpeting and offer home installation for many of their products.

With the demise of Circuit City, retailers like Wal-Mart have upgraded their selections of electronics and high-definition televisions to more effectively compete with specialty electronics stores. According to one report, more than 25 percent of Wal-Mart's sales increase in mid-2009 has come from new shoppers, more than half of whom have household incomes of at least $50,000. Wal-Mart will work hard to keep these new shoppers because this higher-income group spends 40 percent more on their average visit than Wal-Mart's typical shopper.[29] To attract and keep this higher-income segment, Wal-Mart has begun to offer appliances from KitchenAid and Dyson and electronics from Dell, Palm, and Sony and has moved its apparel buying group to New York to become more sensitive to fashion trends.

In addition, competition from web-based retailers now covers virtually all areas of retailing (including new and used autos and real estate), as well as all price lines (from used items sold on eBay to collectibles). Forrester Research forecasts that U.S. web-based retail sales (not counting vehicles, travel, or prescription drugs) will grow to $248.7 billion in 2014, a 60 percent increase from its 2009 level.[30] Forrester projects that the fastest growth will occur in consumer electronics, apparel, accessories, and footwear.

As is the case with traditional supermarkets, the situation affecting department stores is also especially bleak. There are only 10 department store chains left with sales of at least $3 billion in the United States: luxury chains Neiman Marcus and Saks; upscale Nordstrom; mid-tier Macy's and Dillard's; value chains J.C. Penney, Kohl's, and Sears; and regional chains Bon-Ton and Belk. Mervyn's and Goody's both ended operations in 2008.

Like supermarkets, department stores have faced substantial competition at both ends of their market for apparel. There has also been significant competition for "value" shoppers from factory outlets, off-price chains, and closeout web retailers like www.smartbargains.com and www.overstock.com. European chains such as H&M, Mango, and Zara are also able to offer trendy merchandise at very low costs. According to one report, these chains have "[developed] a new category of disposable clothing."[31] And at the high end, department stores face competition from specialty stores with access to fashion designers, on-premises alterations, a well-trained sales staff, and so forth. In cosmetics, a highly profitable segment for department stores, retailers like Sephora and Ulta have been aggressive competitors of department stores. Estée Lauder has also begun to sell cosmetics online. If successful in its offerings, other cosmetics firms would undoubtedly follow suit.

Increased Number of Retail Bankruptcies

As a result of reduced sales, competition from other retail formats, and high operating costs, 26 supermarket chains filed for bankruptcy earlier in this decade. Bi-Lo and Bruno's Supermarkets have also recently filed for bankruptcy protection. In addition to these bankruptcies, a wave of consolidation has swept through the supermarket business. These include the acquisitions of Wild Oats Markets Inc. by Whole Foods, Pathmark by A&P, and Albertson's by Supervalu.

There has also been a large overall increase in retail bankruptcies in other product categories, including restaurants, electronics, furniture, and jewelry retailers. These include such major retail chains as Bennigan's, Bombay, Boscov's Department Store, Circuit City, Crabtree & Evelyn, Dial-A-Mattress, Eddie Bauer, Filene's Basement, Fortunoff's, Friedman's, Goody's Family Clothing, Gottschalks, KB Toys, Levitz Furniture, Linens 'N Things, Mervyn's, Mrs. Fields, Ritz Camera Centers, Samsonite, The Sharper Image, Steve & Barry's, The Walking Company, Whitehall Jewelers, and Wickes Furniture.

Retailers have been especially hard hit by this recession due to high fixed costs for store leases, high interest costs for store fixtures and renovation, and utilities. Unlike manufacturers, retailers cannot reduce labor costs by shutting down plants on a temporary basis or through outsourcing production to suppliers with low-cost manufacturing facilities. According to an analyst with Bernstein Research, this recession will wipe out 5 to 10 percent of all retail stores.[32] Although some retailers have closed stores as a result of bankruptcy, such as Ritz Camera, Circuit City, and Zale Corporation, others like Sears Holding Corp., Starbucks, and Talbots have shut down underperforming stores.[33] According to a report from the CoStar Group, the retail availability rate (which includes vacant locations and locations being marketed by landlords even though the existing retail tenant has not left) was 9.9 percent as of February 2010.[34]

Retailers that are number two or three in market share in their respective markets are particularly vulnerable to bankruptcy or liquidation. This is especially the case for retailers that have increased their debt in recent years when interest rates were low and credit availability was high to fund major store expansions. Retailers owned by private equity firms that were purchased during prior boom years due to their strong cash flow and property assets are also suspect.

The overall effects of the economic downturn have been felt around the world. A major global credit insurer, Euler Hermes, estimates that about 35,000 Western European retail businesses became insolvent in 2009, up 17 percent from 2008. Retailing was the second-worst-hit sector after manufacturing.[35] Among the major recent European retailer bankruptcies were Woolworths, a British chain selling toys and housewares; MFI, a British furniture retailer; The Pier, a housewares chain; and Arcandor, a German retailer whose Karstadt department stores anchor downtown shopping areas throughout Germany.

There are several major concerns with retail bankruptcies and liquidations. Unfortunately, these bankruptcies and liquidations bring down price expectations for the remaining retailers. This forces surviving retailers to reduce their prices (and profit margins) to remain competitive. Store closings also decrease the desirability of many retail locations, particularly malls, making it more difficult for the surviving stores to continue to attract customers. This is especially the case where stores rely on each other to generate store traffic or when one of a mall's major anchor tenants close. And finally, many mall developers are adversely affected. Lower rental income due to both empty stores, as well as lower percentage lease payments from existing retail tenants, may affect the maintenance of retail properties.

Retail Store Positioning and Competitive Strategy

As was discussed earlier, Michael Porter's competitive strategy theory argues that there are two major long-term competitively defensible strategies that retailers can pursue: (1) low cost and (2) differentiation. Low-cost retailers such as Aldi and Costco have succeeded by reducing product choice (this translates into savings due to faster inventory turnover, lower rental costs, and greater bargaining power with individual suppliers), use of a self-service shopping environment, and an absence of services that their consumers view as secondary in importance (such as home delivery, custom cutting of meats, no try-on rooms, and an absence of in-store displays), as well as through low rental costs (due to their ability to generate store traffic). Amazon.com is also a low-cost retailer due to its ability to minimize its inventory investment through drop shipping, the absence of physical stores, and the use of consumer ratings by shoppers and excellent photographic images that can be used by consumers as a substitute for sales assistance.

At the other end of the positioning spectrum are retailers such as L.L.Bean, Nordstrom, Trader Joe's, Wegmans, and Whole Foods. These retailers have succeeded through a differentiation strategy that combines high levels of sales assistance by a dedicated and trained staff, specialized merchandise (much of it being private label), and a shopping environment that is viewed by many consumers as exciting, entertaining, and fun.

In contrast to the cost and differentiation strategies, value strategies pursue elements of cost and differentiation strategies at the same time. Trader Joe's, for example, offers distinctive foreign foods in easy-to-prepare formats. Its products are low cost, and its stores are fun to shop due to its sampling stations (staffed by knowledgeable personnel), free coffee, and the availability of balloons and small shopping carts for children. Costco also offers low prices, as well as a differentiation strategy based on a well-developed private label program, the use of co-branding on many of its private label products, a very liberal return policy, and a treasure hunt atmosphere (due to Costco's use of an opportunistic buying strategy). Amazon.com offers low prices and an extensive selection, suggests books and other products based on a customer's recent purchases, has a simplified checkout procedure, and provides unedited product reviews from past purchasers.

According to Porter's competitive strategy theory, the least-defensible competitive strategy is being "stuck in the middle." These retailers offer no long-term benefit in terms of offering consumers low prices or a highly differentiated retail strategy. This book is offered as a guide to these "stuck-in-the-middle" retailers. The first part of dealing with a "stuck-in-the-middle" strategy is a retailer's recognizing its true positioning in the marketplace. Obviously, what is crucial is the customer's positioning of the retailer, not the retailer's idealized positioning. The second part of the change process is for the retailer to formulate short- and long-term plans to implement the recommended changes.

Recognizing the Need to Change

A central issue to be covered in this section is how a retailer can determine whether a cost, value, or differentiation strategy is most suitable. As in all forms of self-analysis, a retailer needs to honestly evaluate its strengths and weaknesses.

Here are a number of questions a retailer needs to ponder in assessing the use of low cost as a competitive advantage:

- What is the retailer's cost of goods sold as a percent of sales versus its key competitors?
- What are the retailer's operating costs as a percent of sales relative to its key competitors?

- Does the retailer have special competencies in the management of opportunistic buying (bankrupt stocks, manufacturer overruns, closeouts, broken lots, canceled orders, refurbished products, and so on)?

- Does the retailer have opportunities to significantly reduce its costs (through reducing organization hierarchies, subletting extra space, reducing product proliferation, reducing services that are regarded as unnecessary or of low value by its target market, centralizing functions, increasing labor proficiency, using self-checkouts, selling select merchandise on the Web, using drop shipping, shifting to an everyday low pricing format, and so forth)?

- Can the retailer effectively reposition empty or low-performing stores as a discount operation? Can these stores use existing store fixtures to reduce investments? Is the retailer able to effectively manage multiple formats (one of which is a low-cost operation)?

In contrast, there are a number of questions a retailer needs to ponder in assessing the use of differentiation-based strategies as a competitive strategy, as follows:

- Does the retailer's sales personnel have specialized product knowledge or skills that are especially relevant to the goods and services sold (such as "foodies" working in a grocery, sports enthusiasts working in a sporting goods store, or interior decorators working in a furniture store)?

- Is the store's atmosphere viewed as "fun," "entertaining," or "exciting" by its customers? Can the store's atmosphere easily be repositioned as "fun," "entertaining," or "exciting" through sampling stations, demonstrations, or short classes on using equipment?

- Does the retailer have special customer services or can it effectively develop services (such as need assessment, alterations, delivery, installation, troubleshooting, and repair) that can be used as a major competitive advantage?

- Does the retailer have access to unique goods through arrangements with specialized vendors, foreign sources of supply, and private label supplier contacts?

- Does the retailer have the competency and resources to successfully implement a distinctive private label program (including customer need assessment, product development, and product testing and tasting)?

The answers to the preceding questions may suggest that the retailer needs to further develop its core competencies around low cost or differentiation. Some of these questions need to be answered by a store's middle and top management, as well as its board of directors. Others require questioning shoppers via surveys or focus groups.

Formulating Short- and Long-Term Strategies to Effectively Implement Change

According to a *Harvard Business Review* article, retailers should focus their strategies around where the true "headroom" lies. The authors defined *headroom* as "market share you don't have minus market share you won't get."[36] Consumers loyal to your competitors represent market share you will not likely achieve. In contrast, a retailer is most likely to retain its most loyal customers. Headroom represents "switchers" loyal to neither you nor your competitors. The choice of a low-cost, value, or differentiation strategy also has to consider the needs and size of this switcher segment, as well as a retailer's ability to attract and maintain this group of customers.

There are many different paths to developing and implementing repositioning strategies based on low cost, value, or differentiation. These include the use of existing middle management, retaining consultants, hiring executives with specialized talents, outsourcing key tasks (such as hiring a firm with significant private label experience to develop and manage these goods), and merging or acquiring retailers that have special strengths.

There are several major caveats in repositioning for any retailer. One, a retailer may not possess the core competencies to effectively carry out the repositioned strategy. Two, consumers' perceptions about a retailer's key strengths have been formed over years and are very difficult to change. When Sears decided several years ago to sell more costly lines of clothing, its previous customers of inexpensive apparel simply switched to other retailers. To make matters worse, Sears was also unsuccessful in attracting new customers to purchase the higher-cost apparel at its stores. Generally, positioning changes need to occur slowly. This slow pace enables a retailer to communicate and reinforce its repositioned strategy over a long time period.

In pursuing a low-cost strategy, retailers need to be careful that services that a retailer's target market views as critical not be significantly reduced or eliminated. One way of reducing this risk is to use unbundled pricing. In this way, an appliance retailer can charge separate prices for an appliance, delivery, installation, and carting away of the old appliance. This unbundling strategy satisfies the needs of both the low-cost segment (which is willing to do some or all of the services) and full-service customer segments (which are looking to do none of these tasks). Unbundled pricing also enables a retailer to match the price of low-cost retailers that do not provide ancillary services. It also charges customers for only those services that they desire.

A retailer needs to be careful in formulating its differentiation strategy so that its new strategy is not based upon a niche. One way to effectively address a differentiation strategy is to use micromarketing, where stores are clustered into groupings based on their specialized markets. In this way, an appliance chain may offer compact appliances (such as 10-cubic-foot refrigerators) in its central city stores, and 23-cubic-foot refrigerators, lawn mowers, and snow blowers in its suburban and rural store units. A supermarket can utilize micromarketing by offering six-packs of lamb chops for stores in family-oriented neighborhoods and prepared single-serving portions for stores with a high proportion of single residents.

Retailers can also establish different organizational units for each major market segment. This strategy is most difficult to implement since each segment has very different needs that top management needs to recognize and appeal to. Although Aldi and Trader Joe's are both owned by the Albrecht brothers, their strategies are quite different. Aldi appeals more to the extreme value customer who is more willing than the Trader Joe's customer to forgo certain services for a lower price. The Trader Joe's customer is also much more likely to be a "foodie" who loves to experiment with exotic foreign foods, multiple coffees, teas, and olive oils. Likewise, Nordstrom and Nordstrom Rack are different retail operations in terms of their selection, pricing, store service, and store atmosphere. And Publix has a Publix Sabor division with four stores that caters to a Caribbean and South American population with a special selection of foods and all advertising and product information provided in both English and Spanish.

Many bricks-and-mortar retailers have web sites that offer a different selection of goods and services. Some retailers use the Web as a means of promoting the sale of closeouts and broken lots. Others use the Web as a means of selling distinctive merchandise that appeals to markets too small for their traditional store-based channel.

Takeaway Points

- In general, there has been an overall increase in competition from dissimilar retailer types, called "format blurring." Traditional retailers have seen significant competition as consumers increasingly shop at warehouse clubs, Wal-Mart, dollar stores, extreme value food formats like Aldi and Sav-A-Lot, office supply stores, factory outlets, and closeout-based web retailers.

- One of the major long-term changes that has carried over from this recession is the increased concern for all consumers with "value." An effective value strategy can deter the migration of consumers to other outlets. Among the strategies supermarkets need to consider in delivering value are more attractively priced private label products, warehouse "bulk" packages for selected goods (such as paper towels, facial tissue, dishwasher liquid, and detergents), the use of opportunistic buying as a strategy to offer low prices, pretesting goods for durability, and increasing buying power through cooperative buying agreements among noncompeting retailers. Appliance stores can demonstrate value through special purchases, listing certain appliances as "Best Buys" based on features, performance, and price.

- Retailers need to make it easier for consumers to get special values. Specials should be communicated on blackboards in front of each store and can be grouped together as solutions (such as pasta, pasta sauce, ground beef, and Italian bread for a supermarket or an HDTV, a speaker system, and HDMI cables for an electronics store). Coupon offerings can be posted on a store's web site.

- Periods of low growth represent an ideal time for retailers to reexamine their operations for possible sources of additional revenues, as well as for ways to trim expenses. Some obvious areas of potential revenues that need to be examined are subletting unnecessary space to service vendors that can benefit from a store's regular customer traffic base. This can include dry cleaners, in-house bakeries, and a full-service pharmacy within a supermarket; a full-service jewelry shop, a tailor shop, and an electronics retail operation within a department store; and an electronics repair and installation facility within an electronics store. Opportunities for format blurring should also be considered. Electronics that are rapidly dropping in price, such as cellular phones, HDTVs, and netbooks, are suitable candidates.

- Periods of low growth are also an ideal time to reevaluate whether additional services should be continued or separately charged. For example, a furniture retailer may want to consider unbundling charges for delivery, installation, and carting away of one's old furniture. In this way, consumers can select and pay for specific services that they value.

- Periods of low growth generate opportunities due to weak competitors going out of business or closing underperforming stores, increased in-home food consumption (at the expense of restaurants), in-home catering, and in-home entertainment.

- Two major competitive strategies that retailers need to carefully consider are low cost and differentiation. Low-cost retailers base their overall strategy around reducing product choice, self-service shopping environments, and an absence of services that consumers view as secondary in importance, as well as lower rental costs. Differentiation strategies are based on high levels of sales assistance, specialized merchandise, and a fun-based shopping environment. Value-based strategies combine elements of cost and differentiation by including only those services that are worth more to consumers than their cost to a retailer.

• Retailers need to examine their ability to increasingly adopt a low cost or differentiation strategy through honestly assessing their capabilities. Retailers also need to assess opportunities in the low cost and differentiation sector by examining where the true "headroom" lies. Some retailers may choose to appeal to multiple market segments through offering different overall retail strategies.

Endnotes

1. Edward J. Fox and Raj Sethuraman, "Retail Competition," in *Retailing in the 21st Century: Current and Emerging Trends*, Manfred Krafft and Murali K. Mantrala, eds. (Berlin/Heidelberg/New York: Springer, 2006).

2. www.retailerdaily.com/entry/9225/comparable-store-sales-data/, as of April 16, 2010.

3. "U.S. Consumer Spending, Income Remain Sluggish," *Industry Week* (March 29, 2010).

4. Christine Hauser, "Savings Up; Consumer Spending Flat," *Boston Globe* (May 29, 2010), p. B5.

5. Kate Berry and Sara Lepro, "Still No Peak," *American Banker* (May 20, 2010), p. 11.

6. Fred Hiers, "Foreclosures Back Up Again," *McClatchy-Tribune News* (July 16, 2010).

7. Rick Newman, "What Could Derail a Recovery," *Time* (March 2010), p. 56.

8. Paul Flatters and Michael Willmott, "Understanding the Post-Recession Consumer," *Harvard Business Review* (July–August 2009), pp. 108–109.

9. Stephanie Rosenbloom, "For Wal-Mart, a Christmas That's Made to Order," *New York Times* (Business) (November 5, 2008).

10. "Consumer 'New Frugality' May Be an Enduring Feature of Post-Recession Economy, Finds Booz & Company Survey," *Business Wire* (February 24, 2010).

11. "The New Consumer Behavior Paradigm: Permanent or Fleeting?" (Pricewaterhouse Coopers LLP and Kantar Retail), 2010.

12. Katy McLaughlin and Timothy W. Martin, "As Sales Slip, Whole Foods Tries Health Push," *Wall Street Journal* (August 5, 2009), p. B1.

13. Edward J. Fox and Raj Sethuraman, "Retail Competition," in *Retailing in the 21st Century: Current and Emerging Trends*, Manfred Krafft and Murali K. Mantrala, eds. (Berlin/Heidelberg/New York: Springer, 2006).

14. Stephen Dowdell, Meg Major, Jimmy McTaggart, and Bridget Goldschmidt, "Third Annual Outstanding Independent Awards: Family Values," *Progressive Grocer* (January 1, 2007), pp. 22–23.

15. John Schmeltzer, "Squeeze of the Supercenter: New Players Bite into the Market Share of Traditional Grocers," *Chicago Tribune* (December 24, 2007).

16. Motoko Rich, "When Big-Box Store Smiles on a Book, Sleepy Titles Can Become Best Sellers," *New York Times* (July 22, 2009), pp. C1, C5.

17. Jena McGregor, "The Hard Sell," *Business Week* (October 26, 2009), p. 45.

18. Neil Currie, "Do Supermarkets Have a Future?" *Progressive Grocer* (April 15, 2005), pp. 62–79.

19. Kelly Tackett, "Economic Forecast: Outlook to 2013: Food, Drug, Mass," (Columbus, OH: TNS Retail Forward), (November 2008), p. 4.

20. *Wal-Mart Stores Inc. 10-K for the Fiscal Year Ended January 31, 2010*, p. 6.

21. *Costco Wholesale Corporation, Form 10-K for the Fiscal Year Ended August 30, 2009*, p. 4.

22. http://supermarketnews.com/profiles/top75/2009-top-75, as of June 6, 2010.

23. Marianne Wilson, "No-Frills Shopping," *Chain Store Age* (March 2009), p. 26.

24. http://pressroom.target.com/pr/news/consumables/Super-Target/default.aspx, as of June 6, 2010.

25. *Target Corporation 10-K for the Fiscal Year Ended January 30, 2010*, p. 3.

26. *Dollar General 10-K for the Fiscal Year Ended January 29, 2010*, p. 7.

27. *Family Dollar 10-K for the Fiscal Year Ended August 29, 2009*, p. 7.

28. *Costco Wholesale Corporation Form 10-K for the Fiscal Year Ended August 31, 2009*, p. 4.

29. Matthew Boyle, "Wal-Mart's Magic Moment," *Business Week* (June 15, 2009), p. 52.

30. "U.S. Web Retail Sales to Reach $249 Billion by 2014: Study," *Reuters* (March 8, 2010), http://www.reuters.com/article/idUSTRE6274VG20100308, as of June 7, 2010.

31. Maria Halkias, "Shoppers Departing Stores—and May Not Be Back," *The Dallas Morning News* (February 20, 2009), www.dallasnews.com, as of February 23, 2009.

32. Sandra M. Jones, "2009 Predicted to Be a 'Cleansing' Period for Retailers: More Stores Expected to Close or File for Bankruptcy," *Chicago Tribune* (January 2, 2009).

33. http://retailindustry.about.com/od/statisticsresearch/a/storeclosings09.htm, as of September 10, 2010.

34. http://retailtrafficmag.com/news/store_closings_pile_up_02092010, as of September 10, 2010.

35. Mark Potter and James Davey, "Analysis—Worst Still to Come for Europe's Retailers," *Reuters News* (December 12, 2008).

36. Ken Favaro, Tim Romberger, and David Meer, "Five Rules for Retailing in a Recession," *Harvard Business Review* (April 2009), pp. 64–72.

2

Low-Cost Strategies I: Key Elements of a Low-Cost Provider Strategy

Cost-effective retailers can consistently deliver value on the basis of their low prices. A low-cost advantage is appropriate for effectively matching or coming close to matching low prices at directly competing retailers, as well as indirect competition from superstores, limited assortment stores, warehouse clubs, dollar stores, factory outlets, and web-based retailers. It is also an important part of the strategy to win over and retain cost-conscious consumers during a major recession, when many customers become especially frugal. An additional benefit of a low-cost strategy is retaining customers who will have remained cost-conscious after the recession has passed.

As a cautionary note, the use of a low-cost strategy should not be interpreted as a license to compete with retailers such as Wal-Mart solely on the basis of price. Given Wal-Mart's scale of operations, cost efficiencies due to bargaining power, and effective supply-chain management, Wal-Mart will probably always be among the industry's most efficient retailers. The goal in developing a low-cost strategy is to compete by charging a slight premium over Wal-Mart's prices. This strategy recognizes that there are many consumers that would be more than willing pay a small premium for higher levels of customer service and convenience. Likewise, it is quite difficult matching prices at such cost-effective retailers as Aldi, Costco, and Trader Joe's. According to Whole Foods' CEO, matching prices at Costco is difficult without going bankrupt."[1]

Retailers also need to carefully monitor the extent of their cost cutting. Extreme cost cutting results in "cutting muscle instead of fat." This can create a dangerous spiral that can threaten a retailer's long-term survival. Examples of extreme cost cutting include drastic reductions in staff and inventory that destroy customer service levels that are viewed as essential by a retailer's target market or that result in chronic stockouts on key merchandise.

Implementing Low-Cost/Low-Price Strategies

To consistently deliver the lowest prices or prices at the low end of the competitive spectrum, retailers need to pay constant attention to their overall cost structure. One way of securing low costs consists of having an efficient supply chain (maintaining low inventories, using direct store delivery, and communicating product sales data to suppliers on a real-time basis), using low-rent locations, reducing store fixture expense, and using labor more efficiently (through having employees rotate tasks and better matching employee schedules to peak sales periods). Low-cost retailers generally utilize one of several strategies to keep costs low: They focus on just one or two consumer segments (to reduce inventory requirements), deliver the basic product (with few accompanying services), provide one benefit better than rivals do (such as an excellent private label strategy), or have extra efficient operations (with minimal labor) to keep costs low.[2]

The total impact of cost savings can be considerable, especially if the cost reduction strategy is effectively integrated into a retailer's overall strategy. Let's examine how Aldi generated and maintained its low-cost strategy. According to two academic researchers, Aldi's significant cost advantage over its competitors is due more to its in-store efficiencies than its bargaining power with its suppliers.[3] Much of Aldi's cost advantage is from the chain's use of inexpensive locations that minimize rental costs, its use of simple pallets and cut-case displays for fixtures, few signs and displays, the standardization of pricing across all of its stores, as well as lower inventory holding costs due to the chain's small selection. Aldi also does not have in-store banking facilities or pharmacies, but it accepts debit cards (but does not accept credit cards or checks). To save on labor costs, store hours are also limited to the most popular hours of operation. Aldi's web site emphasizes its efforts at wringing out unnecessary costs. It states: "The typical supermarket is a minefield of hidden costs. Along with your groceries, the extra freight of free bags, baggers, and check acceptance is loaded into your cart every time you shop, whether you use those services or not."[4]

The combined effects of these "pile it high and sell it cheap" strategies gives Aldi the distinction of "...operating the leanest low-cost model" in food marketing in the world, according to a marketing professor who has extensively studied the chain.[5] As a result of these cost-saving strategies, Aldi's total costs for logistics, rent, overhead, marketing, and labor account for 13 percent to 14 percent of an item's cost. One estimate is that logistics, rent, overhead, and marketing expenses for Aldi each comprise 2 percent of the chain's revenues, and labor equals 5 percent of revenues.[6] In contrast, traditional supermarkets (including Aldi's four largest competitors in the UK) have total costs for these items of between 28 percent and 30 percent.[7] This low overall cost structure gives Aldi a 15 percent to 16 percent cost advantage relative to these competing grocers. In addition to these cost savings, Aldi receives significant bargaining power with its suppliers due to concentrating its total purchases on 1,400 or so items. This aspect of cost savings is covered in the following chapter.

Aldi's low cost levels enable it to consistently outprice its rivals, including Wal-Mart. According to a market analyst with DJL Research, Aldi's U.S. prices are between 15 percent and 20 percent less than Wal-Mart and 30 percent to 40 percent less than regional supermarket chains.[8] Another report states that Aldi's U.S. prices are generally 15 percent to 25 percent below other big-box retailers or discounters, and 35 percent to 45 percent below full-service super-markets.[9] A study of Aldi's relative prices in Australia by Choice, an Australia-based independent product testing organization, found that Aldi's prices were 44 percent below that of competitors Coles and Woolworths.[10]

Aldi's overall cost-cutting strategy has been so effective that it is credited as a major factor in Wal-Mart's pulling out of Germany. According to a retail consultant, "Aldi literally ran Wal-Mart out of continental Europe, and now they're taking the fight to Wal-Mart in the United States."[11]

Cleverly, Aldi understands that it cannot minimize costs in all areas of its store operations. Although its customers must bring their own shopping bags and also pay a deposit to ensure that grocery carts get returned to the proper location, Aldi makes sure to have adequate personnel at the checkout counters to avoid long waiting lines.

Similarly, Costco uses an overall strategy designed to minimize its overall cost structure relative to competition. According to James Sinegal, Costco's chief executive officer, "Costco is able to offer lower prices and better values by eliminating all the frills and costs histori-cally associated with conventional wholesalers and retailers, including salespeople, fancy buildings, delivery, billing, and accounts receiv-able. We run a tight operation with extremely low overhead, which enables us to pass on dramatic savings to our members."[12] Few departments at Costco (with the exception of jewelry, pharmacy, and optical) are staffed by salespeople. Much of the fine jewelry depart-ment inventory is drop shipped by jewelry wholesalers; this mini-mizes Costco's inventory investment. Costco also does not have try-on rooms for apparel; that subjects the retailer to pilferage and takes up valuable selling space. The facilities are also bare-bones with concrete floors, exposed ceilings, and a lack of signage. Costco's customers are happy to forgo these conveniences due to the significant opportuni-ties for cost savings.

Advantages of Being a Low-Cost Provider

Simply put, a low-cost retailer can make a profit at a price that would result in a loss to most of its major competitors. These higher-cost competitors would consistently lose money by attempting to match the low-cost rival's everyday prices. The low-cost competitive advantage is especially important among price-conscious customers who have little or no loyalty to any retailer, among customer groups most adversely affected by the recession, and by customers that have switched to low-cost retailers. Let's now examine how retailers like Aldi, L.L.Bean, Costco, Stew Leonard's, Trader Joe's, and Wegmans have developed and maintained a low-cost provider advantage.

Key Elements of a Low-Cost Retailer Strategy

Low-cost strategy elements that we will explore include undertaking continuing efforts to keep costs low, minimizing product proliferation, maintaining high market share in served markets, constantly offering customers the best possible price, obtaining the best net price from suppliers, effectively communicating the low-price message to consumers, implementing supply chain initiatives, using everyday low pricing, having low promotional budgets, and better utilizing employees (see Figure 2.1).

Undertaking Continuing Efforts to Keep Costs Low

Retailers need to constantly to resist the temptation to increase operating costs via services that may not be viewed as valuable or important to its store's target customers. These "bad costs" can creep into a retailer's cost structure due to various factors. As many retailers grow geographically, they often impose common store hours over the entire chain, centrally purchase goods (despite local and regional

Figure 2.1   Key elements of a low-cost provider strategy

differences), and include common services across the entire chain (even though many of these services are not equally valued by consumers on a store-by-store basis).[13]

Bad costs can also occur as a result of retailers not keeping up with changes in technology or consumer behavior. Although some retailers may still deliver electronics to a customer's home, many consumers would prefer verifying the product's availability over the retailer's web site and then picking up the item in a nearby local store, knowing it is in stock. The web search and in-store pickup combination gives the customer immediacy, while saving the retailer unnecessary shipping costs. See Table 2.1 for examples of causes and examples of bad costs.

TABLE 2.1   Causes and Examples of Bad Costs

Causes of Bad Costs	Examples of Bad Costs
Overcentralization of operations.	Each store has the same hours of operation, services, variety, and assortment despite local and regional differences in demand.
Retailers respond to reductions in sales by reducing all expenses on a proportionate basis.	Services that customers value, such as sales support, are reduced by the same percentage as services customers view as unimportant, such as layaway or in-home delivery.
Retailers trade up to capture higher-income customers and gain prestige.	The retailer's current customers are more concerned about low prices than receiving such services as alterations and delivery that are viewed as unimportant.
Retailers do not take into account changes in consumer behavior due to technology.	Opportunities in self-checkouts are ignored. Catalogs are continued when more current and extensive information can be contained on the retailer's web site at a much lower cost to the retailer. The Web also has the potential to be more exciting than catalogs due to its capability to be more personal and to use sound and animation.
Retailers do not take into account changes in consumer behavior due to competition.	Retailers do not understand the need to reduce costs due to entry of low-cost competitors in the market area. Bundled pricing enables retailers to compete in multiple segments with separate service mixes and pricing levels for each segment.

Retailers need to continually reduce bad costs through "customer-benefit costing." This process links the cost of each service element (such as product choice, store ambiance, and waiting times at registers) to a benefit that its customers value.[14] Service costs that are high relative to perceived customer benefits need to be carefully reviewed for possible deletion. In contrast, service costs that are low in comparison to benefits may be targeted for expansion.

Retailers also need to constantly drive down all costs through automation, mechanization, and outsourcing of tasks to more efficient suppliers (such as drop shipping special orders from suppliers). Because nearly 70 percent of items sold online by Costco are shipped from its suppliers directly to the customer, Costco's online business occupies only one warehouse (with about 80,000 square feet and a staff of 185).[15] Costco has also installed pneumatic tubes at checkout areas to speed the movement of cash to a store's back office and has added self-checkout lanes in some stores to make them more efficient.[16] Costco is also one of the first retailers to use RFID to track incoming shipments of inventory.[17]

Costco reduces the temptation to increase its services. According to Louise Wendling, country manager of Costco Canada, displaying a sheet set on a bed is something that "Costco would never do. That would constitute an unnecessary cost. We keep everything as simple as possible."[18] Likewise, Costco is also definitely not the place where one would expect to see a mannequin dressed in coordinating clothing or even a try-on room. With the exception of its web-based unit, Costco also does not accept web- or phone-based orders and does not deliver.

Minimizing Product Proliferation

As discussed in the following chapter, retailers need to carefully analyze their variety and assortments. Cost-effective retailers like Aldi, Costco, Stew Leonard's, and Trader Joe's consciously concentrate their sales in few brands, sizes, and varieties. They understand that too much selection in a given merchandise category reduces the store's sales per square foot, inventory turnover, and bargaining power with suppliers. It also significantly increases inventory ordering and holding costs.

Product proliferation has three detrimental issues. One, it increases such inventory holding costs as interest, insurance, inventory storage, and markdown expenses (due to inventory obsolescence, seasonal sales, and so on). Two, product proliferation reduces a retailer's bargaining power and opportunities for quantity discounts due to purchases being spread among too many suppliers and too many small orders. And three, some research findings suggest that a store's offering too much selection can result in high levels of consumer confusion and stress. Chapter 3, "Low-Cost Strategies II: Delivering Low Costs Through Minimizing Product Proliferation," covers this topic in depth.

Maintaining High Market Share in Served Markets

Several of the benchmark retailers have high market shares in their served markets. The concept of served markets argues that Whole Foods' market is a subset of the total grocery market due to the chain's sales concentration on selling organic food, high-quality produce and meats, and prepared foods. Likewise, L.L.Bean has a relatively high market share in outdoor lifestyle clothing and hunting and fishing accessories. Trader Joe's has a very high market share in terms of the market for prepared canned and frozen foods with a foreign influence, such as Middle-Eastern hummus and Indian samosas. Aldi's served market consists of value-based consumers who are willing to trade off loyalty and store atmosphere for significant cost savings.

A high market share in a served market provides a retailer with high bargaining power in its respective markets. High market share also provides a retailer with destination store status. Shoppers may come from greater distances, rely less on advertising, and seek out retail sales personnel that are especially knowledgeable in a given product category. A very high concentration of customers in a given market area may also result in a retailer's better understanding its customer base. Finally, a high market share can also be a strong deterrent to new competitors entering the market area (due to a poorer understanding of the target market's specialized needs or less competency in delivering the specialized services).

One way of demonstrating Publix's high market share is that although it is among the 10 largest grocery chains in the United States, it has store units in only five southeastern states (Florida, Georgia, South Carolina, Alabama, and Tennessee). Until a few years ago, Publix had only Florida-based stores. Similarly, Wegmans operates only in five states (Maryland, New Jersey, New York, Pennsylvania, and Virginia).

Constantly Offering Customers the Best Possible Price

Low-cost providers are committed to offering the best price possible to their customers. Costco's commitment to keeping prices low is so strong that according to two retail consultants, if Costco could not beat a traditional retailer's price, it simply would not offer the item for sale.[19] For years, Costco would not stock disposable diapers because other retailers had customarily used these goods as loss leaders. Few retailers live by this rule!

One of Costco's cardinal rules is that no branded item can be marked up by more than 14 percent and no private label item by more than 15 percent. James Sinegal, Costco's CEO, has warned investors and retail analysts that if Costco increased markups to 16 or 18 percent, the company might slip down a dangerous slope and lose its discipline in minimizing costs and prices.[20] Sinegal figures that the temptation to "get a little more, a little more is the heroin that killed many a retailer. Holding prices down is part of the faith that our customers have in us."[21] According to Sinegal, "We understand why shoppers come to Costco—it's not for fancy displays or a live Santa Claus at Christmas; it's for value. We cannot lose sight of that!!!"[22]

In contrast to Costco's 14 percent to 15 percent markup, supermarkets generally mark up goods by 25 percent, and department stores by 50 percent or more. Although wine stores often use markups of 40 percent gross margin, Costco's markup for wine is its standard 14 percent. As a result, its low wine prices can be easily recognized as excellent values by consumers. In fiscal 2008, Costco sold $1.1 billion in wine in the United States, making it the largest wine retailer in the United States. Said Richard A. Galanti, Costco's chief financial officer, "If we were a country, we would be the third-largest seller of Dom Pérignon champagne in the world."[23]

Analysts that are critical of Costco's low profit margins do not truly understand its overall business model. Costco has purposely kept its markdowns low as a means of keeping its membership retentions at very high levels. Its membership renewal rate for 2009 was 87 percent. Costco's membership fees, which range from $50 to $100 a year, account for 75 percent of its annual operating profits. One indication of the success of Costco's overall retailing strategy is that its membership base has increased by 4.7 percent from 2008 to 2009.

Likewise, Trader Joe's has priced its popular "two-buck Chuck" wine at $2 per bottle, when the firm could have easily raised its price to any point below $5 with little adverse impact on sales. As a result, this offering became the best-selling wine in history (with more than 10 million cases sold over a three-year period). At one point, Trader Joe's sold 1 million cases a month from pallets located near its store entrances.[24] "Two-buck Chuck" has given Trader Joe's tens of millions of dollars in publicity value. This wine has also served as a symbol of Trader Joe's commitment to providing great value to its customers.

Obtaining the Best Net Price from Suppliers

Although the profitability of a product to many retailers is based on promotional allowances, display allowances, slotting fees, and other allowances from vendors, Wal-Mart, Aldi, Costco, Trader Joe's, and Whole Foods do not negotiate for or accept these allowances. Although these firms are known to drive a very hard bargain, their negotiating activity is strictly confined to obtaining the best possible net price from their suppliers. Any retailer that focuses its bargaining on promotional allowances, chargebacks, and guaranteed markups loses sight of its role as a purchasing agent for its customers. Instead, it takes the role of a selling agent for its suppliers. This point will be further examined in Chapter 3.

To get the best price, Trader Joe's offers suppliers volume guarantees (through multiyear contracts) in return for price guarantees.[25] And because Trader Joe's always pays suppliers in full and on time, they like doing business with Trader Joe's. Likewise, Aldi's UK head of buying states that "Aldi offers manufacturers a welcome alternative to the complex web of hidden fees and costs..." associated with selling goods to other major food-based retailers.[26]

Benchmark retailers continually stress the importance of getting the best possible net price from their suppliers. For example, Costco's Sinegal has consistently warned Costco's suppliers not to offer other retailers lower prices than Costco receives. When a frozen-food supplier mistakenly sent Costco an invoice meant for Wal-Mart, Sinegal discovered that Wal-Mart was getting a better price. "We have not brought that supplier back," said Sinegal. "This is not the Little Sisters of the Poor," he said. "We have to be competitive in the toughest marketplace in the world against the biggest competitor in the world. We cannot afford to be timid." Likewise, Costco dropped Bonita, its long-term banana supplier, when Bonita tried to increase its banana prices due to heavy rains and flooding in Ecuador. Costco now purchases bananas from companies located in five different countries; Bonita is not a current supplier.[27] These conflicts reinforce Costco's commitment to low prices for its members. It also shows its suppliers that it is not afraid of flexing its bargaining power in price negotiations.

To emphasize the importance of low price, Costco requires that its suppliers make Costco aware of all alternative pricing terms. If a supplier had a different price for truckload or trainload quantities, Costco would want to analyze each of the options. According to Costco's policy, "suppliers that do not consistently and voluntarily provide this information will be immediately and permanently discontinued."[28]

Similarly, Aldi recently announced that it was seeking a 5 percent price reduction from its suppliers.[29] This was a risky strategy to Aldi because it uses a relatively small number of suppliers for its private label goods. Unlike other grocers, Aldi cannot easily switch from one supplier to another.

Effectively Communicating the Low-Price Message to Consumers

One way of communicating a retailer's low-price message is through its austere atmosphere and customer-service offerings. For example, Aldi's locations are so spartan that it would be virtually impossible for a consumer to mistake an Aldi location for any traditional grocery store. Through requiring that a consumer pay for a paper grocery bag and through using cut-case displays instead of traditional store fixtures, Aldi effectively communicates that every cent of expense is closely watched as a means of getting the best possible price for its consumers.

Costco clearly communicates its low-cost, low-price message through using warehouse facilities and locations, placing goods on industrial shelving, checking consumer receipts to reduce pilferage, and its limited (if at all) use of advertising. Low operating costs are also an integral part of Trader Joe's strategy. It is also no coincidence that most of Trader Joe's stores are located in low-rent locations in "out-of-the-way" shopping centers. Trader Joe's well understands that it can successfully use locations that would spell disaster for other grocers, because it can easily generate its own store traffic. The low-cost strategy at Trader Joe's extends to its choice of packaging on its private labels. Most packaging design is done internally using type from an existing library, colors from a shared palate, and graphic elements from an extensive catalog of home-produced materials.[30]

Costco recently received a lot of media attention by announcing on its web site that it would no longer repurchase Coca-Cola products unless the company would lower its price. According to the web-based notice that Costco labeled "Price Alert," "Costco is committed to carrying name-brand merchandise at the best possible prices. At this time, Coca-Cola has not provided Costco with competitive pricing so that we may pass along the value our members deserve."[31] Ultimately, the square-off over pricing was resolved, and Costco resumed its orders as of December 2009.

Implementing Supply Chain Initiatives

Aldi, L.L.Bean, Costco, and Trader Joe's (like Wal-Mart) only purchase products direct from manufacturers. This strategy gives them better capability to communicate sales and shipment data to vendors and results in both lower inventory levels and lower stockouts.

Costco works hard to reduce supply chain inefficiencies. When the firm realized that its loading docks were often clogged due to truck drivers leaving their trucks as they were being unloaded, Costco revised its unloading procedures. Now truck drivers are given restaurant-style buzzers and must wait in their trucks while they are being unloaded. When drivers receive a signal from the beeper that their truck has been fully unloaded, they can leave the loading dock. Costco estimates that this simple change will save it $7 million in labor costs in 2009.[32] Costco's vendors must also be prepared to satisfy the chain's stringent supply chain requirements. According to one source, "If you sell to Costco, you'd better have 100 percent fill and 100 percent on-time delivery."[33]

Costco has also partnered with its suppliers to wring out unnecessary package and shipping costs. In 2009, it reduced the amount of resin in its Kirkland Signature brand of water by 12 grams of resin per bottle. This tactic reduced both packaging, as well as shipping costs. Several years ago, Costco worked with its milk supplier to redesign the shape of the bottle. This single, simple change eliminated the need to ship more than 500 truckloads of freight annually.[34]

Wegmans constantly communicates the importance of supply chain logistics costs to its suppliers. In 2003, Wegmans began its data synchronization initiative to ensure the accuracy of product information so that invoices, payments, and other business transactions are correct. Wegmans estimates that this process alone has saved the firm $1 million per year for every billion in sales. These savings come from lower freight costs, error-free scanning, and reduced time required to reconcile coupons.[35] Wegmans also collaborates with its suppliers so that they deliver goods at tightly defined times. To underscore the importance of timing, Wegmans fines suppliers for lateness.

The supply chain initiative area is an area where Wal-Mart truly shines. Wal-Mart requires its suppliers to manage their own in-store inventories. To save additional monies, many of Wal-Mart's products are shipped directly to Wal-Mart's stores (without ever spending any time at Wal-Mart's warehouse). In some instances, selected suppliers such as General Electric manage Wal-Mart's inventory of GE light bulbs inside of Wal-Mart's warehouse. This saves both GE and Wal-Mart the costs of stocking duplicate inventories.

Wal-Mart also allows its suppliers to access its Retail Link inventory system to enable suppliers to more quickly replenish inventory and to provide each store with a more appropriate product mix. Wal-Mart is currently seeking to further reduce supply chain costs by requiring key suppliers to adopt radio frequency identification (RFID). RFID can be used to record product movement on conveyors going at the rate of 650 feet per minute. Bar coding is impossible at this speed. RFID also reduces the possibility of errors due to duplicate scanning of the same item. Finally, RFID tags can be used to monitor temperatures of perishables and frozen foods, thereby reducing product spoilage.[36]

Amazon.com is cognizant of the loss of sales and its top customer service image due to out-of-stock situations on popular merchandise. During the past two years, it has developed a "milk run" initiative to keep "hot" items in stock. As opposed to waiting for suppliers to deliver quick-selling items to Amazon.com's warehouses, Amazon.com simply sends out its own trucks to pick up these goods. According to the vice-president for a firm that markets a fast-selling Flip camcorder that was part of a "milk run" operation, this program is "very forward-thinking."[37]

Using Everyday Low Pricing

Aldi, L.L.Bean, Costco, Nordstrom, and Trader Joe's employ everyday low pricing (EDLP). They do not use such strategies as weekly sales, loss leaders, high-low pricing (use of regular versus on-sale pricing), store-based coupons, and customer loyalty programs. Because there are relatively few sales with everyday low pricing, there is less need to communicate special offers to customers. As a result of EDLP, Aldi, L.L.Bean, Costco, and Trader Joe's have limited advertising budgets.

The use of an EDLP program also results in more predictable sales levels, more efficient warehouse and trucking utilization (as sales peaks and valleys are reduced), fewer stockouts, and lower labor costs due to fewer price changes. According to one source, a 200-store chain operating with high-low pricing that puts 3,000 items on sale in a given week needs to generate more than $250,000 in additional weekly sales just to pay the additional labor costs to implement the necessary price changes.[38] An additional benefit of using an EDLP strategy is that cost savings go to all of a store's customers throughout the year, not shoppers that purchase large quantities during sales periods and store these goods in their homes for future use.

Having Low Promotional Budgets

Although Costco does some direct mail (mostly to solicit new members), its corporate marketing budget is miniscule in comparison to other retailers of its size. Costco also does not have a public relations department. According to Joel Benoliel, senior vice-president of membership and marketing at Costco, "If we do a superb job of delivering value to members, they will be our best ambassadors and we don't need to buy time in television, in radio, or magazines and newsprint because the best kind of advertising is word-of-mouth."[39]

Likewise, Trader Joe's word-of-mouth communication is so great that its advertising budget can be 0.2 percent of sales versus 1 percent to 4 percent for a traditional supermarket.[40] Because, in many cases, Trader Joe's does not have enough stores in any one area to use traditional newspaper ads and freestanding inserts distributed by newspapers effectively, it generally uses direct mail advertising and in-store distribution for its newsletter, called the "Fearless Flyer." This 12- to 20-page booklet, which is printed quarterly on low-cost newsprint, contains irreverent descriptions of new and existing products with Victorian era cartoons. Whole Foods' stores spend most of their marketing budgets on signage and on in-store events such as taste fairs, classes, tours, and product samplings.

Better Utilizing Employees

Because payroll and employee benefit costs can account for close to 16 percent of a store's sales, grocery retailers need to pay particular attention to labor utilization. To reduce employee costs, Costco has no sales associates with the exception of consumer electronics and jewelry. These product categories are relatively costly, have technical issues that may need explanation, and are also characterized by high levels of perceived risk on the part of consumers. In contrast, Costco correctly assumes that much of its other merchandise is presold and that consumers are ready, willing, and able to purchase items without the need for any sales assistance.

Trader Joe's effectively utilizes employees through cross training. It is common at Trader Joe's for its crew members who typically stock shelves to serve as cashiers in peak sales periods. Likewise, Aldi operates its 10,000-square-foot stores with small staffs. Although a store will have between 10 and 15 employees, typically only 3 to 5 work each shift.[41] As with Trader Joe's, Aldi workers rotate positions from stocking shelves to operating cash registers, depending upon customer traffic. According to one estimate, as a result of high sales and high employee productivity, the average Aldi store has three times the sales revenue per employee hour than a conventional supermarket.[42]

To further reduce in-store labor costs, most of Trader Joe's fruits and vegetables, meats, and fish products are prepackaged. To successfully sell prepackaged goods to its food-oriented customers, Trader Joe's recognizes that it cannot compromise quality, freshness, or choice.

Takeaway Points

- Through obtaining significant cost advantages, a traditional retailer can better compete on the basis of price against warehouse clubs, superstores, limited assortment stores, dollar stores, factory outlets, and price-based web merchants.

- Traditional retailers do not necessarily have to meet the prices of warehouse clubs, Wal-Mart, limited assortment stores, and dollar stores. There is a given amount of price premium that many customers will gladly pay to the traditional supermarket based on convenience of location, ability to conduct one-stop shopping, broader selections, additional services (such as helpful store personnel, phone- and web-based ordering, and delivery), and extensive store hours.

- Among the potential sources of low-cost provider status are undertaking continuing efforts to keep costs low, minimizing product proliferation, maintaining high market share in served markets, constantly offering customers the best possible price, obtaining the best net price from suppliers, effectively communicating the low-price message to consumers, implementing supply chain initiatives, using everyday low pricing, having low promotional budgets, and better utilizing employees. Each of these strategies needs to be evaluated by traditional retailers.

- Retailers need to continually employ customer-benefit costing. Retailers also need to understand that not only the desirability of specific benefits, but service costs as well are constantly changing due to competition, economic issues, technology, and customer needs. Customer-benefit costing links each service cost (such as product choice, store ambiance, and waiting times at registers) to a benefit that its customers value.[43] Service costs that are high relative to perceived customer benefits need to be carefully reviewed for reductions. In contrast, there may be major opportunities in expanding those low-cost service costs with high perceived customer benefits.

- The mix of unnecessary services and critical services has to be researched on a store-by-store basis. A retailer needs to undertake constant efforts to keep its prices low by continuing to look at its overall cost structure. Costs that can easily escalate are labor costs; rental costs; energy costs for heating, ventilating, and air conditioning; and costs associated with increased customer support services. Retailers also need to explore how the Web can be used to reduce promotional costs.

- A simple way of reducing product proliferation is to limit a store's use of private label products to those that offer true value and/or meaningful product distinctiveness.

- A retailer's value message needs to be constantly communicated to both suppliers, as well as final customers. One way of communicating the value message is to centralize purchasing among stores, to be on the constant lookout for special buying opportunities, to effectively communicate special prices to a store's customers, and to use everyday low pricing for many items. Stores need to reinforce their low-cost provider status to final consumers by showing price savings over regular prices in advertising, or comparing private label prices to that of comparable national brands, or by stating that it will not be undersold.

- Because both employee expenses and inventory management costs constitute major cost areas for all retailers, these areas deserve considerable scrutiny. One way of trimming employee expenses is through hiring of high-quality part-time employees. Part-time employees provide flexibility in adapting to busy time periods, reduce high overtime labor expenses, and provide a firm the opportunity to review an employee's performance prior to making a full-time commitment. Retailers need to become better at attracting and retaining such groups as retirees, homemakers who are free while their children are at school, and college students. The use of flexible scheduling arrangements so that employee staffing better coincides with peak sales periods is also important.

- Inventory management costs can be better managed through vendor-managed inventories, drop shipping programs with selected vendors, quick response inventory management programs, direct distribution, trimmed assortments, and through better communication with suppliers.

- One way of looking at managing expenses is to determine which services are crucial to a target market and which services are viewed as unnecessary. Providing services that a target market is willing to forgo in favor of lower prices is wasteful. On the other hand, not providing services that a target market views as critical may result in customer outrage. Each significant service offering must be reviewed to determine which ones are regarded as either necessary or a significant strategy in differentiating the store among its competitors.

Endnotes

1. Katy McLaughlin and Timothy W. Martin, "As Sales Slip, Whole Foods Tries Health Push," *Wall Street Journal* (August 5, 2009), p. B1.

2. Nirmalya Kumar, "Strategies to Fight Low-Cost Rivals," *Harvard Business Review* (December 2006), pp. 104–112.

3. Nirmalya Kumar and Jan-Benedict E.M. Steenkamp, *Private Label Strategy: How to Meet the Store Brand Challenge* (Boston, MA: Harvard Business School Press, 2007), p. 64.

4. Andrew Martin, "The Allure of Plain Vanilla," *The New York Times* (September 7, 2008), p. B2.

5. Mark Ritson, "Aldi Feeds Off Lean Times," *Marketing* (August 27, 2008), p. 20.

6. Jan-Benedict E.M. Steenkamp and Nirmalya Kumar, "Don't Be Undersold," *Harvard Business Review* (December 2009), pp. 90–95.

7. Nirmalya Kumar and Jan-Benedict E.M. Steenkamp, *Private Label Strategy: How to Meet the Store Brand Challenge* (Boston, MA: Harvard Business School Press, 2007), pp. 64–65.

8. Cecile Rohwedder and David Kesmodel, "Aldi Looks to U.S. for Growth," *Wall Street Journal* (January 13, 2009), p. B1.

9. Kim Leonard, "Stock Limited, But Deals Plentiful at Discount Stores," *McClatchy-Tribune Business News* (October 5, 2008).

10. Rhys Haynes, "Aldi Hits a Super Rich Vein," *The Daily Telegraph* (Australia) (September 13, 2007), p. 50.

11. Miguel Bustillo and Timothy W. Martin, "Beyond the Big Box: Wal-Mart Thinks Smaller," *Wall Street Journal* (April 28, 2010), p. B1.

12. http://www.answers.com/topic/costco-wholesale-corp, as of April 1, 2009.

13. Ken Favaro, Tim Romberger, and David Meer, "Five Rules for Retailing in a Recession," *Harvard Business Review* (April 2008), p. 69.

14. Ken Favaro, Tim Romberger, and David Meer, "Five Rules for Retailing in a Recession," *Harvard Business Review* (April 2008), p. 69.

15. Ester Cervantes, "The Costco Alternative" (January/February 2006), http://www.dollarsandsense.org/archives/2006/0106cervantes.html.

16. Kourtney Stringer, "Costco's Deep Discounts Don't Extend to Its Share Price," *Wall Street Journal* (February 22, 2005), p. C1; and Mya Frazier, "The Private-Label Powerhouse," *Advertising Age* (August 21, 2006), p. 6.

17. Phone interview with James Sinegal, CEO, Costco, June 19, 2009.

18. Marissa Shalfi, "The Costco Commitment," Retail Merchandiser, www.retail-merchandiser.com, as of January 17, 2008.

19. Willard N. Ander and Neil Z. Stern, *Winning at Retail: Developing a Sustained Model for Retail Success* (Wiley: Hoboken, 2004).

20. Steven Greenhouse, "How Costco Became the Anti-Wal-Mart," *New York Times* (July 17, 2005).

21. "Costco Wins Loyalty with Bulky Bargains," *USA Today* (September 24, 2004), *Money*, p. 1.

22. Phone interview with James Sinegal, CEO, Costco, June 19, 2009.

23. Richard Mullins, "Costco Uncorked," *Tampa Tribune* (December 17, 2006).

24. Len Lewis, *The Trader Joe's Adventure* (Chicago: Dearborn Trade Publishing, 2005), p. 120.

25. Len Lewis, *The Trader Joe's Adventure* (Chicago: Dearborn Trade Publishing, 2005), p. 43.

26. "Discounters Woo Disenchanted Suppliers," *Food Manufacture* (September 2007), p. 5.

27. Jena McGregor, "Costco's Artful Discounts," *Business Week* (October 20, 2008), p. 58.

28. Phone interview with James Sinegal, CEO, Costco, June 19, 2009.

29. Chloe Smith and Peter Cripps, "Suppliers Threaten Revolt as Aldi Calls for 5 Percent Drop in Price," *Grocer* (July 11, 2009).

30. Teresa Hale, "What Joe's Knows," *Step Inside Design* (July/August 2004), pp. 68 ff.

31. Emily Fredrix and Sarah Skidmore, "Costco Nixes Cole Products Over Pricing Dispute," *Spartanburg Herald-Journal* (November 18, 2009).

32. Jena McGregor, "Costco's Artful Discounts," *Business Week* (October 20, 2008), p. 58.

33. Mary Ellen Kuhn, "Power Retailing at Costco Wholesale: Shoppers Are Flocking to Warehouse Club Stores and No One Does This Unique Brand of Larger-Than-Life Retailing Better Than Costco," *Confectioner* (December 2004), pp. 12 ff.

34. Edward Teach, On the Record: Richard Galanti, "Because It's the Right Thing to Do," *CFO* (March 2010), p. 40.

35. Joseph Tarnowski, "Technology: Clean In, Clean Out," *Progressive Grocer* (May 15, 2006).

36. Alan Ayers, "Wal-Mart World: RFID: Off and Running," (Columbus, Ohio: Retail Forward, March 2006).

37. Heather Green, "How Amazon Aims to Keep You Clicking," *Business Week* (March 2, 2009), p. 40.

38. William H. Marquard, *Walsmart: What It Really Takes to Profit in a Wal-Mart World* (New York: McGraw Hill, 2007), p. 54.

39. Mya Frazier, "Costco," *Advertising Age* (November 7, 2005), p. S14.

40. "The Cheap Gourmet," *Forbes* (April 10, 2006), pp. 76–77.

41. "Food Lion Launches New Prototype," *Gourmet Retailer* (November 2008), pp. 8–9; Steven Gray, "The Ultra-Lean Grocer," *Time* (November 17, 2008), pp. 108–111; and Waveney Ann Moore, "Aldi to Let Shoppers Bag Savings," *St. Petersburg Times* (Florida) (October 26, 2008), p. 4.

42. Mike Hughlett, "Aldi's Formula for Success: Small Selection, Low Prices," *McClatchy-Tribune Business News* (August 10, 2008).

43. Ken Favaro, Tim Romberger, and David Meer, "Five Rules for Retailing in a Recession," *Harvard Business Review* (April 2008), p. 69.

3

Low-Cost Strategies II: Delivering Low Costs Through Minimizing Product Proliferation

The second part of a retailer's cost containment strategy deals with product proliferation. Too many retailers offer way too much choice in terms of brands, sizes, and varieties. Poor store profitability is often associated with product proliferation due to a retailer's allocating too little space to its most profitable products (that have high inventory turnover or high profit margins) and too much space to products that really don't sell that well (even though they may be partially supported through vendor allowances). Too much inventory also requires larger store formats with higher rental and utility costs.

The issue of product proliferation is so important that Retail Forward, a major retailing consulting firm, has identified this issue as "one of nine top trends for 2009." According to Retail Forward, this trend includes retailers exiting underperforming or noncomplementary categories, reviewing their private label mix and dropping tertiary brands.[1]

Aldi sells 1,300 to 1,400 items in its stores (typically made up of high-volume grocery basics, most often a single brand in a single size).[2] Save-A-Lot, a subsidiary of Supervalu, operates 1,200 stores in the United States (300 corporate-owned and 900 licensed) with assortments of 1,250 SKUs (stock-keeping units). Likewise, Costco, Stew Leonard's, and Trader Joe's have stores that typically stock between 2,000 and 4,500 SKUs. In contrast, the average number of

SKUs for conventional supermarkets is 22,000, versus 30,000 for the average superstore, 52,000 for the average combination store, and 125,000 for the average supercenter.[3] According to the managing director of Aldi for the UK and Ireland, Paul Foley, "We have fundamentally lower costs than the supermarkets. Rivals can't compete with us as long as they've got hundreds of different branded ranges to our single product offer."[4]

Wal-Mart has recently begun to reduce its total number of SKUs by up to 15 percent in its newly renovated stores. Wal-Mart reported that it has reduced the number of brands sold in its U.S. stores from close to 19,000 in 2007 to slightly more than 16,000 in 2010.[5] Remaining vendors will be asked to participate more in cooperative advertising programs with Wal-Mart. Wal-Mart hopes that with fewer products to manage and restock, its employees can spend more time in assisting customers. As an example, Wal-Mart will now stock four tape measures instead of 24. Wal-Mart has reported higher sales, faster inventory turnover, and higher levels of customer satisfaction in these remodeled stores.[6]

Supervalu plans to double the number of its Save-A-Lot stores from 1,197 in 2010 to 2,400 as of 2015. The average Save-A-Lot store contains 1,800 SKUs, about 5 percent of the total in an average supermarket. Like Aldi, about 80 percent of its goods consist of private label products, and it uses spartan fixtures, including cut-case displays. According to Save-A-Lot's president, Bill Shaner, "A typical grocer carries 100 types of mustard. We have just brown and yellow."[7]

Likewise, Walgreen Company has recently announced that it is reducing the types of superglues it stocks from 25 to 11, and Kroger has tested reducing its number of cereal varieties by 30 percent.[8] According to one report, firms like Walgreen, Wal-Mart, and Kroger, as well as a few of the other largest retailers, are expected to reduce their assortment of products by at least 15 percent.[9]

There is anecdotal, as well as research-based, evidence that some retailers can increase their sales productivity through decreasing the number of SKUs. A 35,000- to 40,000-square-foot supermarket in the United States stocks about 40,000 SKUs and generates sales per square foot of about $7 to $8 per week. In contrast, in the UK, the average supermarket of the same size stocks about one-half of the SKUs and generates weekly sales per square foot of about $14 to $15. It appears that "less is more."[10] Although consumers will always say they want more choice, this is often not the case. According to Todd Maute, a vice-president of Daymon Associates, a specialist in private label brand development and growth, "Over half of an average store's 30,000 SKUs are exactly the same. A national brand will come out with a new product, then the next brand, and the next; then private label versions of the product are launched."[11]

Tim Farmer, Costco's merchandising vice-president and general manager for consumer electronics, has stated, "If you go to a big-box store, you'll see 100 to 150 different TVs. You might find 10 to 20 32-inch LCDs alone." In comparison, Costco has five 32-inch panels that were modified for Costco to deliver the best quality and value. "That allows us to have the right product [in terms of panels, number of HDMI ports, and other features] at the right price."[12] If Costco can prosper with the sale of only five models of 32-inch televisions, one has to wonder what had driven some stores to stock dozens of brands, sizes, and varieties of each brand for such typically low-involvement products as yogurt, coffees, pasta sauces, undershirts, computer hard drives, and rechargeable batteries. Similarly, in 2008, Costco sold only 250 items from Kraft Foods' total product portfolio at its warehouse club locations.[13] Not all of these items were available in all Costco locations. Kraft Foods' product selection is enormous and contains hundreds of brands. Fifty of Kraft's brands generate annual sales in excess of $100 million.

In contrast, Best Buy's web site showed that the electronics chain stocked 28 32-inch high definition televisions (from 14 manufacturers), 28 standard-size digital cameras, 85 laptop computers, and 114 different cordless telephones (from 10 manufacturers). Of the

32-inch televisions offered by Best Buy, six were from Samsung and five were from LG.[14] Imagine the difficulty in a salesperson's learning and then explaining the characteristics of each model!

According to a 20th Century Fox Home Entertainment executive vice-president and general manager, "What the clubs do better than just about any other class of trade is the concept of editorial merchandising. You know that if that product is in the club, it's one of the best offerings in that segment, whether it's a DVD collection, classics collection, or a vacuum cleaner."[15] Because these firms offer few options in each product category, they have to be sure that their selection represents products that are bestsellers or that represent excellent value and quality.

Managerial Concerns Related to Product Proliferation

There are some major benefits that accrue to consumers when a retailer can successfully edit its selection to two or three choices in each product category. A carefully edited product selection reduces consumer decision-making times, as well as confusion and stress. An edited selection can also be viewed by consumers as a strong positive signal that the retailer works as the customer's purchasing agent in pre-selecting appropriate offerings among those offered by suppliers. Because three or four products would account for a large percent of a retailer's sales in a product category, customers could assume that the retailer has chosen these goods based on their features, quality, value, durability, customer service, and so on. Consumers can also assume that a retailer with an edited selection also needs to more carefully monitor consumer satisfaction due to the high level of sales and profit contribution of each SKU.

There are several key issues to minimizing product proliferation. Retailers need to understand that they receive no incremental profit through stocking an additional product offering that merely results in a shift in market share within a product category (with no accompanying sales increase). Retailers need to carefully assess whether offering multiple sizes, brands, colors, fabrics, and flavors will actually increase total sales in a given product category or simply result in constant sales being divided among additional goods. If the vast majority of a store's consumers believe that popular priced men's undershirts are a commodity, there is no need to stock five brands or product versions of this product.

Retailers also need to acknowledge that they receive little or no benefit from stocking a large assortment filled with unattractive items. In a research study composed of eight experiments, in five of these experiments, over half of the participants selected the smaller assortment when it was made up of attractive alternatives. The attractiveness of the assortment was more important to these consumers than the number of alternatives.[16]

Increasing assortments can also positively affect sales only within a limited target audience. For example, a wine connoisseur that inquires about a wine's vintage or appellation is a totally different consumer than a drinker of inexpensive table wine. A wine store may need to stock an extensive selection of French, California, and Italian wines for the connoisseur who views wine as a destination product but needs less of a selection for drinkers of table wines who view their wine purchase as a convenience product.

The process of reducing proliferation needs to be based on a retailer's no longer "being all things to all people"; classifying goods into destination, routine, seasonal, and convenience categories; studying relevant data from its point-of-sale system, as well as shopper data (generated from a retailer's loyalty program participants); and more effectively using micromarketing. Let's look at each of these strategies to reduce product proliferation.

There are several ways to limit the natural inclination of retailers seeking to "be all things to all people." Products that do not offer special value, are not truly distinctive, or do not increase total sales in a category should not be given shelf space regardless of trade discounts. An example of this strategy is the statement by Richard Galanti, Costco's executive vice-president and chief financial officer, that, "We don't have to carry three brands of an item."[17]

All of a retailer's inventory should be classified using a four-tier system: destination categories (where the retailer is the customer's first choice for specific products), routine categories (where the retailer is the preferred supplier of routine needs), seasonal categories (where specific items must be in large supply during peak seasonal periods), and convenience categories (where the retailer is the supplier of fill-in products).[18] Stores need to have deep assortments of destination categories. Thus, despite low overall SKUs, Trader Joe's has broad selections of coffees, frozen desserts, vitamins, dried fruits, packaged nuts, and olive oils since its consumers recognize these as destination categories for the chain. Likewise, Nordstrom seeks to be a destination store for shoes. A typical Nordstrom store can carry tens of thousands of pairs of shoes ranging in size from 4 to 14 for women and from 5 to 18 for men.[19] It carries many half-sizes to enable consumers to get better-fitting shoes. In contrast, Nordstrom stores can have limited assortments for convenience categories.

Retailers need to resist the temptation to ask customers if more variety is preferable. Too many consumers will mistakenly argue that choice is a good thing. And although consumers will express concern when one of their favorite items has been discontinued, many will simply purchase a substitute item from the same retailer. Instead of using consumer questionnaires, assortment planners should gather and analyze a variety of data from a retailer's point-of-sale system and financial data (such as sales per square foot, gross margin, GMROI, gross profit per square foot, and inventory turnover), as well as shopper data (generated from a retailer's loyalty program participants and other sources). Field experiments can also help determine the role of increased assortments on a product category's total sales. The time period studied should be long enough to determine the impact of reduced assortment over several buying periods for an item. This assures that a consumer's stocking up on a special purchase does not artificially indicate a real change in behavior.

Retailers also need to be careful to make sure that they are not overly aggressive in pruning products. After cutting selections of many slow-selling products (ranging from freezer bags to $1 packages of brown rice), Wal-Mart recently began to add back about 300 previously eliminated items when it discovered that some discontinued items, like the dollar bag of rice, were destination items for a portion of its customers. After discovering that Wal-Mart no longer stocked their favorite items, these customers did their weekly shopping elsewhere.[20]

As an example of the process to reduce proliferation, L.L.Bean hired two merchandising executives to go through its catalogs to search for redundant merchandise. As a result of their analysis, polo knit shirts are no longer sold in 10 different varieties, ranging from cotton to CoolMax.[21] L.L.Bean was also able to reduce its number of vendors supplying knitted products from 60 to 6 vendors as part of this review process. L.L.Bean found that the direct benefits of reducing its product offerings aside from cost reductions due to better negotiating ability included improved quality control through its more frequent visits to suppliers' factories, as well as more reliable delivery times due to improved communications with suppliers.[22] By reducing the number of vendors, L.L.Bean has also been able to commit more resources not only to product quality, but also to ensuring that factory conditions were acceptable to the retailer.[23]

Retailers can also utilize micromarketing programs that purposely varies selection by store or geographic region. Best Buy, as part of its customer-centricity strategy, categorizes each of its more than 900 stores into customer segments. Its "Barry" segment is a young professional male, "Russ" is a young entertainment enthusiast, "Jill" customers are upscale suburban moms, and "Ray" is a married middle-class male. The fifth segment is small business owners. Best Buy then relates the product assortment and availability to services in each of its stores based on the representation of each segment. Stores with high concentrations of Jill customers may have inexpensive computers for children, whereas stores with high percentages of Russ customers have high proportions of high-end elaborate home entertainment systems.

To retailers, product proliferation has five major disadvantages, as follows:

- The additional costs associated with pricing, record keeping, and carrying additional inventory
- Category management issues
- Stockout concerns
- Reduced overall sales levels
- Consumer confusion/stress concerns

The added costs associated with product proliferation include ordering costs, store rent, utilities, warehousing expenses, item pricing-related costs, the loss of quantity discounts, and the reduced productivity due to ordering small quantities from a multitude of suppliers. Category management issues relate to space allocation decision making, as well as the time required to manage multiple products that consumers may view as direct substitutes for one another. An additional issue is the increased chance of stockouts due to the need to stock large inventories of goods with slow sales levels (to preserve target service levels). As required service levels increase from 90 percent to 95 percent, the additional inventory needed to support this service level rises exponentially.[24] There has also been some research to suggest that sales can increase when consumers have less choice. The consumer confusion issue addresses the difficulty consumers have in first determining what to purchase and in then attempting to locate specific items on a store's shelves (see Figure 3.1).

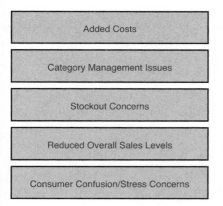

Figure 3.1   Managerial concerns associated with product proliferation

Added Costs Associated with Product Proliferation

Table 3.1 shows that since 1994, the median supermarket size has increased from 35,100 square feet to 46,755 square feet (an increase of 33.2 percent). Some stores have increased in size through adding adjacent space; in other instances, larger supermarkets were built and smaller ones then closed. Although part of the increase in space requirements can be attributed to new departments and services (such as in-store photo processing, pharmacies, florists, and so on), the increase could have been drastically reduced or even eliminated due to scaling down the number of brands and the varieties within each brand that a store stocks.

TABLE 3.1   Median Supermarket Size by Year

Year	Median Size (Square Feet)	Index Number
1994	35,100	100.0
1995	37,200	106.0
1996	38,600	110.0
1997	39,260	111.9
1998	40,483	115.3
1999	44,843	127.8
2000	44,600	127.0

TABLE 3.1   Median Supermarket Size by Year (continued)

Year	Median Size (Square Feet)	Index Number
2001	44,000	125.4
2002	44,000	125.4
2003	44,000	125.4
2004	45,661	130.1
2005	48,058	136.9
2006	48,750	138.9
2007	47,500	135.3
2008	46,755	133.2

Source: "Key Industry Food Marketing Facts," *Food Marketing Industry Information Service* (May 2009).

Let's now look at some of the specific costs associated with product proliferation. The Federal Trade Commission (FTC), in its "Slotting Fees in the Retail Grocery Industry" report, examined the additional costs of stocking a new product in five food categories: fresh bread, hot dogs, ice cream and frozen novelties, shelf-stable pasta, and shelf-stable salad dressing. One regional grocery store chain that responded to the FTC survey estimated the following costs to introducing a new product:

- 10 to 20 people needed to manage shelf space for all stores in a given region.
- $1,000 in labor to stock the item in all shelves in a region.
- $1,200 to move the item into its regional distribution center, because stocking one item could mean moving 30 to 40 products around in a warehouse.
- $600 to add the new item into the retailer's computer systems and ordering and accounting programs.[25]

The total $2,800 for these expenses does not include the 10 to 20 people needed to manage shelf space in a given region. Assuming the shelf management personnel average $35,000 per year including fringe benefits, the total costs to this chain exceed $350,000 (and could even exceed $700,000 if 20 people are required and their salaries and fringes exceed $35,000). These expenses include only five food categories for a regional chain.

According to Milton Merl, a consultant with Accenture Marketing Science, the average shelf facing in a store (depending on part of the country and inventory turnover) costs between $5 and $10 a year to manage. These figures include inventory carrying costs and store labor, but do not include space-related costs such as increased occupancy costs. Says Merl, "The more you add variety, the more fragmented or inefficient the store becomes. We do not need single packs of paper towels in 15 different colors."[26] Assuming that the average supermarket has 40,000 SKUs and grocers like Stew Leonard's and Trader Joe's have 2,000 SKUs, and that each SKU has two shelf facings, the average supermarket has 76,000 additional shelf facings at $7 each; this equals an added expense of $512,000 for store labor and inventory carrying costs. In addition to these costs, the increased number of SKUs also makes it more difficult and more costly to promote products, plan assortments, and to track the sales and inventory levels for all of a retailer's products.

Managing significantly fewer SKUs also means that a retailer's IT and logistics systems can be far simpler and less costly than at a traditional supermarket with 40,000 SKUs. It can also employ fewer buyers. For example, Aldi has 25 buyers in the UK, where its competitors have hundreds.[27] Lower assortments also enable vendors to be more efficient at making products. Manufacturers can concentrate on a few key models with long production runs, have lower setup costs, and generate economies in purchasing raw materials and parts. These savings can be passed onto retailers through lower costs. In turn, the retailers can reduce prices to their final consumers. Herman Miller, a furniture company, is now selling Costco just two of the hundreds of configurations of home-office chairs it produces. According to a Herman Miller spokesperson, "The limited SKUs allow us to be very efficient with our production."[28]

Category Management Issues Associated with Product Proliferation

Product proliferation also causes havoc with category management issues. Due to extreme proliferation, shelf space for a retailer's best-selling products may be reduced due to lack of shelf space for these items and the tying up of equity on slow-moving items. Productivity is also reduced due to increased spoilage for slow-moving perishables and seasonal items.

In contrast, having relatively few products to manage enables a buyer to more effectively monitor the product's sales, competitive developments, special promotions, and crises (such as product recalls or shortages). According to a Costco executive, "If a buyer had to manage a category of thousands and thousands of products, each product wouldn't get the same level of scrutiny that an item does in one of our warehouses. That's simply because our buyers have such a limited number of products that they're responsible for, and so each product receives a tremendous amount of scrutiny."[29]

Stockout Concerns Associated with Product Proliferation

With a fixed amount of space and limited funds for inventory, retailers need to balance variety, depth of assortment, and levels of in-stock availability. This involves trade-offs among these three variables. To conserve inventory, slow-selling items may have to have lower service levels than fast-selling goods. With high levels of product proliferation, a retailer may also have to reduce service levels on all goods, increasing the chance of stockouts on better-selling items. Mark A. Boyer, a perishables category management specialist, notes that over-assortments can also lead to out-of-stocks. Boyer states that if a retailer's out-of-stocks in a category is "...greater than 10 percent, chances are high that over-assortment is a big part of the problem."[30]

The cost of stockouts in terms of lost sales can be very high. One study found that while 34 percent of consumers switched brands as the result of a stockout, 23 percent postponed their purchase, 19 percent went to another retailer, and 18 percent switched items.[31] Thus, a retailer can lose more than 40 percent of its sales (as a result of consumer-postponed purchases and purchasing the good at another retailer).

Reduced Overall Sales Levels Due to Product Proliferation

Some studies suggest paradoxically that less consumer choice can also yield higher sales or profits. Two researchers analyzed data from an experiment involving an online grocer in which 94 percent of the categories offered by the grocer experienced drastic cuts in the number of SKUs due to the retailer's having eliminated slow-selling products. The researchers found that category sales increased as a result of the reduced selection. In total, sales increased an average of 11 percent across the 42 categories studied. Sales rose in more than two-thirds of these categories, nearly half of which experienced an increase of 10 percent or more. Among the households that were loyal to a single brand, size, or brand-size combination that was eliminated, nearly half continued purchasing within the same category.[32]

Similarly, a study conducted by ACNielsen found that not only did consumers have no complaints when 7 percent to 10 percent of the SKUs in various categories were removed, but also the reduced choice improved a category's performance.[33] Procter & Gamble recently reduced the number of soap and skin care offerings by one-third at one retailer and the number of detergents and other fabric care products by 20 percent at another chain. Following the reductions in SKUs, sales grew in each category. According to a Procter & Gamble spokesperson, "In the skin care example, shoppers reported they felt that they had more choices because the selection on the shelf was clearer."[34]

According to Milton Merl, the impact of reduction in a product's selection on sales depends on the product category. In product categories such as skin care and cosmetics, sales can drop by 50 percent if the store doesn't stock a particular brand. However, in other categories such as chilled juice, only about 2 percent of the consumer volume is loyal or exclusive to the brand. In the chilled juice category, consumers are willing to switch within the brand, among the pulp versus no-pulp option, and within the size. Using Nielsen data, Merl found that if a segment has 40 items, the 10 best-selling items are always critical. If these items are eliminated, half of the volume in that category is lost. Beyond these items, most items do not result in additional sales.[35]

Consumer Confusion/Stress Concerns Associated with Product Proliferation

A number of industry reports, as well as academic studies, suggest that product proliferation generates consumer confusion and stress. Because of product proliferation, consumers may find it more difficult to locate specific items, to effectively differentiate among brands, and to assess a product's benefits relative to a retailer's other offerings. One academic study argues that large assortments can be especially confusing for consumers who are uncertain of their preferences.[36] Many consumers have also complained about the complexity of promotional offers or about too much advertising caused by product proliferation.[37] Often, stores have become unnecessarily cluttered as a result of product proliferation. This cluttered appearance not only makes it more difficult for consumers to find items, but also can result in a store's having a downscale image. A *Harvard Business Review* article states that even before the current recession, many consumers felt overwhelmed by the profusion of choices. The authors of the article argue that an appropriate response to this perception is the retailer's use of edited retailing (offering limited collections of coordinated products).[38]

A large body of research suggests that consumers can have difficulty managing complex choices. Many of these studies argue that as the attractiveness of alternatives increases, individuals experience conflict that causes them to then defer decision making, search for additional alternatives, choose a default option, or decide not to purchase.[39] None of these alternatives are desirable from a business perspective. One research study found that megastores can produce "megaconfusion" for consumers, leading consumers to walk away without making any choice at all.[40] Product proliferation can also be a major burden for sales personnel who need to better understand and explain differences between alternatives to consumers.[41]

In a second study, two researchers examined the notion that there are psychologically manageable, as well as psychologically excessive, numbers of choices.[42] The researchers used a field experiment in an upscale supermarket setting with two levels of selection of jams: 24 versus 6. Although consumers who were subject to the 24-item selection option were more attracted to the booth, only 3 percent of them purchased one of these products (versus nearly 30 percent of those in the 6-product choice group).

In a third study, researchers examined the impact of SKU reduction on store choice. This field-based study found that as long as favorite products were available and shelf space remained constant, consumers' assortment perceptions were unaffected by moderate reductions in SKUs. Consumers also reported that stores with fewer SKUs were easier to shop at.[43]

A fourth study suggests that too much choice within a brand can be detrimental.[44] Although the number of brands offered as part of an assortment has a positive effect on store choice for most households, the number of SKUs per brand, the number of sizes per brand, and the proportion of private brands have a negative effect on store choice. According to this study's author, "If retail assortments can be reduced without eliminating brands, the associated reductions in operating costs and out-of-stocks could make SKU reduction an effective and profitable strategy."[45]

A fifth study found that consumers are likely to prefer smaller assortments over larger assortments when both of these assortments are made up of attractive products. Smaller assortments are preferred by consumers when the choice set is comprised of attractive items, whereas larger assortments are preferred when the options are less attractive.[46] The authors of this study argue that in cases where the assortments offered are very attractive, the marginal benefit of a larger assortment is less than when the assortments are not that attractive.

Causes of Product Proliferation

There are a number of causes of product proliferation. Common causes of proliferation include incorrect assumptions by retail executives, trade promotions and discounts, and slotting fee revenues. The first cause can be categorized as demand-sided because it seeks to please as many consumers as possible with a store's variety and assortment. The last two causes are supply-sided, as they are generated by vendor incentives (see Figure 3.2). A careful analysis of these causes should better enable retailers to resist the urge to unnecessarily expand consumer choice. Let's now look at each of these causes.

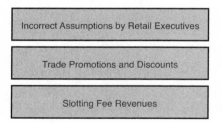

Incorrect Assumptions by Retail Executives

Trade Promotions and Discounts

Slotting Fee Revenues

Figure 3.2   The causes of product proliferation

Incorrect Assumptions by Retail Executives

There are a number of misleading assumptions by retail managers that can lead to product proliferation. These demand-sided orientations assume that increased selection will result in increased sales. Some retail managers erroneously seek to increase store sales and shopper loyalty through having a larger selection than their competitors. In this assumption, called "being all things to all people," executives seek to cater to all market segments. For grocers, these segments can include ethnic, economical, gourmet, natural/organic, private label, convenience (quick-and-easy-to-prepare foods), prepare from scratch, healthy (low salt/low cholesterol/low fat), and diet segments. For clothing-based retailers, these segments can include classic shoppers and fashion-forward shoppers. Retailers need to acknowledge that they cannot effectively compete in all product categories. In doing so, an appliance retailer should realize that it should defer sales of $1,000 espresso machines and $400 coffee grinders to specialty stores and web-based merchants and that selling coffee beans is not an area where it has a competitive advantage. According to Milton Merl, "Despite original ECR research demonstrating that categories with less variety are perceived to have more variety, there still remains a fear factor on the part of the buyer that says, 'If I don't have every conceivable choice, I'll turn the consumer off.'"[47]

Some managers plan and then keep excessive assortments of poor-selling products out of concern for losing shoppers to other stores. In other cases, retailers have expanded their selection of private label products too aggressively. Retailers clearly do not need a private label product in every major product category. One report suggests that while the average supermarket has 2,000 private label SKUs, not all offer superior price/value relationships when compared with national brands.[48]

Trade Promotions and Discounts

Trade promotions and discounts and slotting fees are supply-sided in that they can result in extreme instances of product proliferation due to the lure of supplier incentives. Trade promotions and discounts payments that can significantly increase a store's assortment include display fees (for an end-cap position that gives a product

additional visibility), cooperative advertising allowances (that encourage retailers to promote an item), trade deals (that typically require
that a specific product be placed on sale a specific number of times in
a yearly period), in-store demonstration allowances, volume incentives, and free product discounts.

One estimate is that trade dollars comprise about 7.5 percent of
U.S. retailers' revenues—about two times retailers' pre-tax income.[49]
According to Joel Kozlak, CEO of Thomson Foods in Duluth, "Like
everyone else, I've heard that retailers make more money off these
fees than they do off groceries."[50] Many of these trade discounts are
paid as an upfront bonus or as an off-invoice deduction on the price
of certain goods if certain sales targets are met. Because these sales
targets are based on sales to the warehouse (not sales to the final consumer), trade promotions can result in poor sales performance on a
store level.[51]

According to one source, "Retailers are hooked on the heroin of
this promotional money, and even the few who say they need to wean
themselves from these payments know it is a difficult and arduous
process. Manufacturers would love to find a way to reduce these payments...but, on the other hand, they're used to a system that allows
them to virtually buy real estate in the store."[52]

The presence of trade promotions and discounts, as well as slotting fees, can blur the judgment of stores to buy those products with
large incentives; these are not necessarily the products desired by
consumers. Glen Terbeck, a former Andersen consultant, said, "I am
afraid the retailers for the most part have abdicated the role of
'agents' for their shoppers to the manufacturers because of the significant trade dollars involved. Shoppers today need agents to cut
through the million items active in the market, and present to them
the ones that are appropriate for their needs and likes. Retailers need
to be marketers and merchants, not distributors."[53] Adds a managing
director of 7-Eleven, Inc., "They [large publicly held supermarkets]
are addicted to 'back-door money' such as listing fees, space rentals,

exclusivity agreements, and the like, all of which are obstacles to giving the customer what he/she truly wants."[54]

Slotting Fee Revenues

As with trade promotions and discounts, retailers receive large sums of money from vendors as a result of slotting fees. Through slotting fees, suppliers guarantee shelf space for new products. Slotting fees may also include pay-to-stay fees (that guarantee shelf space for a specific time period for a new product) and failure fees (that guarantee that a manufacturer will compensate a supermarket operator for unsold inventory). In some instances, slotting fees take the format of covering a supermarket's costs for rearranging shelf space and revising its inventory system. Slotting fees can also be required by retailers as payment for in-store allotment, shelf position, or exclusivity for existing brands. Although slotting fees are common in supermarkets, other retail formats require similar payments.[55]

According to Milton Merl, "Quite simply, too many antiquated business models are driving how we look at categories today. Slotting fees make retailers money, period. While what you see is an assortment that may change, it is still too big in most cases to run optimally. Not only are retailers being paid to take product in, they are being rewarded on volume, both of which are short-term strategies that don't take into account the bigger picture."[56]

A major concern of supermarkets accepting trade discounts and promotions, as well as slotting fees, is that these manufacturers' strategies may interfere with a retailer's having the proper mix of goods. One retail analyst has argued that although trade discounts and promotions, as well as slotting fees, provide short-term profits, they may be at the expense of long-term gains. He further states the need for conventional supermarkets to work on a coordinated partnership basis with manufacturers without any fees.[57]

Later on in this chapter, we see that Aldi, Costco, Trader Joe's, and Whole Foods all do not require or accept slotting fees from their vendors. According to one vendor, "They [Whole Foods] could demand considerably more sums of money in terms of slotting and get it, so they are not being pigs." Others agree that Whole Foods is not quick to slap on fees or charges at every turn. Getting into a Whole Foods is a big deal for a natural foods vendor. A single Whole Foods can often be expected to turn 15 times the volume on a SKU versus a typical Jewel or Safeway.[58] Wal-Mart also does not demand or accept slotting fees. Instead, Wal-Mart insists on more favorable prices to propel its successful everyday low-pricing strategy.

Reducing Product Proliferation: The Experience of Aldi, Costco, Stew Leonard's, and Trader Joe's

Table 3.2 shows average sales per SKU for four of the benchmark firms (Aldi, Costco, Stew Leonard's, and Trader Joe's), as well as other retailers. This table uses the average number of SKUs per market since the total SKUs per chain is not available. This table is conservative in that most supermarkets vary the selection to reflect local and regional differences. Average sales per SKU are smaller than indicated to the extent that micromarketing is used by each chain. One would expect that smaller chains like Stew Leonard's would not require micromarketing to the extent of chains with larger regional coverage.

TABLE 3.2   Sales per SKU for Selected Chains (2008 Data Unless Otherwise Indicated)

Retail Chain	U.S. Net Sales	Average Number of SKUs per Unit	Average Sales per SKU
Aldi (2009)	$7.0 billion	1,400	$5.0 million
Costco (global 2009)	$69.9 billion	3,800	$18.4 million
Stew Leonard's	$376 million	2,000	$188,000
Trader Joe's	$7.2 billion	2,500–3,000	$2.4–$2.9 million

TABLE 3.2   Sales per SKU for Selected Chains (2008 Data Unless Otherwise Indicated) (continued)

Retail Chain	U.S. Net Sales	Average Number of SKUs per Unit	Average Sales per SKU
Kroger (2010)	$76.7 billion	30,000–52,000	$1.5–$2.6 million
Safeway (2009)	$40.8 billion	30,000–52,000	$785,000–$1.4 million
Supervalu (2009)	$44.5 billion	30,000–52,000	$856,000–$1.5 million
Winn Dixie	$7.4 billion	30,000–52,000	$142,000–$247,000

This table assumes that Kroger, Safeway, Supervalu, and Winn Dixie have between 30,000 and 52,000 SKUs per supermarket.

The average sales per SKU in this table are conservative because large supermarkets typically manage more than 30,000–52,000 SKUs to be able to reflect local and regional differences in buyer preferences.

Table 3.2 shows that Stew Leonard's sales per SKU average $188,000. With only four stores, Stew Leonard's small number of SKUs gives it the same bargaining power as Winn-Dixie, a chain with revenues close to 20 times higher! Sales per SKU at Costco equal $18.4 million, giving Costco considerable bargaining power with its suppliers.

Table 3.3 shows that stores with comparatively few SKUs generally have high average sales per square foot. Costco has 3,800 SKUs in its average store and sales per square foot of $929 (excluding revenues from membership fees). And both Trader Joe's and Stew Leonard's have between 2,000 and 3,000 SKUs in their average store, yet have sales per square foot in excess of $1,300. (An exception is Wegmans, with 70,000 SKUs in its average store, and sales per square foot of $750). These numbers are high in comparison to the $500 sales per square foot figure for the average supermarket.

TABLE 3.3   Sales per Square Foot of Selected Food Chains and
Average Number of SKUs Per Unit (2008 Data Unless Otherwise
Noted)

Retail Chain	Sales per Square Foot of Selling Space	Average Number of SKUs per Unit
Aldi	$620 est.	1,400
Costco (2009 global data)	$929 (1)	3,800
Publix (2009)	$517	NA
Stew Leonard's	$1,534–$3,750 est.	2,000
Trader Joe's	$1,750	2,500–3,000
Wegmans	$750	70,000
Whole Foods (2009 global data)	$761	NA
Average supermarket	$500	46,852
(1) Revenues exclude membership fees		

Source: "Supermarket Facts," Food Marketing Institute (2008); and author's estimates and
calculations.

The benchmarked retailers are not the only ones looking to
reduce their product assortments. Wal-Mart is experimenting with its
new Marketside store format in Phoenix. These 15,000-square-foot
stores carry 5,000 to 7,000 SKUs. Safeway has opened several of its
The Market stores that stock only 15 percent of the SKUs found in
traditional supermarkets. Half of these SKUs consist of fresh produce, meats, cheese, and prepared foods. Tesco is also using a 10,000-
square-foot format in its Fresh & Easy units with much fewer SKUs
than a typical supermarket.[59]

In the past year, Walgreen reduced the variety of goods in its
remodeled stores from 22,000 to about 18,000 SKUs. In some
departments, like paper goods, the number of SKUs dropped by 30
percent. Despite the reduction in inventory, sales of paper goods
increased. According to Walgreen's vice-president of merchandising,
the increase in sales is due to the paper goods department now being

less confusing to shoppers. An additional benefit of the reduction in SKUs is that Walgreen stores now look much less cluttered due to the lowering of shelf height from 78 inches to 66 inches.[60]

An alternative way of offering increased variety and assortment for retailers, while reducing inventory costs, is drop shipping. In drop shipping, retailers pass on all fulfillment responsibilities to resellers or third parties. Retailers can use drop shipping to increase the sales of specialty items that may have very low inventory turnover. In instances where a consumer wants to inspect a good before purchase, such as a mattress or jewelry, the retailer may stock selected samples for inspection. Magniflex, a maker of European luxury mattresses, offers drop shipping to its U.S.-based dealers. Through its drop-shipping program, retailers can sell mattresses with minimal inventory on hand. The program enables Magniflex to expand its distribution throughout the United States. Costco is an example of a retailer that uses drop shipping. Close to 70 percent of items sold online by Costco are shipped from its suppliers directly to the customer.[61] As with any merchandise, a retailer needs to work out how returns are handled with drop shipping.

Let's now look at how these successful retailers have reduced their store assortment and variety while keeping store productivity at such high levels.

Aldi

Although the average U.S. Aldi outlet is about 17,000 square feet, it stocks 1,300 to 1,400 items. Aldi typically stocks a single brand (95 percent of its sales are its own private label goods) in a single size offering for most products, such as Casa Mamita—its own private label brand of salsa. The selection is also limited for many items. Among ketchups, Aldi sells only one variety, versus Tesco that sells 24.[62] Jason Hart, the president of Aldi's U.S. division, states that "Products have to earn their place on the shelves here because real estate is so precious. If items don't perform, you've got to move it out and replace it with something new."[63] Despite its small number of SKUs, Aldi is careful to have a broad variety. According to an Aldi corporate spokesperson, customers can find 90 percent of their average weekly shopping list at Aldi.[64]

Costco

Part of Costco's genius is the simplicity of its inventory management system. Although a typical supermarket may stock between 30,000 and 53,000 SKUs and a Wal-Mart supercenter may stock over 150,000 items, Costco stocks 3,800 SKUs (the items stocked may vary region to region).[65] Costco's selection also compares favorably with other warehouse clubs such as BJs, which has 7,000 active SKUs.[66] About 3,000 of Costco's SKUs can be found on the selling floor on a day-to-day basis. The balance are treasure hunt items, such as one-time offerings on Coach pocketbooks, plasma televisions, Waterford crystal, and $5,000 necklaces that vary from time to time to generate consumer excitement.[67]

Managing 3,800 items simplifies stock planning; lower inventory levels also reduce buying, handling, and inventory storage costs. Due to its limited selection, Costco's goods have extremely high inventory turnover—14.1 times in its 2009 fiscal year. By narrowing its selections, Costco also has huge sales for each item stocked. This enables Costco to get deeper discounts from its suppliers. Quite simply, no other retailer can deliver the volume Costco does—an average of $18.4 million per SKU in fiscal year 2009. An additional benefit of high turnover is that Costco's inventory is fresh. According to a supplier, "Costco doesn't sell anything that doesn't have an incredibly high turn.... Because it turns so frequently, the opportunity for the meat to stay fresh is very good."[68]

A typical Costco stocks perhaps just four toothpaste brands, whereas a Wal-Mart may carry 60 sizes and brands of toothpaste. According to Costco's CEO, James Sinegal, "We carry a 325 bottle of Advil for $15.25. Lots of customers don't want to buy 325. If you had ten customers come in to buy Advil, how many are not going to buy any because you just have one size? Maybe one or two. We refer to that as the intelligent loss of sales. We are prepared to give up that one customer. But if we had four or five sizes of Advil, as grocery stores do, it would make our business more difficult to manage. Our business can only succeed if we are efficient. You can't go on selling at these margins if you are not."[69]

Costco also uses its limited selection model on its web site, which has only 3,500 items. In contrast, Wal-Mart's web site has over 1 million SKUs, and Sears' site features 150,000 items. According to Ginnie Roeglin, a senior vice-president of E-commerce at Costco, "We will never have hundreds of thousands of SKUs. We have the same discipline online as we do in the warehouse, and you cannot really be the best at what you are doing if you have too much to manage. Others think of it as virtual inventory, so what's the harm, just throw it on the web site.[70] When Costco's chief financial officer, Richard Galanti, was asked how Costco manages to limit its SKUs, he responded that the strict adherence to SKU counts at Costco starts right at the top, with CEO James Sinegal.[71]

Stew Leonard's

Like Costco, Stew Leonard's usually stocks a limited selection of each item, buys directly from manufacturers in huge quantities, and then passes the savings onto its customers. Stew Leonard's stocks only 15–20 different cereal choices as compared with 100 in a typical supermarket. And as with Costco, Stew Leonard's customers are more than happy to accept the trade-off of lower prices and less confusion at the expense of less choice.

To restrict inventory, Stew Leonard's chooses its products based on freshness, quality, and value. And unlike competitors that have extensive offerings of private brands, Stew Leonard's will offer only private labels when they provide better quality and value. For example, when Stew Leonard's was unsuccessful with its private brand cola-based beverages and shaving cream, it simply discontinued these lines.

The advantage of restricted selections can be seen in the high quantities of each item sold. Each year, Stew Leonard's sells 540,000 pounds of butter, 5 million half-gallons of milk, and 1.5 million half-gallons of orange juice.[72] This provides Stew Leonard's with considerable bargaining power with vendors.

Trader Joe's

Because the typical Trader Joe's has approximately 2,500 to 3,000 items, Trader Joe's stores can average 6,000 to 12,000 square feet in size; this is one-sixth the size of the average supermarket. The combination of small facilities and lower selection means that Trader Joe's needs to continually replace items that don't sell well. Let's look at some of the strategies used by Trader Joe's to limit proliferation:

- Like Costco and Stew Leonard's, Trader Joe's keeps its sections narrowly focused by choosing among the bestsellers from its product lines.
- Trader Joe's does not charge stocking fees or slotting allowances to suppliers. It also does not require special promotional support. Taste and delivery execution are more important to Trader Joe's than slotting fees and trade discounts.
- Trader Joe's openly acknowledges that it cannot compete with traditional supermarkets in meats and fresh produce. Because its stores do not have an on-site butcher, baker, or produce person, most meats, breads, and produce are only available in prepackaged varieties. There is also no full-service deli counter at Trader Joe's.
- Although Trader Joe's is extremely successful in specialty frozen foods—particularly ethnic items—it does not sell products such as Cheerios, Coca-Cola, or Bounty towels that are sold everywhere.

Takeaway Points

- Retailers need to recognize that product proliferation raises their operating costs by virtue of additional rent; store labor; air conditioning, heating, and ventilating; and inventory costs. Proliferation also contributes to consumer confusion and stress. There is some evidence that consumer sales may increase, rather than decrease, as a result of reduced assortments. This may be due to increased ease of locating items, as well as reduced consumer confusion.

- Reduced selection can drastically increase a retailer's bargaining power with a single vendor. An additional benefit of reduced selection is that it focuses management's attention on the store's best-selling brands and sizes.

- In the short run, retailers should examine instances of extreme product proliferation and determine the impact on category sales of eliminating marginal products. In the long run, less extreme instances of product proliferation should be determined and reviewed.

- In addition to reviewing national brands, retailers also need to review the selection of their private label products. Like national brands, private label products that do not offer special value, distinctiveness, or high quality should be targeted for pruning.

- All mass market retailers need to acknowledge that they cannot effectively compete in all product categories. Buying committees need to restrict the "being-all-things-to-all-people" inclination. The committees also need to realize that all retailers must forfeit some sales in the quest to minimize product proliferation.

- In some situations, a retailer can gain many of the benefits associated with lower SKUs without loss of sales through arranging of drop shipping directly from manufacturers of slow-selling specialty items. Chain retailers can also stock slow-selling but important items in their central or regional warehouse and ship these items to stores or customers based upon their specific orders.

- Total category sales levels need to be monitored through field experiments to determine the value of increased selections on total category sales.

- Chain retailers should utilize micromarketing programs that purposely vary selection by store or geographic region. Micromarketing results in a store's better matching a community's needs without increasing the total SKUs offered.

- A major issue that retailers must consider is how consumers shop for a given category of merchandise in a specific store. For example, a given brand, flavor, and size can be viewed as so important among consumers that they would shop at another store if the retailer did not stock it. On the other hand, consumer loyalty for some products is so low that they will readily accept a substitute product. All goods should be classified using a four-tier system: destination categories (where the retailer is the customer's first choice for specific products), routine categories (where the retailer is the preferred supplier of routine needs), seasonal categories (where specific items must be in large supply only during peak seasonal periods), and convenience categories (where the retailer is the supplier of fill-in products).

- Trade promotions and discounts and slotting fees are supply-sided in that they result in product proliferation due to the lure of supplier incentives. One way to limit the impact of these promotions is for buying committees to realize that their role is as a "purchasing agent" for their final customers, not as a "selling agent" for their vendors. Products that do not offer special value, are not distinctive, and that do not increase total sales in a category should not be given shelf space regardless of slotting fees, promotional, and trade discounts.

Endnotes

1. Mary Brett Whitfield, "Top Nine Trends for 2009," *Retail Perspectives* (March 2009), pp. 1–3.

2. Marianne Wilson, "No-Frills Shopping Gains Ground," *Chain Store Age* (March 2009), pp. 24–26.

3. Joseph Agnese, *Standard & Poor's Industry Surveys: Supermarkets & Drugstores* (July 26, 2007), p. 15.

4. "Taking on Tesco," *The Grocer* (July 5, 2008), p. 38.

5. "Wal-Mart Cuts Back 12% of Brands," *PLMA E-Scanner* (May 2010), http://plma.com/escanner/may2010.html, as of June 7, 2010.

6. Matthew Boyle, "Wal-Mart's Magic Moment," *Business Week* (June 15, 2009), pp. 51–53.

7. Miguel Bustillo and Timothy W. Martin, "Beyond the Big Box: Wal-Mart Thinks Smaller," *Wall Street Journal* (April 28, 2010), p. B1.

8. Bob Phibbs, "Opinion: Retailers Need to Cut Their SKUs," www.retailcustomerexperience.com (July 9, 2009), as of July 21, 2009.

9. Bob Phibbs, "Opinion: Retailers Need to Cut Their SKUs," www.retailcustomerexperience.com (July 9, 2009), as of July 21, 2009.

10. Neil Currie, "Do Supermarkets Have a Future?" *Progressive Grocer* (April 15, 2005), pp. 62–79.

11. Stephen Dowdell and Joseph Tarnowski, "Going Public with Private Label," *Progressive Grocer* (June 1, 2006), pp. 34–36.

12. Alan Wolf, "Costco Cops Best National Retailer Kudos," *Twice* (October 8, 2007), p. 18.

13. David Sterrett, "Kraft Not Getting VIP Treatment; Grocery-Aisle Giant Holds Only Bit-Player Status at Club Stores," *Crain's Chicago Business* (January 12, 2009), p. 3.

14. www.bestbuy.com, as of June 9, 2009.

15. Jennifer Netherby, "Top Three Wholesale Clubs Celebrate 25 Years," *Video Business* (May 26, 2008), pp. 19–20.

16. Alexander Cherbev and Ryan Hamilton, "Assortment Size and Option Attractiveness in Consumer Choice Among Retailers," *Journal of Marketing Research* (June 2009), pp. 410–420.

17. Elliot Zwebach, "Costco Gets Tough on Suppliers," *Supermarket News* (March 9, 2009), p. 6.

18. Nektina Efthymiou, "Shelved Cases," *Marketing Week* (November 27, 2003), pp. 43–44.

19. Robert Spector and Patrick McCarthy, *The Nordstrom Way to Customer Service Excellence* (Hoboken, NJ: John Wiley & Sons, Inc, 2005), p. 73.

20. Marina Strauss, "In Store Aisles, Less Is More But Customers Can Still Be Particular," *Globe and Mail* (May 18, 2010), www.theglobeandmail.com/, as of June 6, 2010.

21. Sherri Day, "L.L.Bean Tries to Escape the Mail-Order Wilderness," *New York Times* (August 27, 2002).

22. Leon Gorman, *L.L.Bean: The Making of an American Icon* (Boston, MA: Harvard Business School Press, 2006), p. 263.

23. Correspondence from Carolyn Beem, Manager, Public Affairs, L.L.Bean, June 8, 2009.

24. Murali K. Mantrala, Michael Levy, Barbara E. Kahn, Edward J. Fox, Peter Gaidarev, Bill Dankworth, and Denish Shah, "Why Is Assortment Planning So Difficult for Retailers? A Framework and Research Agenda," *Journal of Retailing*, Vol. 85, No. 1 (2009), pp. 71–83.

25. Leonard Klie, "FTC: Slotting Fees Vary Among Product Categories," *Frozen Food Age* 52/6 (January 2004).

26. "The Science of Efficient Assortment," *Grocery Headquarters* (July 2000), pp. 57–60.

27. James Hall, "The Rise and Rise of the Discount King," *The Sunday Telegraph* (London) (August 31, 2008), p. 7.

28. Jena McGregor, "Costco's Artful Discounts," *Business Week* (October 9, 2008).

29. Paul Latham, "Crazy for Costco," *The Hub* (November/December 2007), pp. 19–24.

30. Mark A. Boyer, "Lost in SKUs," *Progressive Grocer* (May 1, 2006), pp. 118–121.

31. Peter C. Verhoef and Laurens M. Sloot, "Out of Stock: Reactions, Antecedents, Management Solutions, and a Future Perspective," in *Retailing in the 21st Century: Current and Emerging Trends*, Manfred Kraft and Murali K. Mantrala, eds. (Berlin/Heidelberg/New York: Springer, 2006).

32. Peter Boatwright and Joseph C. Nunes, "Reducing Assortment: An Attribute-Based Approach," *Journal of Marketing*, Vol. 65 (July 2001), pp. 50–63.

33. Stephen Dowdell and Joseph Tarnowski, "Going Public with Private Label," *Progressive Grocer* (June 1, 2006).

34. Marina Strauss, "In Store Aisles, Less Is More But Customers Can Still Be Particular," *Globe and Mail* (May 18, 2010), www.theglobeandmail.com/, as of June 6, 2010.

35. "The Science of Efficient Assortment," *Grocery Headquarters* (July 2000), pp. 57–60.

36. Sanjay Soo, Yuval Rottenstreich, and Lyle Brenner, "On Decisions That Lead to Decisions: Direct and Derived Evaluations of Preference," *Journal of Consumer Research* (June 2004), pp. 17–25.

37. Al Wittemen, "Average to Apples," *The Hub* (May/June 2007), pp. 38–40.

38. Paul Flatters and Michael Willmott, "Understanding the Post-Recession Consumer," *Harvard Business Review* (July–August 2009), p. 108.

39. See R. Dhar, "Through Uncertainty: Non-Consequential Reasoning and Choice," *Cognitive Psychology* 24 (1992), pp. 449–474.

40. Dana Lissy, "Helping Customers Cope with Product Proliferation," *Harvard Business Review* (May/June 1999), pp. 21–22.

41. Steve McKee, "When Fewer Choices Mean Bigger Returns," *Business Week Online* (November 10, 2006).

42. Sheena S. Iyengar and Mark R. Lepper, "When Choice Is Demotivating: Can One Desire Too Much of a Good Thing?" *Journal of Personality and Social Psychology* 79 (6) (December 2000), pp. 995–1006.

43. Susan M. Broniarczk, Wayne D. Hoyer, and Leigh McAlister, "Consumers' Perceptions of the Assortment Offered in a Grocery Category: The Impact of Item Reduction," *Journal of Marketing Research* 35 (May 1998), pp. 166–176.

44. Richard A. Briesch, Pradeep K. Chintagunta, and Edward J. Fox, "How Does Assortment Affect Grocery Store Choice?" *Journal of Marketing Research* (April 2009), pp. 176–189.

45. Richard A. Briesch, Pradeep K. Chintagunta, and Edward J. Fox, "How Does Assortment Affect Grocery Store Choice?" *Journal of Marketing Research* (April 2009), p. 188.

46. Alexander Chernev and Ryan Hamilton, "Assortment Size and Option Attractiveness in Consumer Choice Among Retailers," *Journal of Marketing Research* (June 2009), pp. 410–420.

47. "The Science of Efficient Assortment," *Grocery Headquarters* (July 2000), pp. 57–60.

48. David Diamond, "Micro Management," *Progressive Grocer* (November 1, 2006), pp. 34–35.

49. Kevin Coupe, "How to Beat the Slotting Allowance Addiction," *Chain Store Age* (July 2004), p. 42.

50. Eric Wieffering, "Product-Visibility Fees Are Hurting Consumers, Some Companies Say," *Star Tribune* (March 7, 2003), p. 1A.

51. Jack G. Kaikati and Andrew M. Kaikati, "Slotting and Promotional Allowances: Red Flags in the Supply Chain," *Supply Chain Management: An International Journal* 11/2 (2006), pp. 140–147.

52. Kevin Coupe, "How to Beat the Slotting Allowance Addiction," *Chain Store Age* (July 2004), p. 42.

53. Kevin Coupe, "How to Beat the Slotting Allowance Addiction," *Chain Store Age* (July 2004), p. 42.

54. "BrainTrust Query: Are Publicly Held Supermarket Chains Headed for Extinction?" *Retail Wire* (August 1, 2006).

55. Guillermo Israilevich, "Assessing Supermarket Product-Line Decisions: The Impact of Slotting Fees," *Quantitative Marketing and Economics* (Number 2, 2004), pp. 141–167.

56. "The Science of Efficient Assortment," *Grocery Headquarters* (July 2000), pp. 57–60.

57. Joseph Agnese, *Standard & Poor's Industry Surveys: Supermarkets & Drugstores* (July 26, 2007), p. 19.

58. Warren Thayer, "Whole Foods Turns 25," *PL Buyer* (October 2005), pp. 70–76.

59. Eileen M. Bossong-Martines, *Standard & Poor's Net Advantage: Supermarkets & Drugstores* (March 2009), pp. 5–6.

60. Amy Merrick and Kelly Nolan, "Walgreen Rides Store Revamp," *Wall Street Journal* (September 30, 2009), p. B2.

61. Ester Cervantes, "The Costco Alternative" (January/February 2006), http://www.dollarsandsense.org/archives/2006/0106cervantes.html.

62. Neil Craven, "Belt-Tightening Shoppers Are Defecting to Discounter Aldi," *Mail on Sunday* (London) (June 8, 2008), p. 53.

63. Jon Springer, "The Secret's Out," *Supermarket News* (August 25, 2008), p. 10.

64. Ike Wilson, "Food Market Boasts 50 Percent Lower Prices," *McClatchy-Tribune News* (December 18, 2008).

65. *Costco Wholesale Club 10-K for the Fiscal Year Ended August 30, 2009*, p. 4.

66. *BJ's Wholesale Club 10-K for the Fiscal Year Ended January 30, 2010*, p. 5.

67. Steven Greenhouse, "How Costco Became the Anti-Wal-Mart," *New York Times* (July 17, 2005), p. F1.

68. Andy Hanacek, "Costco Wholesale: On the Mark," *The National Provisioner* (April 2008), p. 20.

69. Matthew Boyle, "Why Costco Is So Addictive," *Fortune* (October 25, 2006).

70. Mya Frazier, "The Private-Label Powerhouse," *Advertising Age* (August 21, 2006), p. 6.

71. Joseph Tarnowski, "Costco Wholesale Corporation," *Progressive Grocer* (January 1, 2006), p. 46.

72. "Stew Leonard's," www.freeenterpriceland.com/BOOK?STEWLEONARD.html, as of April 4, 2007.

4

Differentiation Strategies I: Effective Human Resource Strategies

A retailer can differentiate itself from its direct and indirect competitors (both retailers with similar formats, as well as other store formats that sell the same or similar goods and services). There are several major benefits to a differentiated strategy. One, a differentiated strategy is difficult for a competitor to copy. Although a competitor can easily match a retailer's price, it is substantially more difficult to compete on the basis of a distinctive private label brand or a strategy based on excellent levels of customer service. Two, economic theory suggests that price competition has less of an effect on retailers that are viewed as distinctive. Three, a differentiated strategy is an excellent source of continued levels of high store loyalty. And finally, consumers should travel greater distances to a retailer with unique appeals. This increases a retailer's sales per square foot in its existing stores, as well as reduces the need for additional stores.

It should not be surprising that an entire chapter is devoted to human resources since employee-related expenses typically account for a large proportion of a typical retailer's total operating expenses. All of the best-practice retailers are well known for their positive human resource policies. Five of these best-practice retailers were included in *Fortune's* 2010 listing of the "100 Best Places to Work For"—Wegmans (ranked 3), Whole Foods (ranked 18), Nordstrom (ranked 53), Stew Leonard's (ranked 64), and Publix (ranked 86). These rankings are based on survey responses from randomly selected employees on such variables as trust in management, camaraderie, and pride in the company.

Whole Foods, Wegmans, Publix, and Nordstrom have been on *Fortune* magazine's "100 Best Places to Work For" list every year since the list began in 1998. Stew Leonard's has been on the list every year from 2002 through 2010. See Table 4.1 for selected data on the retailers listed in *Fortune's* 2010 "100 Best Companies to Work For" study. Let's first look at the strategic benefits of effective human relations strategies. We will then examine some of the hallmarks of each best-practice firm's human resource strategy.

TABLE 4.1   Revenue and Employee Data on Retailers Selected by *Fortune's* "100 Best Companies to Work For"

Company	*Fortune* Rank	2008 Revenues ($ Million)	U.S. Employees	Applicants
Wegmans	3 of 100	$ 4,807	36,770	200,082
Whole Foods	18 of 100	$ 7,954	47,478	617,696
Nordstrom	53 of 100	$ 8,573	45,853	476,139
Stew Leonard's	64 of 100	$ 376	2,037	11,888
Publix Super Markets	86 of 100	$23,929	139,578	584,276

Source: Milton Moskowitz, Robert Levering, and Christopher Thaczyk, "*Fortune's* 2010: 100 Best Companies to Work For," *Fortune* (February 8, 2010), pp. 75–88.

Strategic Benefits of Effective Human Resource Strategies

There are two major strategic benefits of effective human resource strategies: the value profit chain (which describes the linkages between employee and customer satisfaction) and lower human resource expenses due to reduced employee turnover.

The Value Profit Chain—The Relationship Between Employee and Customer Satisfaction and Profits

The value profit chain, developed by three Harvard Business School professors, asserts that value is created by employees that are satisfied, committed, loyal, and productive employees. The value profit chain model is based on a "satisfaction mirror" that suggests that employee satisfaction and loyalty (due to fairness of management, the quality of one's peers in the workplace, employee empowerment, and monetary compensation) translates into high levels of customer service and customer loyalty.[1] According to a business professor at Dartmouth's Tuck School of Business, "It is employees, not management, who interact with customers. And if employees feel good about the company, they will make customers feel good."[2]

The value profit chain concept is based both on the service profit chain (that has found direct relationships between profit and customer loyalty, employee loyalty and customer loyalty, and employee satisfaction and customer satisfaction) and on total quality concepts (which encourage companies to continually measure and benchmark employee satisfaction, customer satisfaction, and business performance).[3] This model assumes the following chain of events: (1) profit and growth are stimulated by customer loyalty; (2) customer loyalty occurs as a result of satisfaction; (3) customer satisfaction is largely influenced by the value of services provided; (4) value is created by satisfied, loyal, and productive employees; and (5) employee satisfaction results from a firm's high-quality support services that enable employees to deliver results to customers.[4]

There is some positive empirical support for the value profit chain model in a retail setting. Two researchers found that within a sample of 800 Sears stores, a 5 percent increase in employee attitude scores resulted in a 1.3 percent increase in customer satisfaction and a 0.5 percent increase in revenues.[5] Two other researchers found that perceived employee commitment had a direct impact on perceived product and service quality for supermarket shoppers.[6] In a third instance, Taco Bell found that the 20 percent of its stores with the lowest employee turnover rates had double the sales and 55 percent higher profits than the 20 percent of its stores with the highest employee turnover rates.[7]

In contrast, other retailer-based studies found only partial support of this model. Although a research study based on a major UK grocery chain found there were correlations between profit, customer loyalty, customer satisfaction, service value, internal service quality, and output quality and productivity, the analysis concluded that there was no support that these were driven by employee satisfaction and loyalty.[8]

Overall Cost Savings Through Reduced Employee Turnover

The second major benefit of an effective human resource strategy is reductions in employee turnover. The Coca-Cola Retailing Research Council estimated that the supermarket industry's annual turnover costs can exceed its entire profits by more than 40 percent.[9] The National Retail Federation estimates retail industry's overall turnover at 59 percent. In comparison, employee turnover ranges from 4 percent to 15 percent at the best-practice firms.

Annual labor turnover at Wegmans is just 7 percent, a fraction of the 19 percent figure for grocery chains with a similar number of stores, according to the Food Marketing Institute (see Table 4.2). Almost 6,000 Wegmans employees—about 20 percent of its labor force—have 10 or more years of service with the company, and 11 percent have worked at Wegmans for over 15 years.[10] More than half of Wegmans' store managers began to work there in their teens.

Similarly, employee turnover is significantly below the industry average at Aldi. According to the president of Aldi U.S., "It's not unusual for cashiers to celebrate 10-, 15-, or 20-year anniversaries with us. In a retail industry known for its high turnover, we have just the opposite."[11]

TABLE 4.2 Voluntary Turnover for Selected Best-Practice Retailers

Company	Voluntary Turnover
Publix Super Markets	5%
Stew Leonard's	6%
Wegmans	7%
Whole Foods	15%
Nordstrom	NA

NA=Not Available

Sources: Milton Moskowitz, Robert Levering, and Christopher Thaczyk, "*Fortune's* 2010: 100 Best Companies to Work For," *Fortune* (February 8, 2010), pp. 75–88; and correspondence from Wegmans.

Let's look at the real benefits of low staff turnover as a result of a retailer's human resource strategies. Data from the Coca-Cola study shows that the total direct and indirect costs of turnover ranges from at least $3,637 for replacing a supermarket cashier earning $6.50 per hour, to $4,857 for an $8-per-hour unionized employee, to $56,844 for a nonunion retail store manager. For the store manager, $34,735 was the direct and indirect costs; the costs for lost customers equaled $22,109.[12] The direct costs of employee turnover include separation costs (exit interviews and separation pay), replacement costs (employment advertising, screening, and new employee orientation), and training costs (both formal and on-the-job). These direct costs are relatively easy to measure. Indirect costs include lost sales due to customer dissatisfaction (from longer waiting lines at checkouts, the difficulty personnel have in locating an item, and so on), reduced suggestion selling, pricing errors, and reduced morale among co-workers due to the additional responsibilities of training new employees. These indirect costs are more difficult to quantify.

The average retention rate in the Coca-Cola study was 97 days, meaning that one-half of the new hires left within that time. In a nonunion environment like Trader Joe's, it costs $2,286 to replace a cashier. When the customers who might be lost due to longer waiting time are factored in, the cost of replacing a cashier jumps to $4,200. One clear implication of this research is that replacing part-time employees is costly. In comparison, the cost of replacing a nonunion department manager is $7,045 and a nonunion store manager is $34,735. Adding the cost of lost customers raises these totals to $9,354 and $56,844, respectively.[13]

The Human Resource Strategies of Best-Practice Firms

Simply put, the objective of any effective human relations program for a retailer should be to hire, continually train, and motivate and retain employees that have fun at work, have a true passion for the goods and services they sell, and enjoy servicing the store's customers. Although each best-practice firm uses a different overall human resource strategy, the impact for each of these retailer's strategies results in a high level of morale among employees, as well as high customer satisfaction levels. According to Neil Stern, vice-president of McMillan/Doolittle in Chicago, "You can create a great marketing campaign, a billion-dollar ad campaign with glitzy flyers, but you can't fake store morale. You want to know about Kmart? Walk into a store and talk to employees. Trader Joe's is just the opposite."[14]

One way of better understanding the crucial role of employees at Trader Joe's is the copy on a hand-painted poster in one of its stores. It says: "We will have well-trained, knowledgeable employees that create a fun store that is clean, WOW merchandised, informative, and one that continually kaizens (continually improves) the customer experience."

Most of the benchmarked companies employ human relations strategies based on having an employee-centered corporate culture, high employee and manager wages and benefits, low top executive compensation, recognition of the importance of continual training, continuous assessment of employees and managers, and the use of employee stock ownership, stock options, and profit sharing as incentives (see Figure 4.1). Let's examine each of these effective strategies.

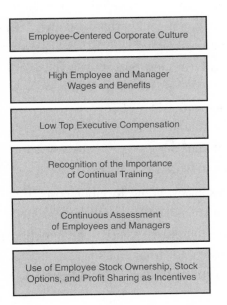

Figure 4.1   Common human relations strategies of best-practice retailers

These strategies are in direct contrast to employee environments characterized by minimal training, poor salaries, low rewards, and high employee turnover, absenteeism, and lateness. This second type of environment can lead to a "cycle of failure" characterized by poor employee morale, poor customer service, and low levels of customer loyalty.[15]

An Employee-Centered Corporate Culture

The human relations strategy of each best-practice firm can be categorized as employee-centered. According to the president of Sesco Management Consulting, a human resources consulting firm, "based on our research, the common denominator [of Wegmans,

Stew Leonard's, Whole Foods, and Publix] is a pro-employee, pro-family, pro-community culture, as these retailers demonstrate."[16] As evidence of its employee-centered philosophy, Wegmans' motto is "employees first, customers second." As part of this philosophy, Wegmans' continually researches the needs of its employees. Recently, it surveyed its 37,000 employees, and 33,000 responded. When these employees were asked, "Does management know what it's doing?" 96 percent of its employee respondents responded with a "Yes" answer. The most common comment to a recent questionnaire was the word "family." Employees viewed the people they work with as an extension of their family.[17] Both Wegmans and Stew Leonard's maintain that good employees are the key to their success. The motto of founder Stew Leonard, Sr. is "You can't have a great place to shop without first making it a great place to work."[18]

With 70 percent of Costco's expenses going to labor costs, the firm has been chastised by some Wall Street analysts who have argued that the firm is too generous with its employee salaries and benefits. Although these analysts want Costco to offer smaller benefits, a stingier return policy, and bigger profits, CEO James Sinegal sides with his customers and staff members. "We're trying to run [Costco] in a fashion that is not just going to satisfy our shareholders this year or this month," he says, "but next year and on into the future."[19] Richard Galanti, Costco's chief financial officer, adds: "From day one, we've run the company with the philosophy that if we pay better than average, provide a salary people can live on, have a positive environment and good benefits, we'll be able to hire better people, they'll stay longer, and be more efficient."[20] Galanti argues that Costco's stores' productivity is the result of high wages and the best benefits among hourly retail workers. As of 2010, Costco's hourly wage was a little over $19 per hour (its lowest starting wage rate was $11 per hour). Full-time employees at Costco reach the top of the pay scale after completing five years with the company.[21] Costco's desire to pay high wages at the same time as being a low-cost provider requires that its employees are highly productive. It also forces Costco's management to be creative in managing its employees, according to James Sinegal.[22]

Similarly, at Whole Foods, shareholders' interests take a back seat to customers and employees. At Whole Foods, profits are seen as a byproduct of treating people well. Each year, members of Whole Foods' teams complete a morale survey that covers such topics as job satisfaction, opportunity and empowerment, pay, training, and benefits. Ninety percent of the respondents to Whole Foods' survey agreed or strongly agreed that "they can do their best work for Whole Foods," and 82 percent agreed or strongly agreed that "they are treated fairly and respectfully at their location." Common responses to the question, "What is the best thing about working at Whole Foods Market?" included "co-workers acting like family, flexibility, work environment, growth and learning opportunities, the products sold, benefits, the team concept, and the culture of empowerment."[23]

Employees have a wide range of discretion at Whole Foods. Instead of using interviews and standardized tests for employee selection, Whole Foods bases employee hiring decisions on the basis of a series of meetings with groups of employees ranging in size from 4 to 14. After the four-week trial period is over, the teams meet again to determine if the candidate is working out or perhaps should be transferred to another group. The trainee needs two-thirds of the team's vote to be a permanent part of the team.[24] In addition to hiring and retention decision making, Whole Foods' employees also are empowered to determine how best to satisfy customers in their local store. As an example, a produce team member recently decided to slice up several kinds of apples as a means of encouraging customers to sample each type.

Because Nordstrom considers its employee-centered culture as an important differential advantage, it relies on its experienced employees to bring the culture to its stores in newer markets. Further evidence of Nordstrom's employee-centered corporate culture is a statement by John N. Nordstrom, a retired co-chairman: "The only thing we have going for us is the way we take care of our customers, and the people who take care of the customers are on the [sales] floor." All tiers of the organization chart at Nordstrom (department managers, store managers, regional managers, general managers, and the board of directors) work to support the sales staff, not the other way around.[25] In response to a survey administered by the Great Place to Work Institute, 94 percent of Nordstrom employees stated that often or almost always, Nordstrom is a friendly place to work.[26]

In 2006 and again in 2008, L.L.Bean was designated by AARP as an "AARP Best Employer for Workers over 50." To attract and retain mature workers, L.L.Bean offers a Healthy Lifestyle Program that offers free health screenings, health coaching, and health assessment on a voluntary basis to all employees. Retirees receive a free lifetime discount on L.L.Bean merchandise and cafeteria foods. L.L.Bean is also viewed as a leader in offering flexible work schedules via its "Swap Book." Workers can trade shifts and accumulate hours in an "Attendance Bank" that can be used for time away from work due to personal reasons. In 2008, 42 percent of L.L.Bean's employees were over 50.[27]

High Employee and Manager Wages and Benefits

According to Darrell Rigby, head of consulting firm Bain & Company's global retail practice, "You cannot separate their [Wegmans] strategy as a retailer from their strategy as an employer." Consider Charles Saccardi, who was hired as sous chef at Wegmans' store in the Rochester suburb of Pittsford, the chain's highest-grossing store at well over $2 million in sales per week. Saccardi's previous employer was Thomas Keller of the French Laundry, the famed Napa Valley restaurant. People like that do not come cheap. Wegmans also thinks nothing of sending a cheese manager on a ten-day trip to London,

Paris, and Italy. Similarly, other benchmark retailers consciously seek to pay higher wages and benefits to attract employees that would otherwise not seek careers in retailing.

High salaries enable the benchmark retailers to better attract and keep higher-quality personnel, to reduce personnel turnover, and to improve employee morale. Jeff Burris, who runs the wine shop at Wegmans' Dulles, Virginia, store, commented, "Just about everybody in the store has some genuine interest in food."[28] In fact, Wegmans has been known to reject perfectly capable job candidates who lack a passion for food. High salaries and fringe benefits also enable Trader Joe's to seek out part-time personnel who are "ambitious and adventurous, enjoy smiling, and have a strong sense of values." One observer mentioned that these qualities are more often associated with Club Med resort counselors than with traditional retail employees.[29]

High salaries are also an important motivator. Research by a Cornell professor found that those employees who were paid above the going rate were more likely to push themselves harder.[30] Firms such as Whole Foods "have found a way to turn higher compensation into a competitive advantage rather than a liability, in the same way Costco has," according to a Bain consultant, "by proving that happy workers provide better service."[31] Similarly, Costco's CEO has been quoted as stating, "We think you get what you pay for. If you hire good people, pay them good wages, and provide good jobs and careers, good things will happen in your business."[32]

Table 4.3 lists average salaries for the current "100 Best Companies to Work For 2010." The table shows that Publix's most common salaried personnel salary is $113,662 (for a store manager). One report states that Publix's salaries for managers are 20 percent to 25 percent higher than the industry average.[33] Likewise, the average pay for hourly personnel is high on a comparative basis. Costco, Trader Joe's, Aldi, Whole Foods, Wegmans, and Stew Leonard's also offer high salaries and fringe benefits.

TABLE 4.3   Average Pay for Salaried Personnel and Hourly Personnel for Most Common Salaried and Hourly Personnel of Selected Best-Practice Retailers

Company	Average Pay Salaried Personnel	Average Pay Hourly Personnel
Nordstrom	$ 49,500: Sales department manager	$39,100: Salesperson
Wegmans	$ 52,922: Store department manager	$29,240: Customer service
Whole Foods	$ 68,405: Team leader	$23,337: Cashier
Stew Leonard's	$ 72,490: Store manager	$30,819: Host/hostess
Publix Super Markets	$113,662: Store manager	$28,379: Clerk

Based on yearly pay rate plus additional compensation for the largest classification of full-time salaried and hourly employees.

Source: Milton Moskowitz, Robert Levering, and Christopher Tkaczyk, "*Fortune's* 2010: 100 Best Companies to Work For," *Fortune* (February 8, 2010), pp. 75–88.

One way of evaluating Costco's compensation program is to compare it to Sam's Clubs'. Costco's average wage is $19.00 per hour, as compared to a full-time worker at Wal-Mart averaging about $12 per hour. (Wal-Mart does not break out Sam's Club earnings.)[34] Though 82 percent of Costco's workers have health insurance coverage, less than one-half of Wal-Mart's have this coverage. Costco's workers pay only 10 percent of their health insurance premium costs versus Wal-Mart's employees being responsible for paying 33 percent of their total health care costs.

Costco's generous compensation package also extends to its retirement programs. Ninety-one percent of Costco's employees are covered by retirement plans with Costco contributing an average of $1,330 per employee (as compared with only 64 percent of Sam's Club employees being covered with Sam's Club's contribution averaging $747 per employee). Finally, after 90 days as a Costco employee, its workers are eligible for a 401(k) program. In a year or after 1,000 hours, Costco matches up to 9 percent of a worker's pay. Costco employees hired after January 1, 2005, are automatically enrolled in the 401(k) program and have 3 percent deducted from their pay.

The average full-time Trader Joe's employee earns $50,000. Part-time workers average between $8 and $12 per hour; and Trader Joe's first-year supervisors average more than $40,000. Its assistant store managers average $95,000 ($67,000 in salary, an average bonus of $14,000, and retirement contributions of close to $14,000); store managers average $132,000 (comprised of an average base salary of $80,000, bonus of $35,000, and retirement contribution of $17,000).[35] In addition, unlike at many retailers, Trader Joe's part-time employees get health insurance benefits (dental, medical, and vision) if they work 900 hours per year (an average of 20 hours weekly). Trader Joe's also contributes 15.4 percent of an employee's salary into a retirement plan. These high wages have been credited as an important contributing factor in explaining Trader Joe's chain's near-zero job turnover.[36]

Similarly at Aldi, employees get high salaries and benefits that are generally 30 percent above the going rate.[37] As a result of Aldi's high salaries and fringe benefits, the chain is able to attract top talent. Aldi reported that in 2007, it had 17,000 college-graduate applicants for 150 positions.[38]

At Nordstrom, all salespeople are paid via commission. Although the average salary for a salesperson is $39,100 per year, there are Nordstrom salespeople who earn over $100,000 per year. In 2007, when the Bureau of Labor Statistics calculated that the average retail salesperson earned $11.79 per hour, Nordstrom's average salesperson earned over $18 per hour. And although the average department manager at Nordstrom earned $49,500, some of the chain's department managers have earnings in the six-figure range.[39]

Aside from high salaries, Whole Foods fully pays for health care premiums for employees who work 30 hours or more per week, has health care coverage for domestic partners, and a personal wellness account for health care expenses. Every three years, its team members select employee benefit package options through participation in a companywide benefits vote.[40] Similarly, Stew Leonard's pays 100 percent of its employees' health care benefits.

Wegmans' benefits even extend to college scholarships for part-time and full-time employees. To be eligible, its employees need to work a minimum number of hours per week, have a good work-related performance, and maintain good grades. There are no restrictions as to suitable courses.

Low Top Executive Compensation

Surprisingly, many of our benchmark retailer firms that pay their employees and middle managers high salaries and fringe benefits often pay their chief executive officer (CEO) relatively low salaries. This list of companies includes Costco, Whole Foods, Publix, Amazon.com, and Nordstrom. Although CEOs can earn as much as 600 times the company's average pay, Costco's James Sinegal currently earns a salary of $350,000, which hasn't changed in close to a decade. According to Sinegal, "I figured that if I was making something like 12 times more than the typical person working on the floor, that was a fair salary."[41] Sinegal also commented, "I just think that if you're going to try to run an organization that's very cost-conscious, then you can't have those disparities. Having an individual who is making 100 or 200 or 300 times more than the average person working on the floor is wrong."[42]

Although Sinegal's stockholdings are worth $128 million, the number of shares of Costco stock he owns is small, considering that it is about 1/2 of 1 percent of the value of the firm that he helped found.[43] His salary is also small in comparison to the $1.01 million earnings for the median salary of a retail chief executive officer.[44] According to Forbes, Sinegal's total compensation in 2009 was $2.58 million.[45]

In comparison, Wal-Mart's chief executive officer, Michael T. Duke, earned $14.5 million in 2009 in salary, bonuses, stock gains, and other compensation. His salary alone was $1.05 million.[46] In an online commentary, *Business Week* intimated that the top job at Costco may be tougher than at Wal-Mart. "Management has to hustle to make the high-wage strategy work. It's constantly looking for ways to repackage goods into bulk items (which reduces labor), speed up Costco's just-in-time inventory, and boost sales per square foot. Costco is also savvier...about catering to small shop owners and more affluent customers, who are more likely to buy in bulk and purchase higher-margin goods."[47]

Nell Minow, editor and founder of The Corporate Library and an expert on corporate governance, said she was shocked to discover that Sinegal's employment contract is only one page in length. "Of the 2,000 companies in our database, he has the single shortest CEO employment contract. And the only one, which specifically says, he can be—believe it or not—'terminated for cause.' If he doesn't do his job, he is out the door."[48]

Similarly, at Whole Foods, through 2005, no executive received compensation of more than 14 times the average salary of all of the firm's full-time team members through 2005. In 2006, this cap was raised to 19 times the average salary of all of the firm's full-time team members. CEO Mackey reduced his annual salary to $1 effective January 1, 2007 (see Table 4.4).

TABLE 4.4   Whole Foods' Top Management Salary Cap Calculation

Year	Average Hourly Wage	Average Annual Wage	Salary Multiple	Top Management Salary Cap
1999	$12.36	$25,709	10	$257,000
2000	$12.84	$26,707	14	$373,900
2001	$13.46	$27,997	14	$391,900
2002	$13.69	$28,479	14	$398,700
2003	$14.07	$29,266	14	$409,700
2004	$14.66	$30,493	14	$426,900
2005	$15.00	$31,200	14	$436,800

TABLE 4.4   Whole Foods' Top Management Salary Cap Calculation (continued)

Year	Average Hourly Wage	Average Annual Wage	Salary Multiple	Top Management Salary Cap
2006	$15.38	$31,990	19	$607,800
2007	NA	NA	19	NA
2008	NA	$34,334	19	$652,400
2009	$16.98	$35,318	19	$671,042

NA = Not Available

Sources: Whole Foods web site as of November 28, 2007; and other sources.

David Livingston, a research analyst, compliments Publix for not providing enormous pay packages to its top officials. "Most of the best-run and successful supermarket companies pay their CEOs modest salaries and their reward comes in their increased equity from growth and profits."[49] William E. Crenshaw, Publix's chief executive officer and director, was paid $777,400 in salary, a bonus of $118,955, and other compensation of $20,350 in 2009—a total of $916,705.[50] In contrast, Winn-Dixie's chief executive officer, Peter Lynch, earned $4.6 million in total compensation (including a base salary of $1.3 million) in 2009 (the third year he led Winn-Dixie out of bankruptcy).[51]

Jeff Bezos, the founder and CEO of Amazon.com, has a salary of around $80,000, an amount that has been constant since 1994, the year he founded Amazon.com. His additional compensation of $1.2 million in 2009 reflected security costs to protect him. In contrast, the median retailing executive had a salary of $1.03 million and total compensation of $5.42 million. When *Forbes* magazine evaluated performance versus pay for executives, it ranked Bezos as 2 of 179 executives.[52] This is *Forbes* magazine's most efficient rank. Bezos owns close to 21 percent of Amazon.com's stock.

Blake Nordstrom's (Nordstrom's president since 2000) 2009 total salary was only $700,000. In addition, he has about two-thirds of his targeted total compensation "at risk" or dependent on Nordstrom's financial performance. In 2008, his total compensation decreased by nearly 25 percent compared with the prior year. Simply put, if Nordstrom does poorly, so does its president. According to the Great Places to Work Institute, "This is the kind of integrity that breeds the intense loyalty that Nordstrom experiences among its employees."[53] Blake Nordstrom's pay-for-performance ranking was 11 among 189 executives according to *Forbes* for 2009.[54]

Forbes' overall executive grading was based on four factors: (1) the company's stock performance (including dividends) relative to its industry peers over six years, (2) annualized stock performance during the chief executive's tenure, (3) stock performance relative to the Standard & Poor's 500 Index during the executive's tenure, and (4) total compensation during the past six years. Jeff Bezos's annualized return over a six-year period was 20 percent; for Blake Nordstrom, it was 15 percent.[55]

The low salary of these chief executive officers demonstrates what Jim Collins calls Level 5 leadership in his *Good to Great* book. Level 5 leaders exemplify humility and value their institution's goals above their own.[56] The relatively low salaries for top executives at these best-practice firms signifies the importance of rewarding executives based on performance. It also demonstrates to employees that there is equity in the firm's overall compensation system. According to Sinegal, "...keeping a lid on CEO base salary and bonus sends a signal that all employees are important. If the CEO is paid 10 to 12 times the highest hourly rate, that is probably pretty fair."[57]

Recognition of the Importance of Continual Training

Table 4.5 lists training data for selected best-practice retailers. Note that training requirements vary from 48 hours per year for salaried workers at Nordstrom, to 50 hours at Stew Leonard's, to 60 hours at Whole Foods, and 65 hours at Wegmans. All Wegmans store employees must complete a group of core courses in customer service, personal safety, and food safety.[58] Depending on their position, employees may be required to complete courses in interpersonal skills, conflict resolution, and interviewing and selection.[59] Employees in seafood, meat, produce, and cheese departments must also complete specific 30- to 55-hour programs. As part of their training, for example, Wegmans' meat department workers must earn certificates in cooking techniques such as braising so they can pass along suggestions to customers.

TABLE 4.5   Training for Selected Best-Practice Retailers

| | Professional Training (Hours per Year) | |
Company	Salaried Workers	Hourly Workers
Nordstrom	48	115
Stew Leonard's	50	50
Publix Super Markets	NA	60
Whole Foods	60	60
Wegmans	65	65

NA = Not Available

Source: Milton Moskowitz, Robert Levering, and Christopher Thaczyk, "*Fortune*'s 2010: 100 Best Companies to Work For," *Fortune* (February 8, 2010), pp. 75–88.

One key to Wegmans' success is the way the firm handles its entry-level workers, particularly teenagers. Through extensive training, attention to team building, scholarship incentives, and vacation and holiday pay, Wegmans is able to make teenagers a cornerstone of its operation.

Stew Leonard's also emphasizes training as an important aspect of its promotion from within. Each month, Stew Leonard's hosts a "team leader Tuesdays" program that teaches future managers how to conduct brief meetings with employees, as well as effective communication techniques. As part of Stew Leonard's management curriculum, management trainees create a new product, train in another department, manage projects, and execute a strategic plan with the assistance of a supervisor. Directors and managers are also responsible for staff development. All managers are also required to take Dale Carnegie relationship courses.

Nordstrom uses coaching, mentoring, and ongoing training so that newly hired workers will understand the firm's corporate culture. Its managers are taught to be "servant leaders." This is demonstrated by the concept that a great leader needs to first become a great servant to those that depend on him or her. At Nordstrom, mentoring and coaching is seen as an important part of one's job. This "each one, teach one" philosophy is in addition to Nordstrom's Future Leaders and New Manager Development Program.[60]

Continuous Assessment of Employees and Managers

Periodic review of all employees (including part-time workers, as well as managers) is a hallmark of the human resource management process at both Trader Joe's and Whole Foods. The continuous review provides benchmarks based on past performance and enables goals to be established and measured for future performance.

At Trader Joe's, managers are reviewed annually and part-time employees every three months, an unusually frequent rate for part-time personnel. A principal with The HR Group in Northbrook, Illinois, stated that perhaps one or two of a hundred firms evaluates part-timers with this frequency.[61] The nature of Trader Joe's evaluations is also highly unusual in that in addition to such common variables as "punctuality" and "thoroughness," employees are evaluated on such traits as "is always friendly," "creates a genuine fun shopping experience," "greets and asks customers if they need assistance while on the floor," "educates self about product features and shares with customers," and "promotes high morale in the store." Each category is scored from one to five. An employee needs to average three or better to get a raise according to one source.[62]

Although Whole Foods also continuously measures performance, it uses team-based measures. This encourages employees to work with teammates who are "effective co-workers" instead of "buddies."[63]

Members of teams that perform well receive up to $2 per hour in additional compensation. A team's current scores are benchmarked to last year's performance and to other teams in the region. Operational measurements include the previous days' sales by team members (often benchmarked against last year's sales or against other teams in the region). Two other important measures of a team's performance are the "Store Tour" and the "Customer Snapshot." The Store Tour measures social interactions, reviews, performance audits, and structured feedback sessions as judged by as many as 40 visitors from another region. The Customer Snapshot, conducted 10 times a year per store, is based on a store's surprise inspection by a headquarters official or regional leader. Each store is rated on 300 different items. The results of the Customer Snapshot are distributed to every store and included in the reward system.

At Nordstrom, continuous assessment is in the form of compensating on a commission basis. Nordstrom's best salespeople are designated as Pacesetters, a title given to the retailer's top 10 percent of its sales staff. In 2009, Nordstrom had 2,361 Pacesetters. Pacesetters receive a cash award, special business cards that show this designation, Nordstrom stock, and a 33 percent merchandise discount for the year (13 percent more than the average Nordstrom employee). The longer one retains his or her Pacesetter status, the greater the benefits received, such as Nordstrom stock. In addition to Pacesetter awards for salespeople, Nordstrom also has special awards for the top store, department, and assistant and support managers in each region.

One of Nordstrom's key performance metrics for its sales personnel is sales per hour. To underscore the importance of this measure, each employee's semi-monthly sales-per-hour productivity numbers are posted in a backroom in a manner that they are visible by all employees. Obviously, no one wants to have scores at the bottom of the performance range!

The Use of Employee Stock Ownership, Stock Options, and Profit Sharing as Incentives

An important incentive is stock ownership, stock options, and other stock incentives that are given to employees, as well as managers. Andrew Wolf, an analyst at BB&T Capital Markets, says ownership motivates the chain's people to do their best. "By being able to share in the success of the company, they have a vested interest in wanting to take better care of it."[64] One simple means of motivating employees is a retailer's communicating that every $1 per share in additional earnings translates into a share's value going up 15 to 20 times based on the stock's price-earnings ratio.[65]

The ownership of stock by employees is central to Publix's human resource strategy. Publix's stock is not publicly traded and is made available for sale only to current Publix associates and board members. Publix is also the largest employee-owned supermarket chain (ESOP) in the United States. George Jenkins, Publix's founder, was so committed to employee ownership that he gave every employee a $2 raise, withheld the money, and put it toward one share of stock for each employee. The chain's current and former employees currently own about 85 percent of the business. (The balance of the shares are owned by the firm's officers and directors, many of whom are members of the Jenkins family.) Publix sells shares in the company to employees and gives them the opportunity to buy more. Anyone who clocks more than 1,000 hours a year and is employed at Publix for more than one year receives Publix stock. And anyone who has worked at the company for at least a year can also buy stock.

There are about 90,000 Publix shareholders, including current and former employees, members of the Jenkins family, and those who were given the stock as gifts. Publix management argues that if it treats the customer well, the firm's stock price will appreciate. "Don't look for a reason why you can't take care of a customer—look for ways you can," says Bob Moore, vice-president for Publix.[66]

Other supermarkets that are 50 percent or more employee-owned include Hy-Vee—46,000 employees (West Des Moines), Price Chopper—22,000 employees (Schenectady), Houchens Industries—9,300 employees (Bowling Green), WinCo—10,000 employees (Boise), Brookshire Brothers—5,700 employees (Lufkin, Texas), and Piggly Wiggly Carolina—5,000 employees (Charleston).[67]

A major advantage of employee ownership is that employee-owners are more concerned over pilferage, spoilage, and fellow worker-owners' work ethic than traditional employees and managers. Worker-owners may also be more willing to work additional hours in peak seasons, volunteer to fill-in for fellow workers when they are absent, shift job assignments based upon a store's needs, and show initiative in store planning and implementation. A second advantage is job security, as it is quite difficult for outsiders to purchase an ESOP though a hostile takeover.

In 2002, an academic researcher summarized the results of some thirty empirical studies conducted over a 20-year period. Most of the studies found a positive correlation between employee ownership and company performance; some found no correlation. None found that equity ownership actually hurt business performance. These are among the specific findings:

- Companies adopting an ESOP saw between a 4 percent and 5 percent increase in productivity the year they became an ESOP; this higher productivity was maintained in subsequent years.
- Employee ownership was associated with greater stability of employment, without any corresponding decrease in economic efficiency.
- Employee ownership was linked to faster employment growth and to higher rates of survival among companies.[68]

As an alternative to a traditional ESOP, retailers can provide incentives to employees via stock options, stock ownership through retirement plans, or profit-sharing arrangements. Whole Foods, for example, awards stock options to store employees (both full- and part-time), not just store executives. Ninety-three percent of all stock options ever issued by Whole Foods were issued to staff below the board level.[69] Currently, nonexecutive employees at Whole Foods hold 96 percent of the firm's stock options.[70]

There is some empirical evidence that links stock option plans to higher corporate performance. One study examined 105 publicly traded companies that provided stock options to at least 75 percent of their employees. In the three years following the implementation of their options plans, these companies improved productivity by 17 percent and return on assets by 2.3 percent per year, on average. Wages were also about 7 percent higher than in comparable companies that did not distribute options widely.[71]

At Au Bon Pain, the chain of French-style bakery cafés, managers have had compensation systems pegged to specific profit goals for their retail locations. Managers could increase their compensation by as much as three to four times by doubling or tripling the profitability of their stores.[72]

Takeaway Points

- Even though it may sound simple, this statement is worth repeating: The objective of an effective human relations program is to hire, train, and motivate and retain employees who have fun at work, have a true passion for the goods and services they sell, and enjoy servicing customers. Happy workers provide better service, which translates into higher levels of customer loyalty and sales.

- Emulating the best-practice firms' human resource strategies means, in many cases, totally rethinking a firm's overall human resource philosophy, as well as developing and implementing new strategies and programs. This chapter clearly questions many of the typical human resource tenets of retailing. With labor costs typically representing over one-half of many stores' total operating expenses, too many retailers have sought to reduce labor costs through paying low wages, hiring high proportions of part-time help, eliminating or drastically curtailing

health care programs, and reducing employee training by sim-
plifying jobs to their basic components.

- Benchmarked companies employ human relations strategies
  based on having an employee-centered corporate culture, high
  employee and manager wages and benefits, low top executive
  compensation, recognition of the importance of training, continuous assessment of employees and managers, and the use of
  employee stock ownership, stock options, and profit sharing as
  incentives.

- Retailers need to carefully review their overall human resource
  strategies and tactics. For example:

  - Does the retailer consistently promote from within?

  - Are workers given time off for important family obligations?

  - Is the manager's pay fair in comparison to top executive
    compensation?

  - Do workers and managers receive continual training to
    stay abreast of important trends?

  - Is employee morale continually measured?

  - Are part-time, as well as full-time, personnel reviewed?

  - Do reviews evaluate customer service issues, as well as
    sales and profitability?

  - Are reviews individual or team-based?

  - Are stock options and other incentives used to motivate
    and reward employees and managers?

- At first glance, the high productivity of these best-practice
  leaders may be seen as a paradox among some retailers. The
  basic question is: How can firms that pay higher-than-industry
  wage rates, have generous fringe benefits, and have costly
  training programs be so efficient? The answer to this seeming
  contradiction is clearly related to reduced costs associated with
  lower employee and manager turnover, higher employee and
  manager productivity, and higher customer satisfaction and
  loyalty levels. Thus, these best-practice retailers received the
  advantages associated with the value profit chain and with
  lower worker and manager turnover.

Endnotes

1. James H. Heskett, W. Earl Sasser, Jr., and Leonard A. Schlesinger, *The Value Profit Chain* (New York: The Free Press, 2003), p. 19.

2. Elayne Robertson Demby, "Two Stores Refuse to Race to the Bottom," *Workforce Management* (February 2004), pp. 57–59.

3. James L. Heskett, W. Earl Sasser, Jr., and Leonard A. Schlesinger, *The Service-Profit Chain to Work* (New York: The Free Press, 1997).

4. Rachel W.Y. Yee, Andy C.L. Yeung, T.C. Edwin Cheng, and Kee-Hung Lai, "The Service-Profit Chain: A Review and Extension," *Total Quality Management*, Vol. 20 (June 2009), pp. 617–632.

5. Anthony Rucci and Steven Kim, "The Employee-Customer Profit Chain at Sears," *Harvard Business Review*, 1998.

6. Manuel Vilares and Pedro Coelho, "The Employee-Customer Satisfaction Chain in the ECSI Model," *European Journal of Marketing*, 2003.

7. James L. Heskett, Thomas W. Earl Sasser, Jr., and Leonard A. Schlesinger, *The Service-Profit Chain to Work* (New York: The Free Press, 1997), pp. 32–33.

8. Rhian Silvestro and Stuart Cross, "Applying the Service Profit Chain in a Retail Environment: Challenging the Satisfaction Mirror," *International Journal of Service Industry Management*, Vol. 11 (Number 3, 2000), pp. 244–268.

9. Matthew Boyle, "The Wegmans Way," *Fortune* (January 24, 2005), pp. 62 ff.

10. Bill Freehling, "Wegmans Called Third-Best Place to Work," *McClatchy-Tribune Business News* (January 22, 2010).

11. Jon Springer, "Small Staff, Low Turnover," *Supermarket News* (August 25, 2008), p. 14.

12. Blake Frank, "New Ideas for Retaining Store Level Employees," The Coca-Cola Retailing Research Council, January 2000, pp. 31, 32.

13. Blake Frank, "New Ideas for Retaining Store-Level Employees," The Coca-Cola Retailing Research Council, 2000.

14. Len Lewis, *The Trader Joe's Adventure* (Chicago: Dearborn Trade Publishing, 2005), p. 147.

15. Leonard A. Schlesinger and James L. Heskett, "Breaking the Cycle of Failure in Services," *Sloan Management Review*, Vol. 32, No. 3 (Spring 1991), pp. 17–28.

16. Jenny McTaggart, "The Most Labor-Friendly Supermarkets Are Keeping Their Employees Happy with More Than Competitive Wages," *Progressive Grocer* (May 1, 2005).

17. Donna Owens, "Treating Employees Like Customers," *HR Magazine* (October 2009), p. 28.

18. Bob Chuvala, "A Stew-Pendous Place to Work," *Westchester County Business Journal* (February 4, 2008), p. 1.

19. "Customer-Centered Leader: Chick-fil-A," *Fast Company* (September 11, 2008), www.fastcompany.com/magazine/87/customer-chickfila.html, as of January 22, 2009.

20. Ann Zimmerman, "Costco's Dilemma: Be Kind to Its Workers, or Wall Street?" *Wall Street Journal* (March 26, 2004), p. B1.

21. Edward Teach, "Because It's the Right Thing to Do," *CFO* (March 2010), pp. 38–40.

22. Phone interview with James Sinegal, CEO, Costco, June 19, 2009.

23. *Whole Foods September 25, 2005 10-K*, p. 9.

24. Tamara J. Erickson and Lynda Gratton, "What It Means to Work Here," *Harvard Business Review*, Vol. 85 (March 2007), pp. 104–112; and Anne Fisher, "Staying Power," *Fortune* (July 7, 2008), p. 142.

25. Robert Spector and Patrick McCarthy, *The Nordstrom Way to Customer Service Excellence* (Hoboken, NJ: John Wiley & Sons Inc., 2005), p. 125.

26. Amy Lyman, "Nordstrom—Great Service for Over 100 Years" (San Francisco: Great Places to Work Institute, 2009), p. 1.

27. "L.L.Bean, Inc.: 2008 AARP Best Employer for Workers Over 50," www.aarp. org, as of April 8, 2009; and Tracie Stone, "Tips for Recruiting and Retaining 50 Plus Workers," *New Hampshire Business Review* (August 1, 2008), p. 10.

28. Matthew Boyle, "The Wegmans Way," *Fortune* (January 24, 2005), p. 62.

29. Irwin Speizer, "The Grocery Chain That Shouldn't Be," *Fast Company* (February 2004), p. 31.

30. Alden M. Hayashi, "What's the Best Way to Pay Employees?" *MIT Sloan Management Review* (Winter 2007), pp. 8–9.

31. Rick Romell, "Costco's Model Is Paying Dividends: Warehouse Club Will Bring Rare Retail Practice of High Wages, Generous Benefits to Grafton," *Knight Ridder Tribune Business News* (March 5, 2006), p. 1.

32. Kris Hudson, "Boss Talk: Turning Shopping Trips into Treasure Hunts—Surprises, Bargains Keep Sinegal's Costco Humming, But Should He Boost Prices?" *Wall Street Journal* (August 27, 2007), p. B1.

33. Frederick F. Jesperen, Megan Tucker, and Dean Foust, "Customer Service Champs," *Business Week* (March 7, 2005).

34. "Costco Versus Sam's Club," *Consumer Reports* (May 2007), p. 17; and Edward Teach, "Because It's the Right Thing to Do," *CFO* (March 2010), pp. 38–40.

35. Irwin Speizer, "Shopper's Special," *Workforce Management* (September 3, 2004), pp. 51–54.

36. "Trader Joe's Retail Explosion," *Display & Design Ideas* (April 1, 2005).

37. James Hall, "The Rise and Rise of the Discount King," *The Sunday Telegraph* (London) (August 31, 2008), p. 7.

38. James Hall, "The Rise and Rise of the Discount King," *The Sunday Telegraph* (London) (August 31, 2008), p. 7.

39. "Nordstrom—Great Service for Over 100 Years" (San Francisco: Great Places to Work Institute), p. 2.

40. "Whole Foods Market Makes *Fortune*'s '100 Best Companies to Work For' List for 12th Consecutive Year," *PR Newswire* (January 22, 2009).

41. Alan R. Goldberg and Bill Ritter, "Costco CEO Finds Pro-Worker Means Profitability," ABC News 20/20, http://abcnews.go.com/2020/Business/story?id=1362779, as of January 22, 2009.

42. Steven Greenhouse, "How Costco Became the Anti-Wal-Mart," *New York Times* (July 17, 2005), p. F1.

43. "CEO Compensation #374: James D. Sinegal," *Forbes.com* (April 28, 2010), http://www.forbes.com/lists/2010/12/boss-10_James-D-Sinegal_OAMI.html, as of June 6, 2010.

44. "CEO Compensation #374: James D. Sinegal," *Forbes.com* (April 28, 2010), http://www.forbes.com/lists/2010/12/boss-10_James-D-Sinegal_OAMI.html, as of June 6, 2010.

45. "CEO Compensation #374: James D. Sinegal," *Forbes.com* (April 28, 2010), http://www.forbes.com/lists/2010/12/boss-10_James-D-Sinegal_OAMI.html, as of June 6, 2010.

46. "CEO Compensation #65: Michael T. Duke," Forbes.com (April 28, 2010), http://www.forbes.com/lists/2010/12/boss-10_Michael-T-Duke_40MH.html, as of June 6, 2010.

47. John Miller, "What's Good for Wal-Mart...," *Dollars & Sense* (January/February 2006), pp. 12–13 ff.

48. Alan R. Goldberg and Bill Ritter, "Costso CEO Finds Pro-Worker Means Profitability," ABC News 20/20, http://abcnews.go.com/2020/Business/story?id=1362779, as of January 22, 2009.

49. Mary Toothman, "Within Their Means: Publix Super Markets' Top Executives Earn Less Than Other Companies' Officers," *The Ledger* (March 19, 2005), p. E1.

50. "Executive Compensation: William E. Crenshaw," *Equilar.com*, http://www.equilar.com/CEO_Compensation/Publix_Super_Markets_William_E._Crenshaw.php, as of June 6, 2010.

51. "Executive Compensation: Peter L. Lynch," *Equilar.com*, http://www.equilar.com/CEO_Compensation/Winn-Dixie_Stores_Peter_L._Lynch.php, as of June 6, 2009.

52. "CEO Compensation #463—Jeffrey P. Bezos," *Forbes* (April 28, 2010), http://www.forbes.com/lists/2010/12/boss-10_Jeffrey-P-Bezos_RYMV.html, as of June 6, 2010.

53. "Nordstrom—Great Service for Over 100 Years" (San Francisco: Great Places to Work Institute), p. 2.

54. "CEO Compensation #373—Blake W. Nordstrom," *Forbes* (April 28, 2010), http://www.forbes.com/lists/2010/12/boss-10_Blake-W-Nordstrom_IRC8.html, as of June 6, 2010.

55. CEO Compensation #463—Jeffrey P. Bezos," *Forbes* (April 28, 2010), http://www.forbes.com/lists/2010/12/boss-10_Jeffrey-P-Bezos_RYMV.html, as of June 6, 2010; and "CEO Compensation: Number 373—Blake W. Nordstrom," *Forbes* (April 28, 2010), http://www.forbes.com/lists/2010/12/boss-10_Blake-W-Nordstrom_IRC8.html, as of June 6, 2010.

56. Jim Collins, *Good to Great* (New York: Harper Business, 2001), pp. 20–21.

57. Michael Bush, "Company Focus: Extravagant CEO Pay Is Back," www.money-central.msn.com/content/P110762.asp, as of December 21, 2009.

58. Rex Davenport, "Wegmans, A Shared Vision," *T+D* (September 2005), pp. 37 ff.

59. Correspondence from Jo Natale, Director of Media Relations, Wegmans Food Markets, Inc., June 7, 2009.

60. "Nordstrom—Great Service for Over 100 Years" (San Francisco: Great Places to Work Institute), pp. 1–2.

61. Irwin Speizer, "Shopper's Special," *Workforce Management* (September 3, 2004), pp. 51–54.

62. Irwin Speizer, "Shopper's Special," *Workforce Management* (September 3, 2004), pp. 51–54.

63. Tamara J. Erickson and Lynda Gratton, "What It Means to Work Here," *Harvard Business Review*, Vol. 85 (March 2007), pp. 104–112.

64. Meg Major, "Publix Florida's Other Magic Kingdom: Employee Ownership and a Culture of Excellence Keep Publix on Everyone's Short List of Best Supermarket Companies," *Progressive Grocer* (February 15, 2003), pp. 22 ff.

65. Corey Rosen, John Case, and Martin Staubus, "Equity: Why Employee Ownership Is Good for Business" (Boston, MA: Harvard Business School Press, 2005), p. 105.

66. Frederick F. Jesperen, Megan Tucker, and Dean Foust, "Customer Service Champs," *Business Week* (March 7, 2005).

67. "The Employee Ownership 100," The National Center for Employee Ownership, www.nceo.org/library/eo100.htm.

68. Douglas Kruse, "Research Evidence on Prevalence and Effects of Employee Ownership," Testimony before Subcommittee on Employer-Employee Relations, Committee on Education and the Workforce, U.S. House of Representatives, February 13, 2003.

69. Alistar Blair, "CEO Pay Heros," *Investors Chronicle* (January 12, 2007).

70. Danielle Sacks, "The Miracle Worker," *Fast Company* (December 2009/January 2010).

71. Corey Rosen, John Case, and Martin Staubus, "Every Employee an Owner," *Harvard Business Review*, Vol. 86 (June 2005), pp. 122–130.

72. James H. Heskett, W. Earl Sasser, Jr., and Leonard A. Schlesinger, The Value Profit Chain (New York: The Free Press, 2003), p. 129.

5

Differentiation Strategies II: Enhancing the Service Experience

According to one source, "An experience occurs when a company intentionally uses services as the stage, and goods as props, to engage individual customers in a way that creates a memorable event."[1] Although some elements of the service experience can be passive (such as consumers seeing an attractive display, or observing a cooking demonstration or a product being made—such as bread being baked), other elements are quite active (such as consumers sampling a product, or taking an in-store course on fly fishing).

Service Industry Research Systems (SIRS), a market research firm, views the service experience from the perspective of emotional and rational factors. Emotional factors include a shopper's perception of the shopping experience from the perspective of the store's ambiance, customer service, and level of trust that a customer feels toward a store's products, services, and store brand. In contrast, a rational factor is the shopper's view of a retailer in terms of its value for the money.[2]

Retailers can provide both passive and active experiences through the way in which items are displayed, sampling stations and demonstrations, and enjoyable employee-customer interactions. As a result of using these strategies, a shopping experience may be described by customers in terms such as "most pleasant," "exciting," and even "fun." Note that these endearing terms are rarely used by customers to describe their experience with most retailers.

Jeff Bezos, Amazon.com's founder and chief executive, distinguishes between customer experience and customer service. "Internally, customer service is a component of customer experience. Customer experience includes having the fastest delivery, having it reliable enough so that you don't need to contact [anyone]. Then you save customer service for those truly unusual situations. You know, I got my book and it's missing pages 47 through 58."[3] Bezos has been described as having an obsession with customers. According to Bezos, "[Customers] care about having the lowest prices, having vast selection, so they have choice, and getting the products...fast. And the reason I'm so obsessed with these drivers of the customer experience is that I believe that the success we have had over the past 12 years has been driven exclusively by that customer experience."[4]

Nordstrom also truly understands the service experience through its principle of "hiring the smile, and training the skill." According to Bruce Nordstrom, the chain's current chairman, "we can hire nice people and teach them to sell, but we can't hire salespeople and teach them to be nice."[5]

According to one retail analyst, "...until recently, most supermarkets hadn't figured out how to turn their stores into shopper destinations for legitimate alternatives to eating at a restaurant or cooking meals at home. By filling those voids with relevant solutions—by connecting food, physically and emotionally, with what shoppers are looking for—retailers like Whole Foods and Wegmans are not only creating high levels of customer satisfaction and loyalty, they are rebuilding long-term relationships previously lost to big-box stores and clubs."[6]

Consumer Satisfaction Studies and Analyst Reviews of the Benchmark Retailers

There are several highly regarded and nationally known studies that regularly monitor customer service ratings: the American Customer Satisfaction Index, *Business Week's* Customer Service Elite, and *Fast Company* magazine's Customer First Awards. *Consumer Reports* recently completed major studies on customer satisfaction with specific supermarkets, big retailers, online clothing retailers, and electronics stores. The findings of most of these studies have been summarized in the Appendix, "Individual and Composite Financial Performance, Customer Service, and Worker Satisfaction Metrics of the Best-Practice Retailers." Generally, high scores on customer service/satisfaction studies have been given to all the benchmarked retailers, except Stew Leonard's. One reason Stew Leonard's was probably not cited in any of these surveys is that it is a four-store geographically focused chain.

The American Customer Satisfaction Index (ACSI) is produced through a partnership of the University of Michigan Business School, the American Society for Quality, and CFI Group, a consulting firm. A retailer's overall ranking on this survey is determined by customer interviews that measure such factors as customer expectations, perceived quality, customer complaints, and customer retention. Publix was found to be the highest-ranking supermarket for customer service by ACSI for 15 consecutive years (since the organization has ranked retailers).[7] In 2009, Publix's customer service score was 86 (its highest score to date). Publix's rating compares favorably with scores of 78 for Kroger, 76 for Whole Foods, 74 for Winn-Dixie, 72 for Safeway, and 71 for Wal-Mart.[8]

Among department and discount stores, Nordstrom had the highest-ranking customer service rating in 2009 with an all-time high score of 83. Costco was tied with Borders for the second-highest specialty store rating (81) in the specialty retail store category in 2009.

Barnes & Noble (with a score of 84) had the highest rating in this category. And Amazon.com, with a 2009 customer rating score of 86, was tied with Newegg for the second-highest rating for Internet retailers (Netflix's rating was 87).[9]

Bloomberg Business Week has compiled a *"Customer Service Champs"* listing of 25 firms (which includes insurance companies, hotels, car manufacturers, car rental firms, and so on). The *Business Week* ratings are based on J.D. Power & Associates rankings, as well as responses to a survey of 5,000 of the magazine's readers. *Business Week* readers were asked to nominate three companies they felt were best and three they thought were worst at providing customer service. Both data sets were combined into "process" and "people" scores. Process scores relate to attributes such as return policies and reservation procedures. People scores deal with friendliness and expertise levels. Five best-practice retailers have placed among the top 25 firms in *Bloomberg Business Week's* latest 2010 study: L.L.Bean (number 1), Publix (number 5), Nordstrom (number 6), Amazon.com (number 11), and Wegmans (number 12).[10]

Trader Joe's, Costco, and Wegmans were the only three retailers of 13 firms chosen by a *Fast Company* panel of experts (from academia, consulting, and organizations), as well as consumer survey respondents, for excellence in customer service. These 13 firms were highly rated on the basis of the total customer experience—the service, quality, design, and brand attributes. According to *Fast Company*, these firms connect on an emotional level, keeping customers satisfied and feeling well served, as well as loyal.[11]

Consumer Reports ratings were based on almost 32,599 responses (covering 48,831 consumer visits) with supermarkets, supercenters, warehouse clubs, and limited assortment stores (between April 2007 and April 2008). Reader scores were based on their overall satisfaction with the shopping experience based on service, perishables, prices, and cleanliness. A score of 100 meant that all respondents were completely satisfied, 80 represented very satisfied, and 60 fairly well satisfied (differences of less than six points are not meaningful); see Table 5.1. Wegmans, Trader Joe's, and Publix were ranked first, second, and third for customer satisfaction among the 59 grocery chains. Interestingly, Costco was ranked seventh, even though it uses a warehouse format, has limited customer assistance (except in consumer electronics and jewelry), and uses few displays. Also noteworthy was that Aldi, an extreme value-based retailer, was ranked 14.

TABLE 5.1   Consumer Rankings of Grocery Chains by *Consumer Reports*

Grocery Chain	Overall Score	Ranking Among 59 Grocery Chains
Wegmans	87	1
Trader Joe's	86	2
Publix	84	3
Costco	81	7
Aldi	79	14
Sam's Club	74	38
Wal-Mart Supercenter	69	56

Source: "Ratings Supermarkets," *Consumer Reports* (May 2009), p. 22.

Other studies of customer service ratings by *Consumer Reports* gave our benchmark retailers high scores. Costco received the highest average customer score for selected big retailers.[12] L.L.Bean received the highest customer satisfaction score for an online clothing retailer; Nordstrom was ranked 4 of 10 retailers on this study.[13] And Amazon.com and Costco.com were ranked 3 and 4, respectively, for customer service by consumers of 14 online electronics retailers.[14]

An IBM survey of over 19,000 consumers found that, on average, only 21 percent of consumers could be classified as an "advocate" for a particular retailer. To be positioned as an advocate, consumers would have to (1) recommend the retailer to friends and family, (2) increase their purchases if the retailer added products sold at other retailers, and (3) continue to purchase goods from that retailer even if another retailer sold the same product more cheaply. For Wegmans, 53 percent of shoppers could be classified as advocates. In addition, 78 percent of Wegmans shoppers that were surveyed stated that this retailer fully met their expectations. Wegmans had the highest scores on both of these dimensions of all retailers studied.[15]

In the IBM survey, Nordstrom was cited by consumers as the leader in the large-format apparel group, with 28 percent of Nordstrom's customers being classified as advocates.[16] Twenty-eight percent of the sampled Nordstrom shoppers (the highest percentage of any store in its group) stated that they would recommend the retailer, would spend more there if the store offered products found elsewhere, and would stay with the retailer even if another store offered competitive goods.[17] According to one source, Nordstrom has "set the bar for American business. If what you do makes you known as 'The Nordstrom of (fill in the blanks),' understand that you have arrived."[18] An *Advertising Age* article stated, "Nordstrom executives long have made it their business to do whatever is necessary to please the consumer—everything from stocking every possible color and size of a pair of shoes to having a sales associate buy an out-of-stock item from a competitor only to turn around and sell it to his or her customer. It is important to note that neither the department store itself nor its products are proffered; instead, it's a very high-end, individualized, and personally gratifying shopping experience."[19]

At L.L.Bean, customer service is so important that its three customer contact centers are open 24 hours a day, 365 days per year. L.L.Bean recognizes that it is important to be available whenever and however its customers want to reach it. L.L.Bean also calls its "customer service" department its "Customer Satisfaction" department.

Leon Leonwood (L.L.) Bean, the store's founder, understood the value of a satisfied customer. He used the following definition of a customer:[20]

- A customer is the most important person in this company—in person or by mail.
- A customer is not dependent on us, we are dependent on him.
- A customer is not an interruption of our work, he is the purpose of it.
- We are not doing a favor by serving him, he is doing a favor by giving us the opportunity to do so.
- A customer is not someone to argue or match wits with. Nobody ever won an argument with a customer.
- A customer is a person who brings us his wants. It is our job to handle them profitably to home and to ourselves.

Employee Dimensions of the Service Experience

This section is organized into two parts: employee and non-employee dimensions of the service experience. The employee dimensions section looks at how employees can contribute to a customer's service experience. These employee dimensions include recognizing the crucial role of employees, empowering employees, and providing customers with "little things that add up to become a lot" (see Figure 5.1).

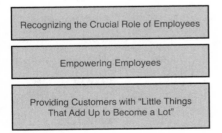

Figure 5.1   Employee dimensions of the service experience

Recognizing the Crucial Role of Employees

Too many retailers either have never learned or forgot the old marketing adage that "all employees with customer contact, regardless of title, serve as marketers." Best-practice retailers recognize the crucial role of all employees that have customer contact in delivering superior customer service, as well as sophisticated product knowledge. As opposed to the Wal-Mart model that focuses on low wages and fringe benefits, these employers typically pay high wages, assess employees on a regular basis, offer extensive training programs, and provide employees incentives for high levels of performance. Often, these firms are able to attract and keep employees who would otherwise not be attracted to careers in retailing. Many of our benchmark grocers, for example, are able to attract "foodies" who love to taste new food products, are excellent cooks, and enjoy sharing their experiences with like-minded customers. These employees are instrumental in providing engaging in-store interactions with customers. Nordstrom has also been successful in attracting and retaining employees with a specific interest in fashion. Likewise, L.L.Bean has been able to attract and retain employees with a specific interest in outdoor activities.

According to Danny Wegman, the president of Wegmans, "How do we differentiate ourselves? If we can sell products that require knowledge in terms of how you use them, that's our strategy. Anything that requires knowledge and service gives us a reason to be."[21] A Wegmans senior vice-president further stresses this point by stating, "The company's focus has shifted from merchandising to culinary education."[22] Knowledgeable employees are "something our competitors don't have and our customers couldn't get anywhere else."[23] The company calls this "telepathic levels of customer service." Product knowledge does not come about without initial, as well as continuous, training. Wegmans' meat and fish department employees must satisfactorily complete a 30- to 55-hour "university" program. Many of the store's department heads also travel overseas to work in French patisseries or tour the French countryside to learn about cheese. The training enables Wegmans' personnel to provide advice on proper cooking times for steak, how to properly grill a fish, or even how to marinate an inexpensive cut of meat to make it more tender and flavorful.

Unlike other retailers that outsource their call centers to distant locations as a means of reducing costs, L.L.Bean's three call centers are all located in Maine, close to the retailer's corporate headquarters. There is no problem understanding accents, with time differences, or with customer service personnel that do not regularly purchase the firm's products. According to L.L.Bean's vice-president of customer satisfaction, "all our call center employees get to experience what the company culture is like first hand, as opposed to from afar."[24] They can also shop at the L.L.Bean main Freeport store and experience many of the new and classic products.

In addition to these call center employees, L.L.Bean has product specialists that are especially trained to handle technical questions relating to cross-country skiing, fly fishing gear, and outdoor apparel. To ensure even better service for specialized inquiries, these call center employees are instructed to refer these special requests to specialists. Specialists go through extensive training and are able to answer the most detailed questions about L.L.Bean's vast array of products.

These retailers realize the importance of both product knowledge and enthusiasm as part of customer service. They understand the role of not only just hiring high-quality personnel, but also the need for continuously training and motivating their employees.

Empowering Employees

One of the constants in most service excellence studies is employee empowerment. Through empowerment, an employee is able to "right a wrong" when a customer seeks to return a defective or spoiled item, when a crucial in-home delivery arrives late or is missing a key ingredient, or when a store's checkout lines are unusually long. The key issue in employee empowerment is that an employee (without a manager's intervention) can handle the service recovery efforts in a manner that both the employee and customer views as fair. For employee empowerment to work properly, the retailer needs to allow its employees to choose among a range of recovery actions at their discretion.

At Trader Joe's, employees are encouraged to open any product a customer wants to taste. They are also told to be honest in recommending products they like, as well as those they do not enjoy.[25] Similarly, employee empowerment is an important part of the corporate culture at Stew Leonard's. According to a Stew Leonard's executive, employee empowerment can include handing out cookies at checkout, offering a crying child a free ice cream, or even gifting a grumpy consumer with a bouquet of flowers.[26] Stew Leonard's cashiers are also empowered to allow a customer who forgot his wallet or credit card to take his/her purchases home and come back to the store later on to pay. Try that at your local supermarket!

The author of a book on Nordstrom states, "What makes Nordstrom unique is its culture of motivated, empowered employees, each with an entrepreneurial spirit. Nordstrom encourages, preaches, demands, and expects individual initiative from these people who are on the front lines, people who have the freedom to generate their own ideas (rather than wait for an edict from above), and to promote fashion trends that are characteristic of that store and region of the country. The best Nordstrom associates will do virtually everything they can to make sure a shopper leaves the store a satisfied customer."[27]

Nordstrom encourages its employees to try new ways of selling and to apply new ways of better serving customers. The only rule that exists at Nordstrom is to "use good judgment in all situations." According to one employee, "I have been amongst retailers for over 50 years. As a supplier and now employee, there is no major retailer that has a better-developed culture in dealing with employees, suppliers, and most important—customers than Nordstrom. I am empowered to deal with any customer situation by using 'good judgment' without going to management." Another employee notes, "Nordstrom is unique in that employees are encouraged to use their best judgment when making decisions on the sales floor as to how to handle customers' requests or situations. If we make a mistake, we are instructed in how we should have handled the situation, but we are not fired, and we are not made to feel dumb or incompetent. We are trusted more here than anywhere I've worked."[28]

Providing Customers with "Little Things That Add Up to Become a Lot"

An important part of the in-store experience is the interaction between employees and customers. At Publix, customer interaction includes such simple things as properly greeting a customer. Publix has a "10 second, 10 feet" rule. This rule encourages employees to greet customers within 10 feet of them or within 10 seconds of noticing them. An important benefit of the "10 second, 10 feet" rule is that it enables customers to ask employees questions without first having to track down the employee.

Another "little thing that can add up to become a lot" is Publix's policy of having employees help customers carry groceries back to their car. Employees are not allowed to accept tips for this service. This service is a major benefit to senior citizens, shoppers with disabilities, parents shopping with children, or simply consumers with extra large purchases. This same philosophy spills over to Publix's pharmacy, which commits itself to having a customer's prescription filled 15 minutes after it is dropped off.

Publix is now testing the use of restaurant-style beepers to alert shoppers that their deli order is ready. Customers are given beepers after they have placed their order. This technology enables customers to continue shopping while their order is being prepared.[29] Another item in the test stage for Publix is curbside delivery for deli items.[30]

Although Costco has no sales associates (except for consumer electronics and jewelry), its stockers and managers are trained to be helpful and friendly. Costco has a "no-pointing policy," wherein employees are required to walk shoppers to the appropriate aisle when asked where an item is located.[31] Similarly, at Trader Joe's, the cashier is trained to ask each customer "if she has found everything she desired at the store." If the answer is "no," the cashiers will leave their station and quickly get an item for the customer. In comparison, at most stores, cashiers leaving their station to help a customer would probably get the cashiers fired!

At Stew Leonard's, one of the "little things that add up to become a lot" is counting customers by day and hour so that it can put the appropriate number of cashiers and baggers on duty so that customers don't have to wait in lines and become frustrated. Says Leonard, "Customer service cannot be a sometimes thing. It must be earned and re-earned every day."[32]

At Nordstrom, employees keep track of their top customers' purchases, email them about upcoming sales, and conduct inventory research online instead of using telephones. Nordstrom is also experimenting with text messaging. According to Erik Nordstrom, the chain's president, "Our focus is less about the latest supercool technology, and more about the customer interaction."[33] A few of Nordstrom's larger stores have a concierge desk where a shopper can receive helpful information as to where to find an item in the store, a restaurant recommendation, or even help in getting a taxi cab.

Nonemployee Dimensions of the Service Experience

The benchmark chains also excel due to a combination of factors that are not directly employee-related. These factors include having a clearly articulated service experience statement, committing to making shopping a fun experience, being viewed as more than just a typical store, having an exciting store atmosphere, offering liberal money-back guarantees, and listening to customers and quickly reacting to their suggestions (see Figure 5.2).

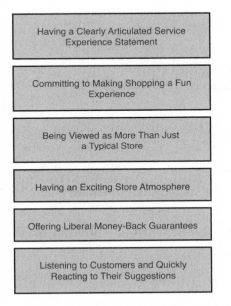

Having a Clearly Articulated Service Experience Statement

Committing to Making Shopping a Fun Experience

Being Viewed as More Than Just a Typical Store

Having an Exciting Store Atmosphere

Offering Liberal Money-Back Guarantees

Listening to Customers and Quickly Reacting to Their Suggestions

Figure 5.2   Dimensions of the service experience that are not employee-related

Having a Clearly Articulated Service Experience Statement

A most effective way to demonstrate a firm's commitment to the service experience is for the firm to have a clearly articulated statement of its customer experience policy. This policy needs to be effectively communicated to all the firm's employees and customers. Publix, Trader Joe's, and Whole Foods each make specific references to the service experience in their 10-Ks, mission statement, or through other visible means.

As stated in its 10-K, Publix's core strategy focuses on the firm's customer service, product quality, shopping environment, competitive pricing, and convenient locations. Publix believes that these core strategies and related strategic initiatives differentiate it from its competition and present opportunities for increased market share and sustained financial growth. The 10-K clearly states that failure to execute these core strategies could adversely affect the firm's financial condition and results of operations.[34]

In its mission statement, Trader Joe's states: "The mission of Trader Joe's is to give our customers the best food and beverage values that they can find anywhere and to provide them with the information required to make informed buying decisions. We provide these with a dedication to the highest quality of customer satisfaction delivered with a sense of warmth, friendliness, fun, individual pride, and company spirit." The operative words used here include "customer satisfaction," "warmth," "friendliness," "fun," "pride," and "company spirit."

Stew Leonard's carves its fundamental customer service policy in stones weighing three tons, at each store's entrance. Rule 1 reads: "The customer is always right." Rule 2 further states: "If the customer is ever wrong, re-read rule 1." The stones are so large that customers and employees cannot avoid seeing the policy each time they enter Stew Leonard's.

Implementing customer service goals at Amazon.com is more difficult than at traditional retailers because Amazon.com uses outside merchants for many of its transactions. Although Amazon.com receives customers' ratings based on their experience with these merchants, Amazon.com is also able to monitor customers' email conversations with these merchants through Amazon's email service. Amazon.com monitors these merchants based on the number of complaints, as well as how often the retailer has to cancel an order due to stockouts. Amazon.com is so committed to excellence in customer service that it will cancel its contracts with merchants that have problems with more than 1 percent of their transactions.[35]

Bill Miller, a fund manager with Legg Mason, has noted that Amazon.com has really only one stated goal since it began: to be the most customer-centric company in the world.[36] As part of accomplishing this goal, it developed such state-of-the-art programs as a one-click buying service, algorithms that offer suggested products, and a two-day, no-additional-fee shipping service for $79 per year. Unlike other web merchants that force consumers to correspond via email when they have a customer service issue, Amazon.com's site clearly identifies its toll-free customer support telephone number.

Committing to Making Shopping a Fun Experience

The benchmark grocers are also committed to providing a shopping experience that shoppers can describe as "fun," as opposed to a "task." According to Whole Foods' CEO, "Americans love to eat. And Americans love to shop. But we don't like to shop for food. It's a chore, like doing laundry.... Whole Foods thinks shopping should be fun."[37] Similarly, Nordstrom's retired co-chairman, John N. Nordstrom, once stated, "When customers first come into the store, we've got about 15 seconds to get them excited about it."[38]

Len Lewis, the author of a book on Trader Joe's, states, "Trader Joe's has created an event out of going to the store. It has taken a bland, boring repetitive chore and created an adventure that begins when you walk through the door."[39] The Hawaiian shirts worn by the employees, the upbeat background music, sampling stations, the cheerfulness of the staff, the hand-made signs with a nautical theme, and the treasure hunt atmosphere (with a constant flow of new and exciting products) all contribute to a fun experience.

Similarly, everything at Stew Leonard's is geared toward making the shopping trip a "fun-for-all-ages" experience. Young children revel at "Stew's Little Farm," with its baby ducks, goats, chickens, sheep, and geese. Children can also talk with employees who are dressed in animal costumes, and see such animated favorites as "Twinkie the Kid" or "Chiquita" banana. Fun for children is also based on unscripted employee-to-customer interactions. Deli staffers might ask children if they want to bite nose and eye holes into bologna slices so they can wear a "mask." According to Stew Leonard, Jr., "We've got every single kid in the store running to get a piece of bologna now.... We call that a 'wow' as in what I like to hear customers saying when they're going through our store: 'wow,' that was fun!"

Stew Leonard's also focuses attention on its adult customers. The store's cash registers "moo" when customers spend $100 or more. At its "Bags Around the World" exhibit, shoppers are given a $3 gift certificate for each photo of themselves submitted with a Stew Leonard's shopping bag in foreign geographic locations.[40] To appeal to children and their parents, Wegmans' stores feature Wkids Fun Centers, a supervised play place where children 3 to 8 can play while their parents shop. *Child Magazine* has named Wegmans as the most family-friendly supermarket in the United States.

An important element of the fun experience is the constant element of surprise. According to business reporter Andy Bowers, "If a normal supermarket is like a mall—filled with familiar, consistent, and humdrum name brands—Trader Joe's is more like a good bazaar, with its eclectic and erratic selection and frequent surprises, both good and bad."[41] Trader Joe's constant stream of new products encourages new customer visits by introducing 10 to 25 new products weekly. These items replace those that did not sell well. Likewise, at Costco, the treasure hunt (continually introducing new products) adds to the element of surprise. Even Aldi offers weekly special non-food buys such as computers, digital cameras, fancy shower heads, and car navigation systems to add excitement to the shopping experience. These products are offered at rock-bottom prices to attract customers to its stores and web site on a weekly basis.

Stew Leonard's generates customer excitement through changing the store experience based on major holidays. On St. Patrick's Day, local Celtic groups perform in its stores. During Halloween season, the chain features hayrides, pumpkin-carving demonstrations, and a "guess the weight of a giant pumpkin" contests.

L.L.Bean features "Walk-On Adventures" in selected stores, covering an introduction to such events as snowshoeing, kayaking, archery, fly fishing, and cross-country skiing. These hands-on demonstrations vary by season and by store. The demonstrations, which typically cost $20 for 90 minutes, take customers out in the field. Not only do these events offer guidance to novices and intermediate-level participants, but also they stimulate additional purchases.

L.L.Bean views its Walk-On Adventures as a major differentiator; it feels that no other specialty retailer offers anything similar to this. According to L.L.Bean's manager of public affairs, "You can buy outdoor gear and apparel at a lot of places, but not all of these places connect the dots through the continuum by providing a vehicle for learning how to enjoy these outdoor activities. Walk-On Adventures are L.L.Bean personified, the brand in action."[42]

Being Viewed as More Than Just a Typical Store

A logical extension to making shopping a fun experience is for a supermarket "to be viewed by consumers as more than just a typical food store." Whole Foods excels at this strategy. It is effectively positioned in consumers' minds as a place to eat lunch or dinner, to meet someone at a cheese and wine sampling, or as a place to take a nutrition class. The store's "Friday Nights at 5" program, for example, is a regularly scheduled wine-and-cheese tasting presentation. Whole Foods' in-store dining and take-out departments typically include a submarine shop, a Mediterranean bar, an Asian buffet, a fruit and grain bar, a cappuccino bar, and a pizza and wings station. Whole Foods' Columbus Circle New York City location has a sushi bar staffed at lunch with 11 employees, a pizza bar featuring 14 kinds of pizza, a coffee and tea bar, a salad bar with 14 items, and a daily hot-lunch bar that includes separate arrays of Asian, Indian, and Latin food. According to Bruce Silverman, a Whole Foods vice-president, "You wouldn't believe how many people I've heard walking around this store, just saying 'Oh my G-d.... This place should be against the law.'"[43]

Wegmans allows consumers to choose among several meal solution alternatives: purchasing the ingredients separately (however, unlike at most supermarkets, Wegmans' recipe ingredients are displayed next to each other in the store), purchasing the prepared meal in a frozen format, or buying the meal hot and ready-to-eat. At its meal stations, Wegmans' chef and employees not only cook featured meals so customers can sample them, but are also available to give customers cooking tips.[44]

At Stew Leonard's newest store, located in Newington, Connecticut, the chain offers free cooking classes aimed at children and adults. Stew Leonard's Children's Cooking Classes aimed at children aged 8 through 12 provides children attendees with a chef's hat, recipe cards, food to take home that they made, and even a medallion at graduation. The adult class covers presentation and plating techniques, knife skills, using essential tools, and how to shop for ingredients.[45] Clearly, the Whole Foods, Wegmans, and Stew Leonard's examples do not sound anything like a neighborhood supermarket!

Having an Exciting Store Atmosphere

Three important components of store atmosphere include lighting/music/signage, enabling consumers to see much of the manufacturing process, and extensive use of product sampling stations. Lighting and music at Whole Foods are not afterthoughts. Whole Foods lights its produce section with the same type of costly fixtures that are traditionally used in art galleries. Classical music is also played. Both Whole Foods and Trader Joe's hire artists to create signs, murals, and graphics to communicate messages, as well as price information. Trader Joe's uses unique signage for each store geared to each specific location. Stores located near oceans, lakes, and rivers may feature nautical themes, while downtown stores often have urban themes. At its Union Square, New York, store, Trader Joe's renamed its sampling station as "Grand Central Sampling Station," because it is within two miles from the major train station.

Stew Leonard's purposely allows consumers to visualize as much of the manufacturing process as possible. Customers can see orange juice fresh-squeezed, coffee beans roasted, bread baked, meat trimmed, and fresh mozzarella cheese made by hand.[46] This "seeing it all being made" not only adds to the drama and educates children, but also enables consumers to validate the store's use of fresh ingredients and the cleanliness of Stew Leonard's facilities.

Wegmans is purposely laid out to resemble an open-air market with displays of fresh produce, fresh-caught fish, artisan breads, and other baked goods that are baked several times a day. Its stores feature chefs in high hats, European-style cafes, 700 varieties of produce, and French patisseries.

Product sampling is also viewed as a crucial factor that contributes to the overall store image of Whole Foods, Stew Leonard's, Costco, and Trader Joe's. Through sampling, customers see the store as a place to go for a "pick-me-up snack" while shopping, to taste new foods, and to get serving suggestions from well-informed and trusted employees. Trader Joe's sampling program generally involves staff members making recipes with three or less Trader Joe's ingredients. This simplifies explaining how a specific recipe is prepared.

At several of its high-profile branches, Nordstrom customers can obtain restaurant reservations. In addition, Nordstrom features a portfolio of full-service and upscale, fast-casual, in-store eating venues including Café Nordstrom, Marketplace Café, and Café Bistro coffee bars. It also recently debuted Blue Stove, a small-plates cuisine and a wine-bar concept. Nordstrom's Blue Stove Boston store, for example, features such selections as risotto with scallops and asparagus, chicken tacos with lime and cilantro, short ribs, and fried calamari. Most of these items range in price between $5 and $12.[47]

Atmosphere is even more difficult for web-based retailers such as Amazon.com. When Amazon.com expanded its product offerings from books, CDs, DVDs, and videos, it was concerned that its home page would resemble a cluttered storefront. Its current storefront welcomes the customer by name, shows past searches, and contains several tabs. According to Amazon's vice-president of site design,

"When you come into a store, you need a soft landing where you can take a breath and orient yourself, as opposed to getting assaulted by a barrage of offers all at once. We created that soft landing online."[48]

Offering Liberal Money-Back Guarantees

A crucial element of the service experience is the store's money-back guarantee. This establishes an element of trust in dealing with a retailer, reduces the risk in purchasing an untried product or brand, and stresses the value of customer satisfaction in maintaining customer loyalty. Although most stores employ money-back guarantees, too many do not properly promote this feature.

The money-back guarantee is central to customer service strategies at L.L.Bean, Publix, Trader Joe's, Stew Leonard's, Costco, and Aldi. L.L.Bean's 100 Percent Satisfaction Guarantee has been part of the firm's strategy since 1912, when the firm refunded money from the sale of a poorly designed Maine hunting shoe due to the rubber bottom separating from the shoe's leather top. The guarantee is simple to understand and, unlike most guarantees, it does not include such disclaimers as "if," "but," or even "normal wear and tear." It does not even have a time limit. Its guarantee statement reads: "Guaranteed. You Have Our Word. Our products are guaranteed to give 100 percent satisfaction in every way. Return anything purchased from us at any time if it proves otherwise. We do not want you to have anything from L.L.Bean that is not completely satisfactory." To L.L.Bean, its guarantee embodies the firm's principles of integrity, honesty, and quality products.[49] The Publix guarantee is also simply stated: "If for any reason a customer is not completely satisfied with his or her purchase, Publix will offer a full refund."[50] There are also no "ifs, buts, and exceptions" to this policy.

Costco, which traditionally had an unlimited return policy, except on computers, changed its policy in 2007 to set a 90-day return limit on electronic goods (televisions, computers, cameras, camcorders, iPods, MP3 players, and cell phones). In turn, Costco has extended the manufacturer's warranties on televisions and computers from one to two years. Likewise, Trader Joe's has a "no-questions-asked" return policy. Unlike most merchants that receive credit on returned manufacturer-branded merchandise, Trader Joe's discards its private label returns.

Aldi goes an additional step. It has a double warranty. Customers unsatisfied with their purchase receive not only their money back, but also receive a replacement product. All they have to do is to bring back an empty package. Nordstrom has close to an unconditional money-back guarantee (except where prohibited by health laws, as in cosmetics). According to chairman Bruce Nordstrom, "If a customer came into the store with a pair of five-year-old shoes and wanted her money back, you have the right to use your best judgment to give the customer her money back."[51]

Some merchants might question that the liberal nature of these guarantees would open the retailer to potential fraud. As a result of these guarantees, they would argue that consumers could return goods used goods that were subject to normal wear-and-tear, or seek to return a good to secure a newer model at no additional charge. Stew Leonard's customer return policy is designed on the assumption that 99 percent of shoppers are honest. The firm believes that if it tried to protect itself from the 1 percent of customers that were dishonest, it would penalize the other 99 percent. Likewise, Richard Galanti, Costco's chief financial officer, argues, "For every customer that abuses this [return] privilege, there are 99 other members that go, 'Wow.'"[52] Costco recognizes that while reducing its liberal return policy would increase the firm's gross margins, it would hurt its customer service reputation. Its liberal long-term return policy is recognized as a crucial factor leading to high membership renewal.

Listening to Customers and Quickly Reacting to Their Suggestions

Effectively listening to customers does not necessarily mean periodically questioning customers via questionnaires, through focus groups, or by employing consumer panels. Trader Joe's, for example, does not have a contact center nor does it engage in extensive consumer research. Instead, it relies on conversations between customers and captains and crew members. Because managers walk around the store and talk directly with customers, they typically understand the positive and negative experiences of shoppers.

Stew Leonard's uses a suggestion box that typically receives over 100 comments per day. According to Stew Leonard, "Big business always makes it sound so complicated. You don't have to reinvent the wheel. You just have to care." Suggestions are typed up and distributed to appropriate managers by 10 A.M. the following day. At that time, store managers must either act on or call the customers about the complaint or suggestions. Copies are also put in staff refreshment areas for all employees to see. In many cases, corrective action is made before a shopper makes his/her next store visit. Stew Leonard's has also used focus groups for years. On a regular basis, a group of customers is invited to spend an hour explaining what they like and don't like about the store. If an idea works, it is implemented on a permanent basis.

A favorite story of Stew Leonard is when he once opened a tuna fish sandwich and complained to his deli manager that there was too much mayonnaise—a costly ingredient. The following week, he noticed that the problem was not addressed. In speaking with the sandwich preparer, he was told that customers wanted a sandwich packed with extra mayo. Stew's comment to the preparer was "Bravo, Mary!"[53]

Optimizing Customers' Web-Based Service Experience

For a web-based merchant, the service experience relates to the delivery speed, the speed with which questions are answered, a customer's ability to quickly find a suitable product, and the accurate portrayal of a good in terms of features, color, and size. L.L.Bean constantly works to get the web-based images more accurate so that customers will better understand an item's true color, texture, and fit. It also seeks to show customers more than just a thumbnail sketch or static view of a product.[54] L.L.Bean's web site enables consumer to chat with its call center personnel through instant messaging and email. In 2008, L.L.Bean added Customer Ratings and Reviews to its product web pages. This feature not only adds value to L.L.Bean's customers, but also to the retailer's designers and merchandisers who read the reviews to obtain customer feedback regarding fit and performance attributes. As of Fall 2010, its site will incorporate a "click and call" component that will prompt L.L.Bean call center personnel to call back any online shopper who desires additional information within two minutes of the shopper's inquiry.[55] According to *Consumer Reports*, the success of L.L.Bean's web site is due to a combination of factors: customer satisfaction with product quality, accurate descriptions, ease of ordering, and customer-friendly return policies.[56]

Amazon.com personalizes the shopping experience for each customer based on his or her past purchases and previous web searches. Instead of using salespeople to change the company's product offering, computer algorithms arrange the offer. A computer engineer and a new mother will face totally different selections of books. As a result of its highly targeted offerings based on individual consumers, Amazon.com has click-through and conversion rates that are far greater than untargeted web advertising content using banner ads and top-seller listings.[57] Amazon.com's site also is personalized in that customers are referred to by their name.

To facilitate consumers' search process, Amazon.com recently added an Amazon Remembers feature for Blackberry users. This application helps consumers keep track of products they see in their daily lives and matches photos taken by the consumer on his/her Blackberry to products available through Amazon.com. Amazon Remembers automatically uploads the product-based photos, sends the matched results to consumers, and then enables the consumer to either purchase the item or "remember it" for a future purchase.[58]

Amazon.com has been a leader in adding customer reviews to its site. Potential customers can look at reactions, comments, and experiences of past purchasers as a guide to their purchasing decisions. These are similar to a blog. And although Amazon.com can screen reviews for profanity and objectivity (such as reviews from a competitor), Amazon.com's site has high credibility due to the large number of one-star reviews for some products.

Recognizing that the checkout process is where a lot of customers drop out, Amazon.com is a pioneer in offering a one-click checkout alternative. Customers need to enter only their name, address, and credit card number once. At subsequent checkouts, all they have to do is choose the one-click option and enter their password.

To ensure a high-level service experience, Amazon.com launched Fulfillment by Amazon, a service in which Amazon.com's partners send boxes of their products to Amazon and let Amazon handle the total fulfillment process. Amazon.com takes the orders, packs the box, answers questions, and even processes returns. In the last quarter of 2008, Amazon.com shipped 3 million of these orders, up from 500,000 in 2007. Jeff Bezos has argued that Amazon.com has launched Fulfillment by Amazon as a means of making the shopping experience more consistent and reliable.[59] In addition, according to a major Fulfillment by Amazon partner, sales are up 40 percent on the items sold through this program and return rates are down 70 percent. Amazon's partners also anticipate savings between $550,000 and $700,000 because Amazon.com is able to negotiate lower shipping rates.[60]

Nordstrom has made its web site appealing through its adding "Design to Inspire" videos to its web site as an experiment.[61] The format is similar to a trunk show that enables consumers to learn more about products from their designer. These videos feature designers discussing a specific style, its design inspiration, occasions that styles are most appropriate for, and how they can be accessorized. For example, one video series features Michelle Smith, the designer of the popular Milly line. In this video, Smith offers suggestions for wearing the same dress at work, as well as out of the office for cocktails.

Nordstrom has also added RSS (Really Simple Syndication) feeds to its web site in 2007. Although commonly used on news media sites, RSS feeds are highly unusual for an apparel retailer to use. Through use of RSS, a Nordstrom shopper can be automatically alerted when a new product she/he is interested in is added to Nordstrom's online store. For example, a shopper interested in Seven jeans can visit Nordstrom's online store. After searching for Seven jeans, she can click on the Fashion Feed button on the web page. After the customer subscribes to the Fashion Feed, any time a new product is added to Nordstrom.com's site that matches this search, the customer will be automatically sent an email. After opening the email, the shopper is taken directly to the new product page.[62]

Takeaway Points

- The quality of the service experience can be a major differential advantage to retailers who know how to effectively plan and implement both employee and nonemployee dimensions. Retailers who truly understand the competitive dynamics of the industry seek to convert shopping from what many family members regard as a chore to a pleasurable, fun experience. This is not an easy task.

- Some ways of effectively managing the store environment to better ensure a more pleasant service experience include the following:
  - Recognizing the crucial role of employees in both providing the proper environment and in service recovery efforts. The service/value profit chain provides evidence of the importance of hiring, motivating, and retaining high-quality employees.
  - Determining how a fun environment can be developed and sustained. This often requires continued innovation and new events throughout the year. One way of accomplishing this goal is to time the experience with holidays and events such as New Year's Eve, Valentine's Day, Mother's Day, Father's Day, Thanksgiving, and Halloween.
  - Extending activities beyond the realm of a typical store. For example, department stores can include shopping days where 10 percent of sales are contributed to a specific charity, demonstrations of new appliances, cooking classes by important local chefs, lessons on wardrobe, and so on.
  - Paying more attention to the store environment. Product sampling stations, organizing products by color, using appropriate music for shopping, and product-related demonstrations all add to a pleasant sensory experience.
  - Considering how a store can "provide little things that add up to become a lot." Possible "little things" for a grocer can include a web site that lists foods for consumers on restricted diets (such as low sodium, dietetic foods), instructing employees to direct consumers to the exact location of a desired item (not the aisle number), directing the next shopper in line to a new register location (instead of having someone jump the line location), and use of reserved parking spots for expectant mothers and families with young children.
  - Carefully listening to customers (both by managers walking around the store and via surveys and suggestion box notations) and quickly reacting to suggestions.

- Continually monitoring customer satisfaction levels (in terms of in-stock levels, waiting lines at registers, responsiveness of store personnel to queries, parking adequacy, store atmosphere, and so on). One common error is managers looking to improve their scores assuming that competitors will stay at their old levels.
- Evaluating the customer's web-based service experience.

Endnotes

1. B. Joseph Pine and James H. Gilmore, "Welcome to the Experience Economy," *Harvard Business Review* (July–August 1998), pp. 97–105.

2. Susan Reda, "Little Is the New Big," *Stores* (November 2007), pp. 32–34 ff.

3. Heather Green, "How Amazon Aims to Keep You Clicking," *Business Week* (March 2, 2009), pp. 34, 38.

4. Joe Nocera, "Put Buyers First? What a Concept," *New York Times* (January 5, 2008), p. C1.

5. Robert Spector and Patrick McCarthy, *The Nordstrom Way to Customer Service Excellence* (Hoboken, NJ: John Wiley & Sons, 2005), p. 91.

6. Al Witteman, "Get Fresh at Retail," *The Hub* (April 2007), pp. 24–25.

7. "Netflix, Amazon, Publix Top in Customer Satisfaction," *Chain Store Age* (March 2010), p. 16.

8. www.theasci.org, as of June 6, 2010.

9. www.theasci.org, as of June 6, 2010.

10. "L.L.Bean Tops *Bloomberg Business Week's* Fourth Annual Ranking of 'Customer Service Champs,'" *Business Wire* (February 18, 2010).

11. Jena McGregor, "Putting Customers First," *Fast Company* (October 2004), pp. 79 ff.

12. "Costco.com Outshines the Rest," *Consumer Reports* (May 2009), p. 8.

13. "Buying Clothes Online," *Consumer Reports* (December 2008), p. 23.

14. "Rating Electronics Stores," *Consumer Reports* (December 2008), p. 26.

15. Cate T. Corcoran, "Shoppers Love Stores Who Love Them," *Women's Wear Daily* (January 17, 2008), p. 17.

16. "Deliver Customer Service," *Women's Wear Daily* (July 28, 2008), p. 20.

17. "Deliver Customer Service," *Women's Wear Daily* (July 28, 2008), p. 20.

18. Craig Reem, "Retail Revolution," *Orange County Metro* (September 15, 2005), p. 41.

19. Jane Stevenson, "Use Merchandising to Build Brand and Attract Consumers," *Advertising Age* (February 25, 2008), p. 17.

20. www.llbean.com/customerservice/aboutLLBean/background.html, as of April 6, 2009.

21. Michael A. Prospero, "Employee Innovator: Wegmans," *Fast Company* (October 2004), pp. 88 ff.

22. Ryann Acton, "Wegmans Thrives on Supermarket Chic," *The Business Journal-Central New York* (July 20, 2007), p. 17.

23. Michael A. Prospero, "Employee Innovator: Wegmans," *Fast Company* (October 2004), pp. 88 ff.

24. Patrick Barnard, "Survey Shows L.L.Bean Is Tops in Customer Service," *Multichannel Merchant* (February 3, 2009).

25. Jena McGregor, "Leading Listener: Trader Joe's," *Fast Company*, www.fastcompany.com, as of April 1, 2007.

26. Bridget Goldschmidt, "At Stew Leonard's, The Personal Touch Is No Marketing Ploy—It's a Way of Life," *Progressive Grocer* (January 1, 2007), pp. 22 ff.

27. Robert Spector and Patrick McCarthy, *The Nordstrom Way to Customer Service Excellence* (Hoboken, NJ: John Wiley & Sons Inc., 2005), p. xiii.

28. "Nordstrom—Great Service for Over 100 Years" (San Francisco: Great Places to Work Institute), pp. 1, 4.

29. Julie Gallagher, "Your Order Is Ready: Publix Tests Deli-Order Beepers," *Supermarket News* (March 20, 2006), p. 38.

30. Susan Reda, "Little Is the New Big," *Stores* (November 2007), pp. 32–34 ff.

31. Marissa Shalfi, "Costco Commitment," *Retail Merchandiser* (January 2007).

32. Bridget Goldschmidt, "Best Grocers to Work For," *Progressive Grocer* (February 1, 2006).

33. Nanette Byrnes, "More Clicks at the Bricks," *Business Week* (December 17, 2007), p. 50.

34. *Publix Super Markets, Inc. 10-K for Fiscal Year Ending December 27, 2008*, p. 3.

35. Heather Green, "How Amazon Aims to Keep You Clicking," *Business Week* (March 2, 2009), p. 38.

36. Joe Nocera, "Put Buyers First? What a Concept," *New York Times* (January 5, 2008), p. C1.

37. Bruce Horovitz, "A Whole New Ballgame in Grocery Shopping," *USA Today* (March 8, 2005).

38. Robert Spector and Patrick McCarthy, *The Nordstrom Way to Customer Service Excellence* (Hoboken, NJ: John Wiley & Sons, 2005), p. 45.

39. Len Lewis, *The Trader Joe's Adventure* (Chicago: Dearborn Trade Publishing, 2005), p. 56.

40. Bridget Goldschmidt, "Stew Leonard's," *Progressive Grocer* (January 2007).

41. Andy Bowers, "An Insider's Guide to Trader Joe's," *Slate* (March 17, 2006).

42. Correspondence from Carolyn Beem, Manager, Public Affairs, L.L.Bean, June 8, 2009.

43. Mike Adams, "Whole Foods Opens 'Food Amusement Park' Grocery Store in Austin, Texas," *NaturalNews.com* (May 28, 2005), www.naturalnews.com/008029.html, as of February 1, 2009.

44. Ryann Acton, "Wegmans Thrives on Supermarket Chic," *The Business Journal-Central New York* (July 20, 2007), p. 17.

45. "Stew Leonard's to Hold Children's Cooking Classes, Adult Cooking Demos," *Gourmet Retailer* (October 30, 2007).

46. Bridget Goldschmidt, "Stew Leonard's," *Progressive Grocer* (January 2007).

47. Alan Liddle, "In Store Feeders Offer Value Bundles, Branded Fare to Sate Shoppers," *Nation's Restaurant News* (July 28, 2008), p. 72.

48. Robert Spector and Patrick McCarthy, *The Nordstrom Way to Customer Service Excellence* (Hoboken, NJ: John Wiley & Sons, Inc., 2005), p. 61.

49. Correspondence from Carolyn Beem, Manager, Public Affairs, L.L.Bean, June 8, 2009.

50. Chris Petersen, "Friendly Aisles: Providing Attentive Customer Service Is the Key to Publix Super Markets' Success in the Southeast," *US Business Review* (January 2006), pp. 160 ff.

51. Robert Spector and Patrick McCarthy, *The Nordstrom Way to Customer Service Excellence* (Hoboken, NJ: John Wiley & Sons, Inc., 2005), p. 122.

52. Mike Troy, "Costco, A Model Business: Long-Term Vision Benefits Customers, Employers," *DSN Retailing Today* (December 19, 2005), p. 16.

53. "Stew Leonard," *Free Enterprise Land*, www.freeenterpriseland.com, as of April 4, 2007.

54. Patrick Barnard, "Survey Shows L.L.Bean Is Tops in Customer Service," *Multichannel Merchant* (February 3, 2009).

55. Michael Arndt, "L.L.Bean Follows Its Shoppers to the Web," *Business Week* (March 1, 2010), p. 43.

56. Buying Clothes Online," *Consumer Reports* (December 2008), p. 23.

57. Greg Linden, Brent Smith, and Jeremy York, "Amazon.com Recommendations: Item-to-Item Collaborative Filtering," *IEEE Internet Computing* (January–February 2003), p. 76.

58. Amazon Announces Amazon App for Blackberry," *Telecomworldwire* (April 10, 2009).

59. Heather Green, "How Amazon Aims to Keep You Clicking," *Business Week* (March 2, 2009), p. 38.

60. Heather Green, "How Amazon Aims to Keep You Clicking," *Business Week* (March 2, 2009), p. 40.

61. David Moin, "Nordstrom Adds Video to Online Shopping Experience," *Women's Wear Daily* (June 23, 2008), p. 3.

62. Cate T. Corcoran, "Nordstrom 'Simplifies' Customer Satisfaction," *Women's Wear Daily* (March 22, 2007), p. 8.

6

Differentiation Strategies III: Developing and Maintaining a Strong Private Label Program

In a similar manner to the store experience, retailers need to develop distinctive private label products that communicate important functional (rational) and emotional benefits. Functional branding benefits relate to a product's physical attributes (such as quality, value, freshness, health, and convenience). Emotional branding benefits represent image-related considerations, such as what a brand name represents to consumers in terms of status, social responsibility, trust, and degree of culinary sophistication appeals.

Too many private labels lack a clearly focused image. Often, a retailer's private label program is viewed by consumers as simply being a lower-cost alternative to a manufacturer's version of the same product. According to Todd Maute, vice-president of Daymon Worldwide, a firm specializing in the marketing of private label products, "Over half of an average store's 30,000 SKUs are exactly the same. A national brand will come out with a new product, then the next brand, and the next; then private label versions of the product are launched."[1]

One measure of the success of a private label is whether the brand is viewed as truly distinctive by its users. According to Brian Sharoff, president of the Private Label Manufacturers Association (PLMA), Wild Oats, Whole Foods, Wegmans, and Trader Joe's have created distinctive store brands that consumers perceive as upscale, all natural, and culinary sophisticated. "These specialty chains have set the standard for what private label has become."[2] Likewise, many consumers perceive private labels from such retailers as Costco, The Limited, Victoria's Secret, Gap, Target, L.L.Bean, Nordstrom, and Trader Joe's as at least the equivalent of major national brands.

Table 6.1 shows that there are major opportunities for grocery retailers to expand their private label programs. When comparing private label penetration rates for the United States and Europe, the U.S. private label market share (as a percent of total category sales) is just 17 percent. The comparable market share is 25 percent or more in Finland, Denmark, Sweden, France, Spain, Germany, Belgium, and the UK. One way of increasing private label penetration in the United States is to promote the fact that private label brands are currently the best-selling brands in one-quarter of the 240-plus grocery categories.[3]

TABLE 6.1   A Comparison of Private-Label Market Shares in Select European Counties Versus the United States

Country	Private Label Sales as a Percent of Total Category Sales
United Kingdom	42
Belgium	41
Germany	38
Spain	32
France	31
Sweden	26
Denmark	25
Finland	25
Netherlands	23
Norway	19
Hungary	18
United States	17

Source: PLMA International/AC Nielsen, "Prepared Foods: A Place of Their Own," (August 2006), p. 14.

The Nielsen Company found that dollar sales of private label goods within food, drug, and mass merchants (including Wal-Mart) were up by 7.4 percent in dollars for the year ending July 11, 2009.[4] According to Nielsen, shopper migration to private labels is at rates not seen since the last recession in 2001. A Nielsen study also found that 63 percent of consumers now state that the quality of most store brands is as good as that of manufacturer brands, up from 60 percent in 2005.[5]

One recent research study in a major academic journal found that part of the market share gains during recessions become permanent as some of those consumers that have switched to these brands remain loyal long after the recession is over.[6] This finding contradicts the popular notion that private brand market share gains in a recession disappear when the economy recovers.

Advantages of a Strong Private Label Program to Retailers

The major advantages to a retailer's having a strong private label program include increased store loyalty, the role of private labels in a store's differentiation strategy, increased channel power over suppliers, and higher profit margins on private labels (see Figure 6.1). We will now explain each of these advantages.

Figure 6.1   Advantages of a strong private label program

Increased Store Loyalty

Unlike manufacturer brands where suppliers typically sell their goods to most channels (including drug chains, dollar stores, warehouse clubs, and supercenters) and to most vendors within a channel, a distinctive private brand is truly unique to a store. High degrees of customer satisfaction with a retailer's distinctive or high-value private label brand should result in high levels of store loyalty. Loyalty to a private label also increases customers' switching costs when they think about shopping at competing stores.

One major research study found that a 1 percent increase in private label purchasing is associated with a 0.3 percent increase of the "market share" of a household's purchases.[7] If a particular household increases its share of purchases of a specific private label by 10 percentage points, the retailer's market share of that household would thereby increase by 3 percentage points.

The Role of Private Labels in a Store's Differentiation Strategy

To have a major impact on a store's image, a store's private label program needs to demonstrate distinctiveness in terms of ingredients (organic, low salt, low fat for food products), recipe (for food products), styling, features, and value. Unfortunately, too many private labels are too similar to manufacturer brands or to other private labels.

At Aldi, distinctiveness is achieved through offering its customers exceptional value through its private labels. According to Aldi's Scotland-based trading director, "We like to source our products wherever we can to give us the freedom to buy what we want in order to fulfill our aim of being 10 percent to 20 percent cheaper than elsewhere. If we take a big brand, we are beholden to their retailing, merchandising, and promotional requirements, which can use up resources. With our own label, we can get similar quality without the extra cost."[8]

Stew Leonard's evaluates its private label alternatives based on a simple test: whether the private label alternative is advantageous to its customers over the national brand options. To be considered, the private label option must have a lower price, use higher-quality ingredients, employ better packaging, and so on. After analyzing these functional attributes, Stew Leonard's then considers how easily it can communicate these advantages to its consumers.[9]

The contribution of private labels to a store's differentiation increases when private labels are sought after due to overall quality and value. This strategy is especially significant when private label goods account for a large proportion of a store's total sales, as with Aldi, L.L.Bean (where about 90 percent of the goods sold are private label), Trader Joe's, Whole Foods, and Nordstrom. Strategies that retailers can use to achieve both functional and emotional distinctiveness for their private label products will be discussed at a later point in this chapter.

Increased Channel Power over Suppliers

Private label brands can provide a retailer with increased channel power over its manufacturer brand suppliers. Retailers can increase their channel power by giving preferred positioning to their private labels, charging lower prices for the private label in comparison to manufacturer brands (often called "fighting against the manufacturer's brand"), and by threatening to or actually replacing a manufacturer brand with a comparable private label version. The increased channel power for a retailer is obviously greatest when a manufacturer's brand is weak relative to the store's private label or other manufacturer brands. Second- and third-tier manufacturer brands are most vulnerable to loss of power by virtue of a retailer's having a strong private label in that product category.

According to Bob Nelson, Costco's vice-president of finance and investor relations, one reason that Costco invests in its private label products is to give it "leverage against vendors, driving its [wholesale] prices down." Costco, as well as its suppliers, fully recognize that Costco is ready, willing, and able to launch its own private label if it can't get the right price on a national brand. When cranberry-juice maker Ocean Spray refused to cut its wholesale prices, Costco launched its own private label of cranberry juice. And when its private label brand sold better, Ocean Spray's cranberry juice was discontinued.[10] Because Costco delivered an average of $18.4 million in sales per SKU in its fiscal 2009, manufacturers cannot ignore its potential as a direct competitor or the loss of this significant sales volume.

The impact of private label products on a retailer's channel power has been demonstrated in two academic research studies. Both studies support the notion that private brands provide additional leverage and bargaining power over national brands. The first study found that a retailer's profit margins for Quaker Oats products increased after the retailer introduced competing private label products.[11] The second study found that a retailer's profit margins on manufacturer brands were higher for product categories where the retailer's private label has a high market share.[12] This study found that in private label categories with high market shares, the supermarket chain has 4 percentage points greater gross margin than on those private label categories that had low market shares. These studies suggest that the existence of a private label brand alternative increases a retailer's bargaining power with the suppliers of competing manufacturer brands. It also suggests that the degree of bargaining power is related to the strength of private label alternatives (as measured by their market share).

The strength of the retailer's channel power associated with a brand is obviously related to the private label's market share relative to manufacturer brands. Manufacturer brands that are "also-rans" are particularly susceptible to strong private labels. This concept has been illustrated by Larry Light, an executive with BackerSpeilvogel-Bates, who coined the phrase, "One, two, three or you're out." This expression means that if a brand were not one of the three top brands in a product category, it would lose out in terms of shelf space, consumer awareness, and manufacturing efficiencies.[13]

Higher Profit Margins on Private Labels

It is generally difficult to make direct comparisons of the net profit on private labels versus manufacturer brands since private labels can involve significant research and development expenses and manufacturer brands often are accompanied by payments and discounts in the form of slotting fees, return privileges for unsold merchandise, promotional allowances (such as manufacturer advertising, cooperative advertising programs, and in-store manufacturer-sponsored promotions), and warehousing support. Furthermore, direct comparisons need to examine the inventory turnover of both types of brands. Private labels may have different inventory turnover rates than national brands.[14] Finally, because manufacturer brands typically sell for more than private labels, even with equal gross profit margins between the two types of brands, manufacturer brands would earn higher profits in dollars.

There is some evidence that retailers receive higher gross profit margins for their private label products in comparison to manufacturer brands. One highly regarded book on private label strategy states that, on average, a retailer's profit margin on private labels is 25 percent to 30 percent greater than on manufacturer brands.[15] Another report indicates that gross margins on private labels average 35 percent to 40 percent on grocery-related items versus an average of 27 percent on national brands.[16] Finally, a literature review of private label brands argues that these brands have higher margins due to three factors: lower costs, lower retailer expenditures for research and development and promotional costs, and lower competition among private label brands within a retailer.[17]

A McKinsey report evaluated brand strength across four types of retailers: superstores (Kmart, Target, and Wal-Mart), department stores (Bloomingdale's, Saks, and Neiman Marcus), general merchandisers (J.C. Penney and Sears), and big-box stores (Circuit City and

Best Buy). This study found that retailers with strong private label brands (measured on the basis of quality, distinctiveness, and consistency) had higher sales per square foot than retailers with weaker private labels. According to the McKinsey analysis, consumers also visit high-brand-strength stores more frequently, have larger purchases per shopping trip, or pay price premiums at these stores.[18]

Private Label Strategies of Successful Retailers

According to the editor-in-chief of *Progressive Grocer*, Trader Joe's is "the most effective store brander in the country right now."[19] Other standout store branders cited by the *Progressive Grocer* editor are Whole Foods, Wegmans, Wild Oats, and HEB's Central Market.[20] A *Consumer Reports* study found that 64 percent of its survey respondents were highly satisfied with Trader Joe's brands.[21] This was the highest ranking of any supermarket, supercenter, warehouse club, and limited-assortment store studied. Private label brands of Whole Foods, Wegmans, Costco, Publix, and Raley's also received high scores in the *Consumer Reports* study.[22]

Let's now look at the successful branding strategies of our benchmark retailers. This section is organized into two parts: functional and emotional distinctiveness.

Functional Distinctiveness Strategies

Functional distinctiveness concerns how a private label product performs in terms of its durability, performance, features, value, taste (for foods), and health-related attributes (for foods). We will see how successful food retailers have developed functional product distinctiveness through such strategies as offering cut-up fruits and vegetables, frozen foods that taste great, foreign taste treats, an unusual combination of ingredients, extensive testing of private label goods, and special formulated foods that are salt-, gluten-, and/or sugar-free (or have reduced levels of these substances). We will also examine how Nordstrom's Product Group designs and contracts with manufacturers to produce its extensive line of private labels and how Trader Joe's, L.L.Bean, and Amazon.com extensively test their private label products.

A private label can achieve functional distinctiveness through focusing on product quality over pricing appeals; conducting consumer research to deliver distinctive products; searching for opportunities in fast-growing healthy, organic, "green," and ethnic markets; working closely with suppliers on product research and development; round-the-world sourcing; extensive testing of private label goods; and constantly reevaluating the sales success of private labels (see Figure 6.2). Let's examine how our benchmark retailers deliver functional distinctiveness on their private label brands based on these strategies.

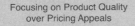

Focusing on Product Quality
over Pricing Appeals

Conducting Consumer Research to
Deliver Distinctive Products

Searching for Opportunities in Fast-Growing
Healthy, Organic, Green, and Ethnic Markets

Working Closely with Suppliers on Product
Research and Development

Round-the-World Sourcing

Extensive Testing of Private Label Goods

Constantly Reevaluating the Sales
Success of Private Labels

Figure 6.2   Elements of a functional distinctiveness strategy for private brands

Focusing on Product Quality over Pricing Appeals

Although private label products are typically sold on the basis of price, many of the benchmark retailers are primarily concerned with developing private labels based on taste, quality, and freshness. To these retailers, private label products that do not meet these criteria are not considered, regardless of their low price or potential profitability. This process assures that quality is always tantamount to price issues. Several of these retailers have begun to develop private label products that are functionally superior to and more costly than their manufacturer brand rivals.

As an example of this process, Costco is especially concerned with the taste of its private label goods. According to Thomas Aquilina, a retail consultant, "They [the Costco buyers] want to taste the product before they do anything else. If the taste isn't first-rate, the process will stop right there. After taste criteria are met, the buyer will start talking price."[23] The same quality orientation applies to anything that has the Costco private label on it.[24]

All of Costco's Kirkland private label products are based on a clear quality proposition: Kirkland products can be priced below those of national brands, but also above their price levels, depending on consumers' perception of value. Richard Galanti, Costco's executive vice-president and chief financial officer, has argued, "For years, supermarkets demanded price points. You take something as basic as a can of tuna: Throughout the '80s and '90s, every time the cost went up [the manufacturer would] make it a 5.1-ounce can instead of a 5.2-ounce can." [Grocers said] "Let's do less filet and more of a chunk because we've got to sell something 3 for $5 on a special."[25] Costco approached the proposition differently. "We've upped the quality," Galanti said, and "upped the price above the branded item and we're selling more units. Because it's the best tuna you could buy."[26] Costco's private label brand, Kirkland, accounts for about 15 percent of Costco's total sales and includes 500 products ranging from trail mix to champagne.[27] According to James Sinegal, Costco's private brands have the potential to account for 20 percent of its SKUs and 30 percent of the chain's total sales.[28]

Although Aldi acknowledges the importance of the price in its private label products, the head of Aldi-Australia states that "We are hard discounters who start with brand quality first. And that is absolutely where we start. We always look at quality first and then we will have a look at who can make that product best for us."[29] To make sure its products will have high consumer acceptance, Aldi benchmarks its private label products against the market share leading product in a given product category. Aldi then gets manufacturers to replicate or improve on the market leader. In many instances, the Aldi private label brand is often made by the manufacturer of the market leading brand in that category.[30]

Some foreign retailers have also begun to offer premium private labels that can exceed their manufacturer brand counterparts in independent ratings. These premium private-label brands include Loblaws's President Choice (Canada), Tesco's Finest (UK), Marks & Spencer's St. Michael (UK), Pick & Pay's Choice (South Africa), and Albert Heijn's AH Select (Netherlands).

At Stew Leonard's, the concept of product quality is seen from the perspective of freshness (and is applied to a wide variety of products: milk, fresh-squeezed orange juice, scratch-baked goods, fresh-cut fruit, or even homemade mozzarella). According to a Stew Leonard's executive, "Eighty percent of our products are either made fresh onsite or bought fresh every day."[31] Stew Leonard, Jr., son of the company's founder, states that "We started as dairy farmers, and from the very beginning, there was a real emphasis on fresh, because you can't store milk for a month."[32] This is in stark contrast to most grocery stores whose top management often has packaged goods industry experience. As part of the freshness philosophy, Stew Leonard's empowers its employees to reject shipments of fruits that do not meet the store's top-quality standards. If a store runs out of strawberries because it could not find a high-quality supply, the department manager indicates on a sign that it could not find strawberries of sufficiently high quality to be sold at Stew Leonard's.

An important part of Trader Joe's branding philosophy relates to product safety. After major reports on product safety issues and Chinese ingredients, many customers felt uneasy about purchasing Chinese food products. As of April 2008, Trader Joe's discontinued all single-ingredient Chinese food products, such as garlic, frozen organic spinach, ginger, and edamame.[33] The dropping of these products was Trader Joe's way of stating its overall concern for product safety and consumer health, above sales and profits. As further evidence of concern for consumers, all of Trader Joe's private label products are free of artificial colors, flavors, and preservatives.

Conducting Consumer Research to Deliver Distinctive Products

Many of the benchmark retailers take an active part in the development of their private label products as evidenced by extensive consumer research undertaken to develop new products. These firms are known to first determine which products the customer wants and then find a manufacturer to make it. This is in contrast to the selling philosophy in which the retailer contracts with a manufacturer to make a private label product and then tries to promote it.

According to a management consultant, Trader Joe's is one of most successful private brand programs in the United States—on par with Sainsbury and Tesco in the UK—when it comes to quality. According to Frank Dell, president of Dellmart & Company, a food and consumer products consultant, "[At Trader Joe's] it's never apples to apples, it's always apples to apples with a twist. Not the supermarket model which seeks to replicate national brands at a slightly lower price."[34] Gretchen Gogesch, president of Integrale LLC, an innovation-based consulting firm, states that retailers could learn a lot from the way Trader Joe's defines its image and products. Says Gogesch, "Dare to have a unique point of view. Customers appreciate it and are drawn to it."[35] Joe Coulombe, the founder of Trader Joe's, was once quoted as saying, "You can take any product, no matter how dull a commodity it may seem, and dig into it. You can find something different that can be exploited." Examples of Trader Joe's products that can be categorized as "everyday products with a twist" include wild salmon in cans, microwavable scrambled egg whites, chocolate-coated sunflower seeds, peanut butter-filled pretzels, and multi-grain pretzel nuggets sprinkled with sesame seeds.

The concept of an "everyday product with a twist" can be easily illustrated by looking at retailers in a number of industries. Brooks Brothers, for example, has a line of Advantage chinos® that is specially treated cotton to repel stains and to retard creasing. It also does not require ironing when washed. Realizing that men prefer different styles and have different body shapes, these pants are available in three different combinations of pleated and two plain fronts (such as slim, straight, and relaxed fits). To further minimize the need for tailoring, these pants are available in 1-inch multiple waist sizes (from 30-inch to 40-inch widths), whereas most competitive manufacturers only have even waist sizes). The slacks are also precuffed.

Wegmans sells about 8,000 products that are part of its private label brand. Some are unique, such as Wegmans Basting Oil, which contains grape-seed oil, garlic-oil extract, and freeze-dried parsley and thyme. This product targets the gap between the need for high-quality home-cooked foods and limited time for cooking based on work and family obligations. Similarly, Wegmans uses packaged convenience as a theme for many of its products, such as prechopped onions, celery, and cleaned leeks.

L.L.Bean uses extensive interviews with customers and product concept development meetings with focus groups to develop new products that meet specific customer requirements for outdoor clothing and gear.[36]

Searching for Opportunities in Fast-Growing Healthy, Organic, "Green," and Ethnic Markets

Outlaw Consulting, a market research firm that focuses on social and style trends, recently conducted a research study to determine what "Gen Y" consumers, 21- to 29-year-olds, view as the "top 15 green brands." The top five brands, in order, were Whole Foods (1), Trader Joe's (2), Toyota (3), Honda (4), and Google (5).[37]

According to a new products analyst with Mintrl International, Trader Joe's employs savvy buyers who constantly look out for products that fit the chain's philosophy, as well as its commitment to sustainability, organics, and innovation.[38] Trader Joe's buyers especially seek out opportunities at natural and organic food trade shows. Its buyers also visit Whole Foods. According to the analyst, "One of the interesting things is that they're [Trader Joe's] able to take niche products, or products you can only find in a small specialty shop, and bring them to a wider audience."[39]

Trader Joe's, Whole Foods, and Wegmans elicit a "feel-good" perception among consumers. Trader Joe's, as an example, stopped selling ducks after animal rights activists complained about the manner in which ducks were slaughtered. All Ahi tuna sold at Trader Joe's are caught without nets. Whole Foods is also deeply committed to the environment. It will not stock Chilean sea bass (the product has been seriously overfished) or lobsters. (Whole Foods does not like how they are stored after being caught.) It also refuses to sell commercial veal from tethered calves and foie gras from force-fed ducks.[40] Additionally, Whole Foods monitors the production and environmental practices of its seafood suppliers and fully supports the seafood sustainability work of the Marine Stewardship Council.

Similarly, Wegmans has worked with Environmental Defense (a major environmental advocacy organization) and its farmed seafood suppliers to help improve practices within the aquaculture industry. Since 2007, Wegmans has sold shrimp from Belize whose supplier has eliminated the use of antibiotics and other chemicals, avoided damaging sensitive habitats, treated the waste water, and reduced the use of wild fish to feed shrimp. Wegmans continues to work with its other shrimp and salmon suppliers to help them reach similar standards.[41]

In addition to environmental issues, Trader Joe's will not sell goods that contain genetically engineered ingredients or trans fats. The chain also sells a large selection of organic and natural items, and all its varieties of dried apricots do not contain any sulphur. Likewise, Whole Foods features minimally processed foods that are free from artificial preservatives, colors, flavors, sweeteners, and hydrogenated fats. Whole Foods will also not sell any products that contain preservatives or trans fats. According to Scott Van Wrinkle, managing director of research for Adams Harkness, an investment banking firm, "Probably more than any other retailer, Whole Foods is about something."[42] Grocery consultant Bill Bishop has commented, "What everyone is really looking for is a mother. Whole Foods assumes the responsibility of taking care of you in a somewhat materialistic way—everything in their store has been edited."[43]

Aldi, the extreme value grocery chain, has a Fit & Active line of 60 products (including cereal bars, yogurt, salad dressing, and packaged meats). The "Fit Facts" listing for each of its Fit & Active branded products uses color graphics to display the product's calories, fat, sodium, and sugar levels. In addition, this listing also lists whether or not the product is a good source of fiber. Fit & Active is the first private label brand to include these guideline daily amounts as part of its packaging.[44]

Publix was one of the first grocery chains to offer a private label for Hispanic products, according to Ron Johnston, the publisher of *The Shelby Report*, a monthly journal for grocers.[45] In addition, Publix has a GreenWise brand with its own monthly magazine called *Publix Green-Wise Market*. This magazine includes features concerning nutrition and has advertising from natural food vendors, as well as coupons. Publix recently introduced bathroom and facial tissue made from 100-percent recycled paper.

These retailers have established and maintained an image among consumers as the ever-watchful editor of a selection of merchandise offered by suppliers. They have a reputation that they are looking out for their consumers in terms of offering products that are healthy, that are environmentally sound, and that one can feel good about serving to his or her family. The pervasive feeling is that the retailer is looking at the ingredient listing so the consumer does not have to.

Working Closely with Suppliers on Product Research and Development

Research and development is often needed to taste test foreign products for their acceptability in a domestic market, or to determine consumer acceptance of different package sizes or ingredients. Because many retailers do not have the staff or financial resources to develop new private label products on their own, they need to work closely with their suppliers. Suppliers may be small firms with a limited market presence or large firms that are manufacturers of major national brands that hope to profitably use their excess capacity.

Trader Joe's buyers spend a lot of time working with manufacturers to develop niche products. Marie Forsyth, Trader Joe's product manager for snacks and candy, "...[has] emphasized the importance of being able to work with the supplier hand-in-hand in sort of an artisan basis, working with small batches and tinkering to find [just the] right product." The Winter 2007 issue of *Trader Joe's Fearless Flyer* states, "Our frozen foods buyer is known in the industry as someone who really likes to roll up his sleeves and get involved in the process. Really. It's not uncommon for him to be in the kitchen with a renowned chef, adding ingredients and modifying recipes until their creation is just right. Our involvement in every step of this process—from selecting ingredients to formulating recipes—is one of the reasons you'll find so many things in Trader Joe's that you won't find anywhere else."

Nordstrom's Product Group (NPG) consists of close to 500 employees that design, source, and merchandise its private label apparel and footwear brands. These brands include Classiques Entier, Caslon, and other Nordstrom labels. Nordstrom's private label merchandise is available in its Nordstrom and Rack stores, as well as in its catalogs and online. In 2008, NPG has developed a Wentz line of T-shirts for a limited time, as well as hooded jackets, denim jeans, and accessories. The Wentz line is named for Pete Wentz, the bassist in the multiplatinum brand, Fall Out Boy. To aid in the promotion of its Wentz line, Nordstrom developed a limited edition CD-DVD entitled "Making Mischief," which features video footage of Wentz's design collaboration, as well as 10 unreleased tracks from Wentz.[46]

Similarly, L.L.Bean is working with Alex Carleton, a well-known fashion designer, on a new line of clothing called L.L.Bean Signature. According to Carleton, "The Signature DNA is classic American sportswear staples with updated fits—more body conscious and less restrictive."[47] The L.L.Bean Signature line is priced 20 to 30 percent above traditional L.L.Bean clothing and is aimed at a more style-conscious consumer. In addition to developing more modern inter-pretations of men's blazers and ladies shirtdresses, the Signature line includes new versions of such L.L.Bean classics as the Boat and Tote bag. Carleton designed clothing for Abercrombie & Fitch and Polo Ralph Lauren before beginning his own brand in 2002.[48]

Round-the-World Sourcing

Trader Joe's 15 to 20 buyers have relationships with hundreds of vendors and are constantly scouting the market for unique items.[49] These buyers seek out finished goods other retailers are not selling or find specialized ingredients for their own recipes. At Trader Joe's, uniqueness is often based on a product's ethnicity (such as a Bulgarian eggplant spread, Sicilian olive oil, French crème brulee dessert, and

Italian pasta available in specialized shapes). About 25 percent of Trader Joe's suppliers are located overseas. To underscore a product's ethnicity, Trader Joe's uses the Trader Giotto's brand for Italian items, Trader José's for Mexican foods, Trader Ming's for Chinese foods, Trader Darwin for vitamins, and Trader Joe-San for Japanese foods. Foreign sourcing has an additional advantage, as it is difficult for competitors to replicate Trader Joe's due to difficulty in establishing and maintaining relationships with product manufacturers worldwide.

Although Nordstrom's Product Group sources its manufacturing throughout the world, it requires its suppliers to fully meet its standards and business practices guidelines involving legal practices, health and safety issues for workers, and environmental responsibilities.

Extensive Testing of Private Label Goods

Category managers at both Trader Joe's and Aldi more closely resemble product managers at a manufacturer of branded goods like Heinz or Campbell due to their high involvement with initial and subsequent taste testing of recipes and ingredients. At Trader Joe's Boston and Monrovia offices, panels of up to 20 people sample products in development and others already sold in its stores. According to Jon Basalone, Trader Joe's senior vice-president for marketing, the panel approves about 10 percent of the products it samples.[50]

Often, products go through multiple taste tests and revisions before the product is placed in Trader Joe's stores. For example, although the tasting panel has gone through five different variations of dried tortellini, it still has not approved a product version. Some combinations of ingredients were not filling enough, others were too filling, and still others didn't properly cook.[51] Likewise, a Thai peanut snack was repeatedly given to Trader Joe's taste-testing panel, which finally agreed to stock the good after the proper balance of salt, spices, citrus, and heat was obtained.[52]

Although Aldi's customers are price-conscious, it does not mean that the food retailer will sacrifice taste or quality for price. Aldi's

Australian unit conducts two internal sampling sessions each day to test existing and proposed products. It also uses outside consultants to advise the firm about product quality.[53] Aldi carefully tests all of its products in its test kitchens to ensure that its private label products meet or exceed the quality and taste of manufacturer brands. Blind taste testing is routinely done by Aldi's UK managing director and seven members of its buying committee against competitive brands, some of which are much more costly. For example, Aldi recently tested six variations of a curry that were evaluated by a panel on the basis of the distinctiveness of the tomato and onion flavors, as well as the sauce's appearance. Even though the Aldi alternative was priced at 30 percent of the cost of the Tesco product, the Aldi product outscored similar products sold by Sainsbury, Asda, and Tesco.[54] In circumstances when the Aldi product did not have the highest-ranking score, the taste testers would determine the reasons and then make appropriate suggestions to the supplier. Similarly, Aldi uses its test kitchen in its U.S. headquarters location for taste testing of all of its food and beverage products six times per year against major national brands. Products that do not perform well are earmarked for immediate improvement by its suppliers.[55]

Aldi's system obviously works! A British independent market research firm recently found that Aldi's private label offerings were viewed, on the basis of taste tests by consumers, as at least as good as manufacturer brands in 14 of 15 product categories tested.[56] As additional evidence of Aldi's concern for quality, despite its low prices, eight Aldi products were recently highlighted for their exceptional value at the Quality Food Awards, the UK's equivalent of the Oscars of the food industry.[57] The high quality of Aldi's private label products was also confirmed by a market research firm that analyzed the results of consumer tests (conducted in 26 product categories by Germany's leading consumer safety group, Stitf ung Warentest). This firm found that 81 percent of Aldi's private label products were rated as good to excellent as compared with 74 percent of the national brands.[58] Aldi is so convinced of the overall quality of its private label goods that it offers a "double guarantee." It offers to gladly replace its private label product *as well as* refund the product's purchase price, if the consumer is not "100 percent satisfied with the product."

Although Aldi likes to stress its private label brands, it will not stock a private label that does not meet or beat a comparable manufacturer brand. Among the few national brands available at Aldi are Hershey chocolate bars, Arizona iced tea, and Pringles potato snacks. According to Aldi's vice-president of corporate purchasing, these manufacturer brands would not be available at Aldi if the chain could find a way of making similar products with the same taste and quality.[59]

L.L.Bean operates its own independent laboratory to test materials, construction, and design of its private label goods. L.L.Bean continually tests, revises, and retests goods in laboratory and field environments against their competitors to ensure that they meet the retailer's high standards, as well as the expectations of consumers.[60] In addition to laboratory testing, L.L.Bean has a group of 1,300 independent field testers—adults, as well as children—who evaluate new products. In addition, L.L.Bean personnel are involved in using new goods. Explains L.L.Bean's president, Chris McCormick, "We get into the field as much as we can at L.L.Bean and do the same things that our customers are doing. We use our own products so that we have a better idea of how they're performing."[61] Established products are also tested to ensure that the quality of materials and construction continue to meet the company's high standards. After selection, product quality is confirmed through customer-based surveys.[62]

Amazon.com uses an independent testing laboratory to test the quality of its Pinzon-branded cookware line. The laboratory performs extensive testing to confirm the cookware's meeting specific standards for stability; bottom flatness; resistance to torque, heat, and fatigue; boil dry; and soak testing. It is not surprising that *Cook's Illustrated* magazine rated a Pinzon cookware set as a "Best Buy."

Constantly Reevaluating the Sales Success of Private Labels

Retailers need to constantly reevaluate their private label offerings in terms of taste tests with new manufacturer brands, opportunities for new products (such as ethnic products, co-branding opportunities, and health-related products), and so on. Obviously, poor-selling private label products need to be either modified or discontinued. This process takes on added significance for grocers with relatively few SKUs (such as Aldi, Costco, Trader Joe's, and Stew Leonard's), because these firms cannot afford to devote valuable shelf space to poor-selling goods. Eliminating poor-selling products also opens up opportunities for a stream of new goods.

To add excitement, Trader Joe's constantly changes its portfolio of private label products. Because Trader Joe's introduces 1,000 new products each year, yet stocks only about 3,000 in its stores, it must constantly stop marketing poor-selling products. As soon as Trader Joe's realizes it has made a buying mistake, store managers stop reordering the poorly selling product and then wait for their current supply to run out.

Emotional Distinctiveness Strategies

A brand's emotional distinctiveness relates to what a brand name means to consumers. Typical emotional distinctiveness variables include a brand's image, positioning, packaging, and promotion. In total, emotional distinctiveness translates into such attributes as a brand that a good cook would consider purchasing, a brand committed to ecological issues, or a brand that can be trusted.

L.L.Bean believes that its brand is more than a selling proposition or marketing device. It is the embodiment of all that the company stands for.[63] Research by L.L.Bean found that positive associations with the L.L.Bean brand were "excellent customer service," "a company I can trust," "sells high-quality items," and "good for outdoor items."[64] The core values statement of L.L.Bean reflects its unique positioning:

- **Outdoor heritage**—The enduring worth of our natural environment and the physical and spiritual value of the outdoors experience.

- **Integrity**—The physical quality of our products; telling the truth; and guaranteeing satisfaction 100 percent; L.L.'s Golden Rule.

- **Service**—Treating customers like human beings with the best, personal service we would all like to receive; and meeting all our responsibilities to our employees, owners, and communities.

- **Respect**—Respect for all people involved in our enterprise and trusting them to be honest and straightforward; valuing their talents and points of view.

- **Perseverance**—L.L.Bean is in it for the long term; in good times and bad, we will not yield in our values.[65]

Trader Joe's brand also stands for a series of values among consumers. Laurie Demeritt, president of the Hartman Group, a marketing research firm, states that consumers seem to respond to Trader Joe's almost as if it were a real person. "And because they see Trader Joe's as a person, they trust that the products are safe (pesticide-free), organic, and sustainable—and most important, taste good. Consumers think they can relax because T.J.'s has done all the research."[66] Coles, Woolworth, and Aldi stores are other examples of store names that connoted "trust" in the Australian market. A 2006 study by Maxus Retail in the Australian market found that Coles, Woolworth, and Aldi stores had higher levels of predisposition and trust than the manufacturer brands stocked by these stores, with the exception of Colgate.[67]

Too often, private labels have no or weak emotional distinctiveness levels. A grocer can build emotional distinctiveness through using co-branding, recognizing the importance of packaging, and telling a story about what makes one's products unique (see Figure 6.3).

Using Co-Branding

In *co-branding*, a private label brand is paired with a strong national brand. Although the co-branded product is still distinctive to

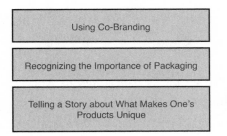

Figure 6.3   Elements of an emotional distinctiveness strategy for private brands

the retailer, it adds the cache, image, and market strength of the manufacturer brand to the good. Costco commonly pairs its Kirkland private label brand with a national brand that has a strong, positive, and premium image, such as the Starbucks name coupled with Costco's Kirkland brand coffee. Although the Starbucks brand name imparts a prestige image to Costco's private label, the Kirkland brand shows its connection with Costco and differentiates the product from the national brand alternative.

Costco now has a dozen co-brands, including Starbucks coffee, Newman's Own products, Jelly Belly candy, Quaker Oats cereal, Post cereal, Whirlpool appliances, Borghese cosmetics, and Stonyfield dairy products. When Costco co-brands with such upscale suppliers, it makes sure that co-branded merchandise is offered at lower prices than comparable merchandise and has comparable quality.[68] Where there are no strong national brands, Costco has established Kirkland as the key product in the category.[69] Similarly, Target uses co-branding with major designers (such as Michael Graves Design, Kitchen Essential from Caphalon, Mossimo, and Liz Lange for Target) to impart a positive, fashion image for its private label products. And Amazon.com has a line of kitchen utensils and tools called Tom Douglas by Pinzon. Tom Douglas is a well-known Seattle chef, cookbook author, and restaurateur.

Recognizing the Importance of Packaging

Private label packaging is often neglected. In too many instances, the packaging for private label products is bland, nondistinctive, and dated in appearance. One gets the impression that packaging is erroneously viewed as unimportant and not given the attention and resources it deserves.

Publix recognizes that part of branding is packaging, as well as effective promotion. In 2000, Publix conducted a corporate identity audit to better examine its logos and retail environment. As a result of this program, three departments were provided with new branding identities: deli, bakery, and pharmacy. Publix recently revamped its private label packaging with sleeker graphic lines and brighter colors. According to an article in the *New York Times Magazine*, "Publix products have their own look: clean, clever—and with lots of white space and simple but crisp typography—vaguely upscale." And according to Tim Cox, Publix's director of in-house creative-service department, the style of private brand at Publix is to "separate itself from what else is happening on the shelf." Publix's distinctive packaging for canned vegetables shows a spoon with a few peas or corn kennels; its aluminum foil boxes feature little animals (a turtle, a swan, and a moose) made of foil.[70] The packaging design also won praise from *Package Design Magazine*, *Private Label Buyer*, and *HOW*, a graphics-design business magazine. *HOW* named Publix "in-house design group of the year" in 2005.[71]

Although other firms outsource their private labeling promotional program, Publix has a small in-house army of packaging designers, promotions personnel, copywriters, and advertising staffers devoted strictly to private labels. Publix also promotes private labeling programs through in-store promotions. In its Publix Brand Challenge regional promotion, consumers who purchased certain national brands received the Publix private label version free of charge (instead of using in-store sampling of its private labels). In this manner, consumers could do a side-by-side taste comparison in their homes using traditional recipes and other ingredients.[72]

Telling a Story About What Makes One's Products Unique

Blaine Becker, an executive with a market research company, states that customers have a hunger for information about private brands concerning their ingredients, where they are produced, and what standards are being adhered to.[73] The story can be communicated as part of the label, through periodic promotions, via store signage, or on the store's web site. Effective stories can be based on a product's ingredients (natural), sourcing (a local farmer), recipe (a 100-year-old secret recipe), and health characteristics (low salt).

Trader Joe's clearly excels in this area by providing such information through its quarterly *Fearless Flyer* newsletter and web site. The 12- to 20-page *Fearless Flyer*, which is distributed via direct mail and in-store, contains irreverent descriptions of new and existing products with Victorian-era cartoons. Central to the *Fearless Flyer* strategy is its focus on stories that "foodies" want to read, as opposed to just a low-price message. The Winter 2007 issue of *Fearless Flyer* (page 3) shows off the unique selling proposition of many of its items with informative material. Its Wild Pacific Silverbrite Salmon Fillets is an excellent example: "Talk about a value! Our Wild Pacific Silverbrite Salmon Fillets are from the new catch, fished from the icy cold waters off Alaska. Much of the salmon you find in grocers' freezers has been frozen, shipped to China for processing, frozen again, and shipped back to the States for sale. Not ours. We think that process interferes with the fish's flavor and texture, so we're only selling 'once frozen' salmon in our freezers."

Trader Joe's web site also contains similar stories of new products. For example, its All Natural Ground Chicken "is flavorful and versatile, perfect for a variety of memorable meals, including chili, tacos, meatloaves, burgers...you name it. Plus it is low in fat—a truly lean, healthy protein. Even better? It's all natural, meaning there are no antibiotics or hormones added ever."

One of Stew Leonard's featured private brand products is Naked Chicken, a 100-percent natural chicken with no antibiotics or preservatives. To effectively communicate its new product's positioning, it chose the Naked Chicken brand name. To reinforce its image, Stew Leonard's retail promotions for Naked Chicken include demonstrations, tastings, a new Naked Chicken costume character, in-store banners, emails to customers, and five weeks of $1 off coupons.

L.L.Bean, a common winner in the *Multichannel Merchant's* catalog awards competition, often uses the "telling a story" strategy. In a recent L.L.Bean Kids Catalog, its fitness fleece pullover was described as follows: "Our lightest fleece is made of stretchy polyester microfleece—just the right weight to starve off chilly breezes or cool night air. And a special treatment helps it resist pilling with every wash. Sleeve pocket holds miniature treasures."[74]

It's comparatively easy to tell a story about a product by virtue of its superior materials, workmanship, or features. The story can relate to the products using recycled ingredients, the firm's superior testing facilities, its skilled workforce, the product's lack of artificial ingredients, and so on. Too few retailers use this important marketing differentiation-based strategy.

Takeaway Points

- Effective private labels assist a retailer to achieve store loyalty, be positioned as distinctive due to its own brands, increase its channel power with suppliers, and have greater control over profit margins.
- The best-practice retailers studied take a brand manager's (not a retailer's purchasing) perspective to developing and managing effective private labels. The successful retailers are able to develop distinctive goods by conducting consumer research, working closely with key suppliers, worldwide sourcing, and product testing. This is in sharp contrast to reacting to a supplier's plan to simply sell a firm a less-costly version of chicken soup. Thus, those retailers with successful private label

programs treat these products as brands—not simply as goods sold with the retailer's brand designation.

- There are two critical elements to developing a private label strategy: functional and emotional distinctiveness:

  - For *functional distinctiveness*, a retailer would question whether its private label soup is organic, is low salt, contains a large quantity of chicken so it can become a meal, or is comprised solely of white meat chicken. The manager would then subject the soup to a series of taste tests. And most probably, the recipe would have to be revised several times until the proper combination of chicken, noodles, salt, and fat was obtained.

  - *Emotional distinctiveness* translates into such attributes as a brand that a good cook would consider purchasing, a brand committed to ecological issues, or a brand that can be trusted. There are too many private labels with no emotional distinctiveness. Unfortunately, all they mean to most consumers is a discounted copy of a national brand. Retailers can develop emotional distinctiveness for their products through co-branding with a highly regarded national brand, through packaging and promotional strategies, and through "telling a story about their private labels" on the product's label, through periodic promotions, via store signage, or on the store's web site. Appropriate stories may relate to the good's special ingredients, the origin of the product's design, a product's being made in small batches by highly skilled workers, or the use of a small local manufacturer using specially trained personnel.

Endnotes

1. Stephen Dowdell and Joseph Tarnowski, "Going Public with Private Label," *Progressive Grocer* (June 1, 2006), pp. 34–36.

2. Sonia Reyes, "Saving Private Labels," *Brandweek* (May 8, 2006), pp. 30–34.

3. Stephen Dowdell and Joseph Tarnowski, "Going Public with Private Label," *Progressive Grocer* (June 1, 2006), pp. 34–36.

4. "As Consumers Seek Savings, Private Label Sales Up 7.4 Percent," *Nielsen News* (August 13, 2009), http://blog.nielsen.com/nielsenwire/nielsen-news/as-consumers-seek-savings-private-label-sales-up-74-percent/, as of June 7, 1010.

5. Mike Hughlett, "Shoppers Pick Up Store Brands," *McClatchy-Tribune Business News* (November 21, 2008).

6. Lien Lamey, Barbara Deleersnyder, Marnik G. Dekimpe, and Jan-Benedict E.M. Steenkamp, "How Business Cycles Contribute to Private-Label Success: Evidence from the United States and Europe," *Journal of Marketing* (January 2007), pp. 1–15.

7. Marcel Corstjens and Rajiv Lal, "Building Store Loyalty Through Store Brands," *Journal of Marketing Research* (August 2000), pp. 281–291.

8. Cate Devine, "Nattle of the Budget Buys: Co-op, Lidl, and Aldi Are All Set for Big Expansion in the Next Few Years," *The Herald* (Glasgow) (July 18, 2008), p. 19.

9. Bridget Goldschmidt, "Third Annual Outstanding Independents Awards: Stew Leonard's Hands On," *Progressive Grocer* (January 1, 2007), pp. 86–88.

10. Mya Frazier, "The Private-Label Powerhouse," *Advertising Age* (August 21, 2006), p. 6.

11. Pradeep K. Chintagunta, Andre Bonfrer, and Inseong Song, "Investigating the Effects of Store Brand Introduction on Retailing Demand and Pricing Behavior," *Management Science* (October 2002), pp. 1242–1267.

12. Kusum L. Ailawadi and Bari A. Harlam, "An Empirical Analysis of the Determinants of Retail Margins: The Role of Store Brand Share," *Journal of Marketing* (January 2004), pp. 147–165.

13. Kate Newlin, "Private Label: The Prestige Brands of Tomorrow?" www.retailcustomerexperience.com (July 30, 2009), as of August 2, 2009.

14. Nirmalya Kumar and Jan-Benedict E.M. Steenkamp, *Private Label Strategy: How to Meet the Store Brand Challenge* (Boston, MA: Harvard Business School, 2007), pp. 110–114.

15. Nirmalya Kumar and Jan-Benedict E.M. Steenkamp, *Private Label Strategy: How to Meet the Store Brand Challenge* (Boston, MA: Harvard Business School, 2007), p. 111.

16. Joseph Agnese, *Standard & Poor's Industry Surveys: Supermarkets & Drugstores* (July 17, 2008), p. 13.

17. Michael R. Hyman, Dennis A. Kopf, and Donghae lee, "Review of Literature— Future Research Suggestions: Private Label Brands: Benefits, Success Factors, and Future Research," *Brand Management* 17 (March 2010), pp. 368–389.

18. Terilyn A. Henderson and Elizabeth A. Mihas, "Building Retail Brands," *McKinsey Quarterly* (August 2000), pp. 110–117.

19. Stephen Dowdell, "Private Goes Private," *Progressive Grocer* (November 1, 2006), pp. 6–9.

20. Stephen Dowdell, "Private Goes Private," *Progressive Grocer* (November 1, 2006), pp. 6–9.

21. "Win at the Grocery Game: Shop Smarter," *Consumer Reports* (October 2006), p. 38.

22. "Win at the Grocery Game: Shop Smarter," *Consumer Reports* (October 2006), p. 38.

23. Mary Ellen Kuhn, "Power Retailing at Costco Wholesale: Shoppers Are Flocking to Warehouse Club Stores and No One Does This Unique Brand of Larger-Than-Life Retailing Better Than Costco," *Confectioner* (December 2004), pp. 12 ff.

24. Phone interview with James Sinegal, CEO, Costco, June 19, 2009.

25. Mike Duff, "A Private Label Success Story," *DSN Retailing Today* (December 19, 2005), p. 56.

26. Mike Duff, "A Private Label Success Story," *DSN Retailing Today* (December 19, 2005), p. 56.

27. Marissa Shalfi, "Costco Commitment," *Retail Merchandiser* (January 2007).

28. Phone interview with James Sinegal, CEO, Costco, June 19, 2009.

29. Christopher Webb, "Aldi's Simple Recipe for Success," *The Age* (Melbourne, Australia) (July 26, 2008), p. 5.

30. Christopher Webb, "Aldi's Simple Recipe for Success," *The Age* (Melbourne, Australia) (July 26, 2008), p. 5.

31. Bridget Goldschmidt, "At Stew Leonard's, the Personal Touch Is No Marketing Ploy—It's a Way of Life," *Progressive Grocer* (January 1, 2007), pp. 22 ff.

32. Bridget Goldschmidt, "At Stew Leonard's, the Personal Touch Is No Marketing Ploy—It's a Way of Life," *Progressive Grocer* (January 1, 2007), pp. 22 ff.

33. "Trader Joe's to Exclude Some Food Imports from China," *USA Today* (February 11, 2008), p. 1A.

34. Trader Joe's Is Not Your 'Average Joe,'" *Private Label Buyer* (June 2002), pp. 14 ff.

35. Mary Gustafson, "Trader Joe's Remarkable Journey: Its 50th Year in Business, Trader Joe's Still Manages to Thrill Its Customers and Impart Its Personality into Every Part of Its Business," *Private Label Buyer* (November 2008), pp. 42–46.

36. www.llbean.com/customerservice/aboutLLBean/background.html, as of April 6, 2009.

37. "Outlaw Consulting Announces Top 15 Green Brands," *Internet Wire* (July 30, 2008).

38. Mary Gustafson, "Trader Joe's Remarkable Journey: In Its 50th Year in Business, Trader Joe's Still Manages to Thrill Its Customers and Impart Its Personality into Every Part of Its Business," *Private Label Buyer* (November 2008), pp. 42–46.

39. Mary Gustafson, "Trader Joe's Remarkable Journey: In Its 50th Year in Business, Trader Joe's Still Manages to Thrill Its Customers and Impart Its Personality into Every Part of Its Business," *Private Label Buyer* (November 2008), pp. 42–46.

40. *Whole Foods 10-K for Year Ended September 24, 2006*, pp. 6–7.

41. Correspondence from Jo Natale, Director of Media Relations, Wegmans Food Markets, Inc., June 7, 2009.

42. Michael Sasso, "Publix 'Wises Up' on Organic Food," *Knight Ridder Tribune Business News* (May 13, 2005), p. 1.

43. Daniel McGinn, "The Green Machine," *Newsweek* (March 21, 2005), pp. E8 ff.

44. Kathie Canning, "Retailer of the Year: Aldi Inc: A Frugal Force," *PL Buyer* (April 2009), www.privatelabelbuyer.com, as of December 25, 2009.

45. Paul Owens, "Publix Super Markets to Offer Hispanic House Brand," *Knight Ridder Tribune Business News* (January 5, 2005), p. 1.

46. Julee Kaplan, "Wentz to Do Nordstrom Exclusive," *Women's Wear Daily* (March 18, 2008), p. 4.

47. Max Padilla, "Out and About; Shopping; Updating the Classics," *Los Angeles Times* (March 21, 2010), Image Section, p. 6.

48. "L.L.Bean Offering Updated Style," *Women's Wear Daily* (October 13, 2009), p. 3.

49. Len Lewis, *The Trader Joe's Adventure* (Chicago: Dearborn Trade Publishing, 2005), pp. 46–47.

50. Elizabeth Lee, "Private-Label Grocery Brands Go Upscale," *Cox News Service* (October 22, 2006).

51. Elizabeth Lee, "Private-Label Grocery Brands Go Upscale," *Cox News Service* (October 22, 2006).

52. Julia Moskin, "For Trader Joe's, a New York Taste Test," *New York Times* (March 8, 2006), Dining Out, p. 1.

53. Christopher Webb, "Aldi's Simple Recipe for Success," *The Age* (Melbourne, Australia) (July 26, 2008), p. 5.

54. James Hall, "The Rise and Rise of the Discount King," *The Sunday Telegraph* (London) (August 31, 2008), p. 7.

55. Kathie Canning, "Retailer of the Year: Aldi Inc: A Frugal Force," *PL Buyer* (April 2009) www.privatelabelbuyer.com, as of December 25, 2009.

56. Mark Ritson, "Aldi Feeds Off Lean Times," *Marketing* (August 27, 2008), p. 20.

57. Tom Rawstorne, "Look Out, Tesco...The Germans Are Coming!" *Daily Mail* (London) (July 14, 2008), p. 32.

58. Jan-Benedict E.M. Steenkamp and Nimalya Kumar, "Don't Be Undersold," *Harvard Business Review* (December 2009), pp. 90–95.

59. Mike Hughlett, "Aldi's Formula for Success: Small Selection, Low Prices," *McClatchy-Tribune Business News* (August 10, 2008).

60. Correspondence from Carolyn Beem, Manager, Public Affairs, L.L.Bean, June 8, 2009.

61. www.llbean.com/customerservice/aboutLLBean/background.html, as of April 6, 2009.

62. Leon Gorman, *L.L.Bean: The Making of an American Icon* (Boston, MA: Harvard Business School Press, 2006), p. 266.

63. Leon Gorman, *L.L.Bean: The Making of an American Icon* (Boston, MA: Harvard Business School Press, 2006), p. 266.

64. Leon Gorman, *L.L.Bean: The Making of an American Icon* (Boston, MA: Harvard Business School Press, 2006), p. 267.

65. Leon Gorman, *L.L.Bean: The Making of an American Icon* (Boston, MA: Harvard Business School Press, 2006), pp. 274–275.

66. Mary Gustafson, "Trader Joe's Remarkable Journey: Its 50th Year in Business, Trader Joe's Still Manages to Thrill Its Customers and Impart Its Personality into Every Part of Its Business," *Private Label Buyer* (November 2008), pp. 42–46.

67. "Will Grocery List Get Shorter?" *B&T Magazine* (October 20, 2008), p. 8.

68. Katia Watson, "Costco: What's the Buzz?" *Retail Forward* (December 2006), pp. 1–8.

69. Mike Duff, "A Private Label Success Story," *DSN Retailing Today* (December 19, 2005), p. 56.

70. Rob Walker, "Shelf Improvement," *New York Times Magazine* (May 7, 2006), p. 20.

71. Rob Walker, "Shelf Improvement," *New York Times Magazine* (May 7, 2006), p. 20.

72. Carol Angrisani, "First Run: To Support Their Brands, Retailers Are Putting More Theater into Their Private Label Promotions," *Supermarket News* (August 28, 2006), p. 24.

73. Stephen Dowdell, "Private Goes Public," *Progressive Grocer* (November 1, 2006), pp. 6–9.

74. Hershell Gordon Lewis, "Competitive Benefit Is King," *MultichannelMerchant.com* (September 2008), p. 16.

7

Implementing Cost-, Differentiation-, and Value-Based Retail Strategies

Cost-Based Strategies

There are three overall types of cost-saving opportunities. The first form deals with obtaining better prices due to high bargaining power. In general, large retailers with centralized purchasing organizations or that concentrate their overall purchases in a small number of SKUs are best able to secure the lowest prices. Retailers with strong private label brands are also able to use these as means of negotiating better prices for manufacturer-branded merchandise.

A second form of cost-based strategy is through a retailer's reducing bad costs. Some bad costs are incurred by chains that overly centralize strategies across the United States, or by retailers that do not change their strategies as a result of advances in technology or changes in consumer behavior. In other cases, low-cost retailers incur bad costs through adding services that may not be desired by its cost-conscious customers.[1]

The third form of cost savings involves making proper trade-offs between lower costs and reduced levels of customer service. These may include staff reductions that result in increased waiting times at cash registers, installing self-checkouts, or out-of-stock situations on slow-moving merchandise caused by inventory reductions. This is the most objectionable form of cost savings due to its impact on potential sales and customer satisfaction levels. See the following sidebar, "Cost-Based Strategies."

Cost-Based Strategies

Bargaining power-based strategies:

- Negotiating better prices and terms with key vendors through centralizing orders for multiple units or through development of private label products.

- Centralizing orders for purchases by chain retailers.

- Engaging in cooperative buying joint ventures with noncompeting retailers.

- Reducing the number of vendors to increase bargaining power with each vendor.

- Developing private label brands to increase bargaining power with national brand vendors.

- Taking full advantage of opportunistic buying situations caused by special offers from regular and nonregular suppliers.

- Taking full advantage of forward buying opportunities.

Increasing efficiency:

- Controlling costs via effective supply chain management. Among the strategies to be considered include vendor-managed inventory, quick response inventory management, and better use of communication linkages between the grocer and its supply chain management partners and direct store delivery, and use of lower rent locations.

- Using highly efficient heating, ventilating, air conditioning, and lighting equipment.

- Scheduling personnel to coincide with a store's busiest periods. The use of high-quality, part-time personnel, such as early retirees, mothers with school-age children, and so on, may be a helpful strategy.

- Better using space in front of the store for fruits and vegetables and other seasonal merchandise (such as outdoor furniture).

- Allocating shelf space effectively based on product sales levels and profit margins.

- Reducing product proliferation by pruning items with low inventory turnover.

- Studying category management solutions relating to variety and assortment planning for manufacturer brands, as well as private labels.

- Motivating workers to be more efficient and effective through bonuses and stock option incentives tied to store productivity measures.

- Using the Web more effectively. Examples include selling slow-selling merchandise on the Web, promoting specials via the Web, explaining an item's key features on the Web to save in-store sales personnel time, handling basic customer support issues, reviewing in-store stock levels for selected merchandise, and enabling customers to order merchandise on the Web and then pick it up in the store.

- Reducing the temptation to increase operating costs by adding services that are not relevant to your target audience.

- Benchmarking store performance against the most efficient in the chain. Study those elements that contributed to best practices both within the chain and throughout an industry.

Trade-offs between lower costs and potentially reduced sales and customer satisfaction:

- Using low-rent locations and second-use locations (where other merchants installed flooring, lighting, and store fronts) for new stores; selectively using used fixtures from closed stores or fixtures that were purchased from used fixture vendors.

- Enabling customers to use self-checkouts. This may be more applicable to consumers with few items.

- Charging additional fees for services that now are bundled into a store's pricing structure. Services that should be examined include order fulfillment, delivery, and custom cutting of beef.

- Studying store hours. One solution is to close earlier on certain days or perhaps even to have one store open 24 hours a day within a specific geographic area.

Although cost-cutting is a natural response to the current competitive and economic environment, retailers need to be cautioned against tentative and conservative cost-cutting strategies. Research conducted by the Boston Consulting Group has found that companies that have used modest cost reductions as an initial response to an economic downturn are prone to overreacting later on by cutting prices more than necessary.[2] A second concern associated with cost cutting is that some retailers may be tempted to take a short-run approach by eliminating essential customer services as opposed to making long-term structural changes (such as revising improved supply chain relationships).

Traditional retailers that pursue a cost-based strategy need to effectively communicate that they are capable of delivering competitive prices to their customers. Retailers cannot effectively pursue a cost-based strategy by quietly matching other retailer's prices. Unfortunately, too many consumers now view supercenters, dollar stores, warehouse clubs, and factory outlets as the real cost leaders. Many consumers have also begun to regularly shop in these stores as alternatives to traditional retail formats. Through effective communication, retailers can potentially overcome their higher price image and lower the perceived pricing gap with these discounters. This communication can be in the form of a "We will not be undersold" plaque that is prominently displayed in the store's interior, on all freestanding inserts, and on the store's web site. Retailers can also aggressively show the comparable savings through use of its private label brands. This can be done on an individual item or total shopping basket basis. Retailers should consider using their in-store flyers and web sites to communicate elements of their pricing strategy, such as buying direct from manufacturers, using local suppliers to reduce transportation costs, selling bulk packages, and passing cost savings from special buying opportunities onto consumers (see the following sidebar, "How to Effectively Communicate a Store's Competitive Pricing Strategy").

An example of such a strategy is Target, which for years used its "Expect More, Pay Less" motto. Despite this motto, recent research by Target showed that consumers view Target as pricier than Wal-Mart, even though its prices were only a few cents apart on most items.[3] And although for years, Target's promotion and merchandising focused on the famous designers behind many of its apparel and houseware products, Target management now realized that it needed to emphasize that "good value can be chic" as well.

Target has recently used the message "Fresh food for less green," and "Quality cuts, lean prices," in its Philadelphia-based advertising campaign for its food marts.[4] According to a Citigroup retail analyst, "While Target did cut some prices on some merchandise, its marketing onslaught is mostly responsible for changing consumer perception [that its prices are competitive with Wal-Mart]."[5] To reinforce its new strategy, Target devoted 75 percent of its advertising budget to price-related appeals in Christmas 2009, versus 25 percent in Christmas 2008.

How to Effectively Communicate a Store's Competitive Pricing Strategy

- Place a "We will not be undersold" plaque prominently in the store's interior, on all freestanding inserts, and on the store's web site.

- Offer highly selective assortments of bulk packages (similar to warehouse clubs). These assortments should include high-turnover goods such as paper towels, toilet paper, plastic storage bags, vitamins, party supplies, dishwasher liquids, chicken breasts, and so on. Stores need to consider whether these bulk packages should all be located in a special aisle location, or whether these items should be next to traditional package sizes.

- Better demonstrate cost effectiveness of private label merchandise by showing direct price comparisons between private labels and national brands. These price comparisons can be either on an item-by-item basis or on a total market basket level.

- Offer prepackaged bags of produce and vegetables in outdoor bins outside a store's main entrance. These appeal to cost conscious shoppers. Higher grades of the same produce would be available in the store. Similarly, general merchandise retailers can use sidewalk sales to illustrate special purchases, closeout merchandise, and odd lots.

- Negotiate special coupon offers with vendors that are only valid in your store.

- Grocers can work with a dietician to plan meals based on lower-priced cuts of meat, lower cost fish, fruits and vegetables that are in-season, and so on. Use these meal ingredients in specials.

- Provide special offers that can be made to loyalty club members with a given number of points (based on purchases). This strategy rewards a store's best customers while not giving these buying opportunities to "cherry pickers." In a more

sophisticated version of this strategy, a store can ask its loyalty
club members to classify themselves based on their distinct
needs. The retailer can then provide special offers to consumers based on their preferences.

- Use the Web to communicate special buys. Web-based specials can be sent to a select group of customers via email or can
  be available to all potential customers on the store's web site.

- Take full advantage of opportunistic buying situations caused
  by special offers from regular and nonregular suppliers. Pass
  on savings from special buys to increase store traffic and to
  reinforce a retailer's price image.

- Consider using everyday low pricing for many items.

- Use in-store flyers to communicate pricing strategies. These
  can include special stories about buying direct, private-label
  buying strategies, and purchasing from local farmers to
  reduce transportation costs at the same time as improving
  product freshness.

A major issue is whether special buys and the communication of
offers should be made to all potential customers or to a more select
group. A retailer may want to restrict some offers to its loyalty card
members or to a selected group of customers. Although the restricted
offering may have less impact on the store's overall low-cost image, it
better assures its loyal customers of getting access to a limited offering, as well as rewards only its most loyal customers. The restricted
offering alternative also limits purchases by customers who buy only
sale items.

Differentiation-Based Strategies

Chapters 4, 5, and 6 focused on differentiation strategies targeted
to consumers concerned about atmosphere, unique merchandise,
and high levels of customer service. To successfully achieve a differentiation strategy, a retailer needs to foster a "fun-based," in-store

service experience, sell unique products (including private labels), offer superior levels of customer support, and secure customer trust. See the following sidebar, "Differentiation-Based Strategies," for a listing of differentiation-based strategies based on these dimensions.

Differentiation-Based Strategies

Differentiation based on atmosphere:

- Remove impediments to a pleasant experience—long lines, rude salespeople, stockouts, and difficulty in locating sale items.

- Include exciting departments in the store such as coffee bars, fresh pasta bars, salad bars, sound rooms, and so on.

- Show how fresh food is made. Let customers observe bread being baked, fresh pasta being prepared, beef being cut and aged, coffee being roasted, and so forth. This also validates the store's cleanliness.

- Plan a series of events throughout the year, such as wine and cheese tastings, demonstrations by local chefs, book signings, trunk shows, and so on, to generate continuous excitement.

- Generate a fun atmosphere for all age groups through product samplings, a petting zoo, and events based on local holidays (for example, Celtic dancers on St. Patrick's Day, hayrides for children, and fresh-dipped chocolate on St. Valentine's Day).

- Encourage staff to provide food samples for young children (based on a parent's approval).

- Plan and implement a well-lit, well-fixtured store interior. Consider using appropriate background music.

- Use sampling stations to show off fresh vegetables, special cuts of meat, and private label products. Also provide demonstrations of new appliances, digital cameras, netbooks, and so on.

- Display fruits and vegetables in an artistic manner showing their diverse colors.

Differentiation based on merchandise:

- Develop private label products that are distinctive based on recipe, contents, features, durability, or health benefits (low cholesterol, fat, or salt).

- Sell distinctive lines of manufacturer brands.

- Edit merchandise offerings of vendors to items with high quality, ease of use, and distinctive features.

- Communicate the advantages of your private label or exclusive merchandise products by "telling a story" about the products on the product's label, on store signage, or on the Web. Tell customers what is so special about these products in language they can identify with and understand.

- Develop attractive packaging for private labels.

- Provide demonstrations showing private labels, as well as national brands.

- Provide free samples of private label and national brands for cooking at home.

Differentiation based on customer service:

- Empower employees to "right a wrong."

- Have store personnel help customers load heavy packages into their vehicles. A no-tipping policy should be enforced.

- Allow customers to order merchandise using the Web, or to verify that a local store has the desired quantity of goods in stock.

- Train employees to take customers to the exact aisle location, not shelf aisle, when they are asked for the location of an item.

- Hire employees that have a passion for being with people, love to help others, and enjoy good food.

- Hire employees with a passion for the products you are selling ('foodies" for a supermarket, "tennis buffs" for a sporting goods store, and "techies" for a computer/electronics store).

- Educate employees through special classes, field trips to vendors, or free samples to take home.

- Employ a staff dietician that can help customers with special food needs.

Differentiation based on trust:

- Pretest and pretaste all products offered for sale. Refuse to sell poor-quality merchandise regardless of their sales potential or ability to generate store traffic.
- Offer rain checks if sale merchandise is out of stock.
- Offer an unconditional "no questions asked," "no ifs, ands, or buts" money-back guarantee.
- Specify a written policy relating to no preservatives, no artificial ingredients for foods, and no wood furniture from nonrenewable sources.
- Place nutritional information on all private label food products.
- Co-brand a retailer's private label with an established national brand.
- Employ well-informed sales personnel trained to offer the most suitable goods for customers based on customer needs. Sales personnel should be compensated primarily on salary (as opposed to commission), so they will honestly assess a customer's needs and not oversell.
- Clearly communicate information on product recalls to affected customers.
- Compensate employees based on salary, not commissions. In this way, the incentive to oversell no longer exists.
- Refuse to sell merchandise that would be objectionable to the retailer's target audience.
- Develop safety standards that are higher than Food and Drug Administration and Department of Agriculture requirements.

One way to assess a store's differentiation strategies is for managers to "think like a shopper." Appropriate questions in this area are as follows:

- Would you recommend this store to your best friend?
- Would you serve the store's private label brands at a dinner party?
- What are the real differential advantages of your store from a shopper's perspective?
- How compelling are these differential advantages?
- Does the store look and feel differently from its major competitors?
- Does the retailer impart a sense of trust via its product testing programs, "no-questions-asked" returns policy, product ingredient screening, and so on?

A major benefit of "thinking like a shopper" is that managers can view themselves in their role as purchasing agents for their customers, not as intermediate destinations for their supplier's output. In this context, sales to final customers, not trade deals, become the sole criterion for stocking a vendor's goods. "Thinking like a shopper" also suggests that managers consider competition to include all potential competitors from discounters to full-service specialty stores.

Many differentiation strategies require unique resources that are difficult for competitors to copy. Although there is no doubt about the success of Aldi's, Trader Joe's, Costco's, and L.L.Bean's private labeling program, many traditional retailers do not have the capability and resources to work closely with suppliers, to source goods on a worldwide basis, and to effectively test and revise items.

In planning a differentiation strategy, it is important to realize that the competitive landscape is ever changing. Thus, strategies that could be viewed as a significant competitive advantage one year, may be no more than a "me too" strategy in a later year. Examples of these include Aldi offering more healthy products and products that can be viewed as gourmet, Amazon.com expanding its private label products, and Wal-Mart's purchase online and pickup in store options.

These important aspects of a differentiation strategy are worth emphasizing: employees count, all private brands are not created

equal, treat your store as a brand—positioning counts, develop and
maintain customer trust, the in-store experience counts, and deliver a
highly-integrated multichannel experience (see Figure 7.1). We will
now examine each of these.

| Employees Count |
| All Private Brands Are Not Created Equal |
| Treat Your Store as a Brand—Positioning Counts |
| Develop and Maintain Customer Trust |
| In-Store Experience Counts |
| Deliver a Highly Integrated Multichannel Experience |

Figure 7.1   Important components of a differentiation strategy

Employees Count

As described in Chapter 4, "Differentiation Strategies I: Effective
Human Resource Strategies," the value profit chain explains the link-
age between employee satisfaction, customer satisfaction, and store
profitability. To simplify this model, employee satisfaction drives the
profit equation. As a consequence, retailers need to pay employees
more, better empower them, and build an environment of rewarding
excellent performance. Industry analysts that argue that retailers like
Costco, Wegmans, or Nordstrom should pay employees less do not
understand the service/value profit chain model and the real impact
of employees on customer loyalty.

Part of the "employees count" notion is to reward employees
based on stock ownership and other incentives geared to corporate

performance. Although Publix goes to the extreme of being an ESOP, other retailers can adopt incentives based on an overall store or teams meeting or exceeding specific sales, profit, and customer satisfaction targets. This continually energizes employees and gets employees to act as managers (by coming in early in peak seasons, watching over team members, and rotating jobs, when required). Another successful employee incentive model is to reward sales and profit performance only in instances where customer satisfaction targets have also been met. This assures that financial objectives are not made at the expense of reduced levels of customer service.

All Private Brands Are Not Created Equal

As was discussed in Chapter 6, "Differentiation Strategies III: Developing and Maintaining a Strong Private Label Program," the most successful private labels have become destination brands due to some combination of distinctiveness, quality, and value. Retailers need to view themselves as brand managers that can understand market needs, translate popular foreign products to American tastes, and work with suppliers on developing products that are truly distinctive in terms of taste, features, quality, and styling.

There are tremendous opportunities for retailers via private branding. One major opportunity is for a retailer to develop private labels aimed at different market segments. A "good" alternative should be sold on the basis of price differentials with the top-selling manufacturer brand. In contrast, the "best" option should have a quality advantage in comparison to the top-selling national-branded alternative.

Treat Your Store as a Brand—Positioning Counts

Like their nondistinctive private brands, too many retailers are also "plain vanilla" in terms of their overall image. Among the benchmarked retailers, clearly Trader Joe's represents adventure, a foreign food experience, and a place where a time-pressed homemaker can assemble an interesting meal rather quickly. Whole Foods represents a store that excites a "foodie" with its selection of high-quality and fresh fruits and vegetables, meats, and fish products. Likewise, Stew Leonard's represents freshness, fun, and value. Both Trader Joe's and Whole Foods also portray environmental stewardship qualities. Aldi represents extreme value. L.L.Bean represents all that is needed to enjoy the outdoors. L.L.Bean is a trusted source of outdoor clothing and lifestyle accessories. Nordstrom is a full-service, fashion-based department store. And Amazon.com represents the Web's hassle-free department store for books, hobby, and household needs. The store positioning for all of these retailers has also stayed relatively constant since its founding in 1912. L.L.Bean, for example, throughout its history has positioned itself as an outdoor company. Its overall positioning has not changed despite new marketing channels and the addition of many new product lines.[6]

Through treating a store as a brand, managers should examine their store's enduring values, differentiation strategies, target market, and so on. The brand concept also compels store management to protect the brand from short-run strategies that could become detrimental to the brand's image in the long term.

Develop and Maintain Customer Trust

Retailers need to communicate to consumers that they truly care for them from a financial, safety, product performance, and time perspective. This can be done through carefully editing the goods offered for sale. Customer trust can be portrayed through the following:

- Pretesting and pretasting all products offered for sale. The firm should refuse to sell products that do not meet its standards, regardless of customer demand or profitability.
- Listing all reviews (negative, as well as positive) on the firm's web site.
- Developing and implementing a written policy relating to no preservatives, no artificial ingredients for foods, and no wood furniture from nonrenewable sources.

- Placing nutritional information on all private-label food products.
- Employing well-informed sales personnel trained to offer the most suitable goods for customers based on customer needs.
- Clearly communicating information on product recalls to affected customers.
- Compensating employees based on salary, not commissions. In this way, the incentive to oversell them no longer exists.

The In-Store Experience Counts

The in-store experience perception can range from outrage at one extreme, to satisfaction, and to delight at the other extreme. Outrage can occur as a result of long register lines, out-of-stock situations on popular items, and poor levels of customer service. In contrast, delight is characterized by positive, memorable, and unexpected experiences. The idea with delight is to make shopping a fun-based activity, not drudgery. Obviously, fun may mean different things to different people. To many people, product demonstrations, in-store classes (such as learning how to fish with flies, or how to install a kitchen faucet), book signings, blind taste testing for foods and wines, and an especially knowledgeable and helpful staff all contribute positively to the in-store experience. Fun also needs to be portrayed differently to different age groups and throughout the year with appropriate seasonal promotions. Clearly, retailers need to think more about promotions based upon fun as opposed to promotions based around price.

Deliver a Highly Integrated Multichannel Experience

Retailers need to view multichannels as complementary, as opposed to competitive with one another. L.L.Bean and Nordstrom are multichannel retailers. L.L.Bean's goods are sold via catalogs, on the Web, as well as in retail stores. According to *Multichannel Merchant* magazine, "L.L.Bean seamlessly transfers its catalog message to the web channel."[7]

Nordstrom also offers seamless integration across its full-line stores, catalogs, and web site. Web-based orders can be picked up at a local Nordstrom customer service department within one hour of a customer's placing the order. This saves both Nordstrom and the customer shipping costs. It also gives the customer the ability to take home the ordered good immediately and to more easily return merchandise to the store. Nordstrom's management information system has also recently been upgraded to reflect inventory availability at multiple channel locations and warehouses. This enables Nordstrom to fulfill customer orders at the store level from inventories at Nordstrom's Cedar Rapids, Iowa, online warehouse, if necessary.[8]

Value-Based Strategies

An obvious question is whether a firm can move in the direction of offering lower costs and increasing differentiation simultaneously. One way to combine cost and differentiation strategies is to focus on value from a customer's perspective. Value-based strategies seek to combine product quality, differentiated goods, and the customer service experience with relatively low prices (which may be due to cost reduction strategies).

According to a study by The Nielsen Company, "good value for money" is the most important factor U.S. and global consumers use when deciding where to shop for groceries. Sixty percent of U.S. consumers ranked "good value for money" as the most important factor in choosing a grocery store.[9] On a global basis, 85 percent of shoppers ranked good value first (with the most avid value-seeking customers living in the Philippines, Singapore, German, India, and Austria). Among U.S. respondents, the second most important factor in choosing a grocery store was its selection of high-quality brands and products (listed among 28 percent of the respondents). The third most critical factor was closeness (cited by 23 percent of the respondents).

The Nielsen Company found that U.S. consumers evaluate a number of factors in deciding what stores offer good value for the money. These are the most important factors:[10]

- Use of frequent promotions and discounts (cited by 80 percent of the respondents).

- A store's reputation for delivering low prices (cited by 72 percent of respondents).

- Prices published in the store's own flyers (cited by 71 percent of respondents).

- A store's promise to have everyday low prices (cited by 70 percent of respondents).

- Having price discounts for loyalty card members (cited by 63 percent of respondents).

- Providing price comparisons across retailers (cited by 59 percent of respondents).

- Providing private label offerings (cited by 53 percent of respondents).

Although each of the items cited clearly represents a component of value, there are some interesting inconsistencies (such as the frequent use of promotions and discounts versus a store's promise to have everyday low prices).

Another approach to defining the components of value is to further explore the conceptualization of "value" as described in the value profit chain. The value profit chain model defines value for customers as:[11]

$$\text{Value} = \frac{\text{Results} + \text{Process Quality}}{\text{Price} + \text{Customer Access Costs}}$$

See the following sidebar, "Elements of Value," for a discussion of the value components.

Elements of Value

$$\text{Value} = \frac{\text{Results} + \text{Process Quality}}{\text{Price} + \text{Customer Access Costs}}$$

Results:

- Product overall quality, including warranties
- Product taste, freshness, performance, health characteristics (low salt, low fat, low cholesterol)
- Product testing by manufacturer and retailer
- Product convenience (ease of use)
- Superior product styling

Process Quality—Positive customer service elements:

- Ease of finding items
- Use of carefully edited product assortments
- Ease of navigating store
- Wide aisles
- High in-stock positions
- Short waiting lines
- A "fun" in-store experience (sampling stations, cooking demonstrations, fashion shows, book signings)
- Home delivery availability
- Installation availability
- Assistance in loading products into car
- Delivery at promised time interval
- Positive customer services (high levels of customer support, high-quality salesperson interactions)
- Free alterations to garments
- Exchange privileges, money-back guarantees
- Excellent service recovery (a sales clerk offering a substitute item instead of a rain check for an out-of-stock item or a free takeout dinner to compensate for an overcooked dinner that was recently purchased)

Price:

- Low final purchase cost (also private label versus comparable national brand cost) including delivery charges, assembly costs, credit terms

Customer Access Costs—Costs in terms of consumer frustrations:

- Warehouse club membership fee
- Parking fees while shopping
- Inconvenient store locations
- Inadequate parking availability; long distance from parking area to store
- Inability to use one-stop shopping due to limited selections
- Poor store hours

Let's look at each of the four components of value: results, process quality, price, and customer access costs. Elements of results include a product's overall quality (including warranties), product convenience (prewashed, precut, "heat-and-eat," ease of setup or installation), product health (low salt, low fat, low cholesterol, product safety), and presentation (styling). The concept of results extends beyond the product to focus on solutions, not individual components. A supermarket can extend the results portion of value through bundling the ingredients for a soup with a recipe, through selling products that are grown by local farmers, or through focusing on an individual's special dietary needs (low fat, vegetarian, low salt, or low sugar). To an electronics store, results include rewriting directions to installing a television to simplify the process, including the store's technical service department phone number in all television boxes, and bundling necessary HDMI cables with all televisions (as opposed to selling them separately). To an apparel store, results can include free alterations to garments purchased at full price and moderately priced alterations for merchandise purchased on sale. One of the ways that Aldi, Amazon.com, L.L.Bean, and Trader Joe's add to the results element of value is through extensive product testing.

Process quality includes positive customer services (high levels of customer support, high quality of salesperson interactions), successful service recovery efforts (what the store will do when things go wrong), ease of finding items, short waiting lines, high in-stock positions for advertised specials, a "fun" in-store experience, and adequate parking. According to a research study sponsored by Cadbury Adams USA, almost one-half of the 300 grocer respondents viewed the front-end checkout experience (a process quality attribute) as very important in customer decisions to visit their stores.[12] Process quality is assessed by most consumers on the basis of their expectations on these service components. These expectations may significantly differ depending upon the store format. Thus, waiting lines are expected to be short in convenience stores relative to warehouse clubs or supercenters.

Best-practice retailers such as Aldi, Amazon.com. L.L.Bean, Costco, Publix, Trader Joe's, Wegmans, and Whole Foods provide high process quality by virtue of their high customer satisfaction scores in *Consumer Reports, Business Week*, and in American Customer Satisfaction Index scores (as described in the Appendix, "Individual and Composite Financial Performance, Customer Service, and Worker Satisfaction Metrics of the Best-Practice Retailers"). Part of the reason for high process quality is the service experience; the other part is the low number of SKUs in comparison to competition. The 1,300 to 2,500 SKUs at Aldi, Costco, Stew Leonard's, and Trader Joe's simplify the shopping experience.

Amazon.com excels in this area through making its web site especially easy to use. According to the chief marketing officer at Landor Associates, a branding consultant, "It is pretty unprecedented that their [Amazon.com's] brand has ascended so quickly without a large marketing budget. It's not about splaying their logo everywhere. They [Amazon.com] are all about ease of use."[13] Adds the head of technology research for an investment firm, "By investing back in the user experience, you [Amazon.com] get[s] high loyalty and repeat usage."

Price is the final purchase cost including such elements as delivery charges and credit terms. One way for appliance retailer specialty stores to effectively price match mass merchandisers and discounters is to unbundle prices for delivery, installation, and disposal of old appliances. Similarly, a local computer store can charge a price for a new computer, an additional fee for loading software and transferring files from one computer to another, and yet another fee for an extended warranty. This strategy enables the retailer to appeal to both price and service-oriented customers. It also allows customers to decide which costs are relevant to them and which are "bad costs" that are not worth their additional expense. Aldi, Costco, and Trader Joe's are benchmark retailers with low prices relative to their competitors. Low-cost operations and heavily edited selections of merchandise contribute to their ability to outprice most competition.

Customer access costs include negative customer experiences such as warehouse club membership fees, parking fees while shopping, inconvenient retail locations, difficulty in locating sale items, difficulty in navigating narrow aisles, and poor parking access. Very large stores, discount operations located in industrial parks or isolated locations, and downtown stores with insufficient parking all have high access costs. These costs can be measured in terms of wasted time, parking fees, and consumer frustration. One away of significantly reducing customer access costs is through web-based ordering and home delivery services. As a category, all warehouse clubs have high access costs by virtue of their yearly membership costs, inconvenient locations, and large parking lots.

In this value model, results and process quality comprise the numerator of value. Both results and process quality are viewed as significant benefits by consumers. High process quality can also be used by a retailer to reinforce a product's superior quality or to level the playing field by adding superior customer support to a product of slightly lesser overall quality (results). In contrast, price and customer access costs are the denominator of the value equation. This notion reinforces the concept that the lure of low prices can be offset by high access costs due to poor parking, inconvenient locations, parking fees, or limited store hours.

Retailers need to study results, process quality, and customer access costs to seek out opportunities for differentiation based on these components, as well as their strengths and weaknesses relative to same and different format competitors. Costco and other warehouse clubs, as well as Aldi, may be particularly strong in price, yet weaker in customer access costs. Amazon.com, L.L.Bean, Stew Leonard's, Nordstrom, Wegmans, and Whole Foods excel in results, process quality, and customer access costs. And Trader Joe's excels in most of the dimensions.

The value model also provides a framework for retailers to reposition themselves on the value equation. This can be accomplished through increasing results (such as pretesting of goods), improving process quality (better training the retailer's sales personnel), lowering prices (which enables price reductions with little impact on critical customer service), and reducing access costs (through enabling customers to purchase goods online and pick them up in-store). Especially effective are retail strategies that can simultaneously result in cost reductions and improvements in process quality and access costs. Many of these strategies are based on improved multichannel retailing efforts, private label strategies, supply chain initiatives, and removal of bad costs (including product proliferation). See the following sidebar for details.

Retail Strategies That Can Simultaneously Result in Cost Reductions and Improvements in Process Quality and Access Costs

- Enable customers to order goods on the Web.
- Allow customers to determine inventory availability at nearby stores via the Web.
- Enable customers to order online and then pick up the merchandise at a local store (instead of having the goods delivered to the customer's home or office location).
- Increase integration among store, Web, and catalog operations.

- Reduce bad costs that add little to the customer experience.

- Add services that have value relative to costs: "little things that add up to become a lot."

- Reduce product proliferation.

- Lower costs due to supply chain initiatives.

- Reduce out-of-stock goods through improved inventory management.

- Increase value due to unique private label goods.

Retailers should understand that the elements within the value equation are constantly changing. One academic researcher argues that cost-effective competitors (such as Wal-Mart and the warehouse clubs) have succeeded by getting customers to accept fewer store-related benefits due to their lower prices.[14] Outlet malls have also been successfully used by factory outlets to reduce access costs through locating similar stores together.

Retailers must continually evaluate the value equation through customer-benefit costing. They also need to understand that not only the desirability of results and process quality, but price and customer access costs as well, are constantly changing due to competition, economic issues, technology, and customer needs. The elements of the value equation differ by market target. Customer-benefit costing links each element of results and process quality to a cost component. Retailers then need to determine the value of each service component relative to its cost.

Auditing a Store's Cost, Differentiation, and Value Strategies

One way to assess a company's competitive responsiveness is a cost, differentiation, and value audit. The audit form poses a series of questions relating to these strategies. This audit suggests areas for improvement, develops a means to evaluate the person or committee responsible for strategic planning, and provides a framework to assess a firm's overall competitive positioning. Key aspects of the audit are the retailer's contingency plans, its view of competition, its means of reducing product proliferation, its human resources strategies, its in-store experience, and its branding strategies. A cost, differentiation, and value audit form is contained in the following sidebar, "A Cost, Differentiation, and Value Audit Form."

A Cost, Differentiation, and Value Audit Form

Does the retailer...

- Have a short-term plan that reflects the current economic environment?
- Have a long-term plan that reflects the current economic environment?
- Have adequate contingency plans if the current recession is more prolonged or deeper than anticipated?
- Monitor market share among similar format retailers?
- Assess market share among all stores that sell similar product lines?
- View competition from a generic perspective?
- Effectively communicate its low-price message?
- Seek to reduce costs through supply chain initiatives?
- Seek to reduce costs through the effective use of the Web, in-store flyers, and word-of-mouth communication?
- Reduce costs through eliminating product proliferation?
- Plan assortments using a destination goods, routine goods, seasonal goods, and convenience goods category management model?
- Measure employee satisfaction levels?
- Have an employee-centered human resources strategy?

- Seek to hire the best available personnel through paying above-average industry wages and fringe benefits?

- Utilize continual training for managers and workers?

- Provide incentives through stock ownership, stock options, and bonuses?

- Seek to improve employee retention?

- Empower its workers?

- Measure customer satisfaction levels?

- Have a well-thought-out and communicated service experience statement?

- Seek to provide a "fun" experience in the store?

- Monitor important elements of process quality (such as aisle width, waiting lines, and delivery times)?

- Make the store atmosphere an exciting one?

- Promote its liberal money-back-guarantee policy?

- Listen to customers and react to their suggestions in a timely manner?

- Have a private label strategy policy that first focuses on product quality and then looks at price competitiveness?

- Systematically look at opportunities in the healthy, organic, green, and ethnic segments?

- Practice close collaboration with key suppliers?

- Taste test all new products?

- Utilize co-branding with major manufacturer brands?

The audit can be implemented by the chief executive officer or owner of a retail store, a planning coordinator, a team comprised of category managers from multiple departments, or an independent consultant. Although the planning coordinator and category manager committee are most familiar with the overall firm, there may be some concern as to their objectivity.

Takeaway Points

In reading these, it is important to ponder how a retailer can change. Changing slowly enables a firm to test the effect of a new strategy, to get employees to better understand a new corporate culture, or to develop a more creative private label strategy. For example, although most firms will at first not offer stock incentives to employees, they might initially consider some type of profit-sharing plan based on a business unit's or store's overall performance on stated goals:

- There are three potential positioning strategies for all retailers: low-cost-based retailers that seek to offer the best prices, those that offer high levels of customer support and differentiated goods, and a middle area (where stores do not offer differentiated products, high service levels, or low prices). This discussion parallels Michael Porter's concept of the differentiators, the cost conscious, and those "stuck in the middle," offering neither low prices, or a differentiated experience and differentiated products.

- The appeal of the low-cost-oriented retailer is its capability to consistently offer low prices. This strategy is often based on a retailer's capability to appeal to price-conscious consumers due to lower-cost locations, less selection, self-service merchandising, and savings due to efficient supply management. Wal-Mart is an example. A pure value-oriented retailer such as Wal-Mart may ask the customer to give up customer service or selection for low prices. Several of these retailers such as Aldi, Costco, Stew Leonard's, and Trader Joe's have also achieved significant cost efficiencies due to reduced selection. This strategy reduces inventory carrying costs, utility expenses, and rental costs at the same time as increasing the stores' bargaining power with suppliers.

- The argument for differentiation states that traditional retailers need to offer something unique, such as special levels of customer support, specialized products, and alterations, as well as high levels of customer excitement (through demonstrations, trunk shows, and customer sampling opportunities).

- Retailers "stuck in the middle" are not distinctive on any of the prior grounds. Many old-line retailers are strategically "caught in the middle," unable to match the price levels and cost structure of a Wal-Mart or that of a retailer that excels in terms of superior service, as well as distinctive goods.[15]

- The choice of Aldi, Amazon.com, L.L.Bean, Costco, Nordstrom, Publix, Stew Leonard's, Trader Joe's, Wegmans, and Whole Foods as benchmark retailers is also based on these retailers' strategy of differentiation. What makes our benchmark retailers so successful is that they have redefined the retail experience on the basis of high levels of customer support and differentiated goods. Retail Forward found differentiation to be based on product, service, the in-store experience, and other factors.

- Retailers need to better understand where they excel. Is it low operating costs, the capability to deliver a superior in-store customer service experience, or success in managing a broad spectrum of private labels?

- Traditional retailers can compete with value-based stores on several dimensions. They can communicate weekly specials more effectively by showing actual reductions from normal prices, through taking full advantage of special buys, through having merchandise in key areas that is price competitive with major discounters, and by explaining their special values.

- Although being able to compete on the basis of price may be the ticket to remaining in business in the short run, in the long run, each retailer needs some distinctiveness-related strengths. Each chain needs to rethink its distinctiveness in terms of branding, the in-store customer experience, and assortments in select merchandise categories and then develop a plan so that it can consistently deliver them.

- Much of the success of any differentiation plan is based on a store's employees. The strategies of the best-practice firms need to be carefully studied in terms of the implications of employee salaries and fringe benefits on employee morale, employee turnover, and its ultimate effect on employee productivity and customer satisfaction.

- Retailers need to understand that the elements within the value equation are constantly changing.

- Customer-benefit costing links each element of results and process quality to a cost component. Retailers need to determine the value of each service component relative to its cost.

- Larger retailers need to consider developing a portfolio of store formats ranging from limited assortment stores to smaller neighborhood-based formats. The multiple format approach enables the retailer to better reach multiple segments, to reduce the risk inherent with a single format, and to increase sales in mature locations.

- A store needs to continually audit its use of effective marketing strategies. The audit needs to honestly convey its areas of weakness, as well as its strengths.

Endnotes

1. Ken Favaro, Tim Romberger, and David Meer, "Five Rules for Retailing in a Recession," *Harvard* Business Review (April 2008), p. 69.

2. David Rhodes and Daniel Stelter, "Seize Advantage in a Downturn," *Harvard Business Review* (February 2009), pp. 50–58.

3. Michelle Conlin, "Look Who's Stalking Wal-Mart," *Business Week* (December 7, 2009), p. 32.

4. Michelle Conlin, "Look Who's Stalking Wal-Mart," *Business Week* (December 7, 2009), p. 32.

5. Michelle Conlin, "Look Who's Stalking Wal-Mart," *Business Week* (December 7, 2009), p. 33.

6. Correspondence from Carolyn Beem, Manager, Public Affairs, L.L.Bean, June 8, 2009.

7. "L.L.Bean: B-to-C—Multichannel Merchant of the Year," *Multichannel Merchant* (September 2008), p. 25.

8. Joanna Ramey and Mina Williams, "Gap, Nordstrom Talk Growth at Annual Meetings," *Women's Wear Daily* (May 19, 2010), p. 11.

9. "'Good Value' Seals the Deal of Store Choice: Study," www.progressivegrocer.com, as of December 18, 2007.

10. "'Good Value' Is the Top Influencer of U.S. Grocery Store Choice, Nielsen Reports," *The Nielsen Company News Release* (December 17, 2007).

11. James L. Heskett, Thomas W. Earl Sasser, Jr., and Leonard A. Schlesinger, *The Value Profit Chain* (New York: The Free Press, 2003), p. 26.

12. Joseph Tarnowski, "Lasting Impressions," *Progressive Grocer* (November 15, 2007), pp. 16–21.

13. Spencer E. Ante, "At Amazon, Marketing Is for Dummies," *Business Week* (September 28, 2009), p. 53.

14. Nirmalya Kumar, "Strategies to Fight Low-Cost Rivals," *Harvard Business Review* (December 2006), pp. 104–112.

15. James Tillotson, "Whole Foods Market: Redefining the Supermarket Experience," *Nutrition Today* (March 1, 2006).

Appendix: Individual and Composite Financial Performance, Customer Service, and Worker Satisfaction Metrics of the Best-Practice Retailers

Introduction

Here we explore the financial performance of each best-practice retailer. Justification is provided for each retailer's being chosen as a "best-practice" firm. The best-practice retailers represent a diversified group that includes six food-based retailers (Aldi, Publix, Stew Leonard's, Trader Joe's, Wegmans, and Whole Foods), a warehouse club (Costco), a specialty retailer (L.L.Bean), a department store (Nordstrom), and a web-based retailer (Amazon.com). The six food-based retailers range from extreme value merchants (Aldi) to specialty food retailers (Trader Joe's and Whole Foods) and also include traditional supermarkets (Publix, Stew Leonard's, and Wegmans). And although Costco sells a broad spectrum of goods and services, it also derives a large proportion of its sales from food-related merchandise. Interestingly, of the ten retailers studied, six firms are privately held (Aldi, L.L.Bean, Publix, Stew Leonard's, Trader Joe's, and Wegmans). Of these firms, Publix is also employee-owned (Publix). None of these firms has a unionized staff.

These successful stores are also different in terms of their overall sales levels (see Table A.1). The smallest retailer is Stew Leonard's, with annual revenues of $376 million from four stores. The largest is Costco, with 534 stores and annual revenues of $69.9 billion. The use of Stew Leonard's as a best-practice grocer shows that even comparatively small retailers can be successful. As we saw in Chapter 3, "Low-Cost Strategies II: Delivering Low Costs Through Minimizing Product Proliferation," Stew Leonard's derives bargaining power not from its overall size, but from its concentrating sales in much fewer SKUs than the traditional supermarket.

TABLE A.1   Size of Benchmarked Retailers

	Net Sales	Number of Locations
Aldi (2008)	$ 6.2 billion (a)	1,000 +(a)
Amazon.com (2009)	$24.5 billion	NA
L.L.Bean (2008)	$ 1.6 billion	13
Costco (2009)	$69.9 billion	534
Nordstrom (2009)	$ 8.3 billion	184
Publix (2009)	$24.3 billion	1,104
Stew Leonard's (2008)	$376 million	4
Trader Joe's (2009)	$ 8.0 billion	344
Wegmans (2007)	$ 4.8 billion	75
Whole Foods (2009)	$ 8.0 billion	284

(a) U.S. data

NA = Not Available

Sources: Company 10-Ks; "*Fortune*'s 2010 Top Places to Work For;" and author's estimates.

The first part of this appendix discusses the performance of each of the 10 firms on an individual basis. The second part makes the case for choosing these firms as a reference group based on their composite financial performance, high customer service, and work environment scores.

Individual Performance Metrics of the Best-Practice Retailers

In 2009, *Fortune* combined the former "America's Most Admired Company Survey" with the "World's Most Admired Company Survey" into one overall measure. The top 50 list overall was obtained by the Hay Group (*Fortune's* partner) as a result of asking 4,170 executives, directors, and security analysts to select 10 companies they most admired. Three of the best-practice companies—Amazon.com, Costco, and Nordstrom—were ranked numbers 5, 21, and 30, respectively on *Fortune's* 2010 listing of the "World's Most Admired Companies.[1] For the industry stars survey, the Hay Group asked executives, directors, and analysts to rate companies in their own industry on nine criteria (ranging from investment value to social responsibility). A company's score must be in the top half of its industry to be included. The industry stars include Amazon.com (ranked 2 among Internet services and retailing firms), Publix (ranked 2 among food and drug stores), Nordstrom (ranked 3 among general merchandise retailers), and Costco (ranked 1 among specialty retailers).[2]

In another report, Retail Forward, a major retail consulting firm, listed eight retailers that have effectively differentiated themselves: Target, Trader Joe's, Whole Foods, Urban Outfitters, Chico's, Nordstrom, IKEA, and Apple.[3] Three of these eight retailers (Trader Joe's, Nordstrom, and Whole Foods) were included among my benchmarked retailers.

Let's now examine each of the 10 benchmarked retailers based on individual performance metrics.

Aldi

Although Aldi (the "AL" is short for Albrecht, and the "DI" for discount) is owned by Karl and Theo Albrecht, who also own Trader Joe's, Aldi has a very different overall retail strategy. Aldi sells goods on the basis of low price and has an extremely low-cost operating model (requiring customers to bag their own goods, pay an additional fee for a store-supplied bag, and to even return shopping carts to get a refund on their twenty-five cent deposit).

In the early 1990s, Aldi stores were often made fun of by competing retailers and major brand manufacturers because its stores were unattractive and aimed at customers who could not afford to purchase groceries at traditional food stores. Despite being the object of jokes, Aldi's sales, profits, and market share continued to increase. Recently, Aldi was ranked as Germany's third most-respected brand, behind Siemens and BMW.[4]

Like L.L.Bean, Trader Joe's, Stew Leonard's, and Wegmans, Aldi is privately held, so getting concrete financial data is difficult. Aldi operates more than 8,000 stores worldwide, with more than 4,000 stores in Germany (organized into two divisions—North and South), as well as stores in Denmark, France, Poland, UK, Hungary, Switzerland, Austria, and Australia. More than 90 percent of German households shop at Aldi, and Aldi's and other discounters' market share in Germany have been estimated at 40 percent of total grocery store sales.[5] Aldi's overall success in the German market has been so formidable that several market analysts have argued that Aldi was the prime reason for Wal-Mart's withdrawal from the German market in 2006.[6]

Recently, Aldi announced plans to invest £1.5 billion (about $2.19 billion U.S. dollars) in a five-year expansion plan that would increase its number of UK stores from 400 to about 1,500 and its stores in Australia from 167 to 650. Aldi opened 75 stores in the United States in 2009. It plans to open an additional 25 stores in 2010. According to one source, Aldi USA is one of the fastest-growing retailers in the world. Since 2000, Aldi USA has grown an average of 12.2 percent annually. Its sales growth was 21 percent in 2008 and 13.7 percent in 2009, with sales increases of 8 percent per year since 1998.[7] The growth rate could have been even faster except that Aldi's long-term strategy is to finance all growth from current profits as opposed to debt.

Another indication of Aldi's success is a comment about Aldi made by Sir Terry Leahy, Tesco's chief executive. Sir Leahy, in his keynote address at the World Retail Congress, commented that Aldi "...had a grocery offer unmatched by any chain globally." He added: "Aldi has a unique formula which has enabled it to achieve a consistent rate of growth over a sustained period of time. I really admire that."[8]

Amazon.com

In 2009, *Business Week* magazine ranked Amazon.com as number 23 on its "The Business Week 50: The Best Performers" listing. *Business Week* chose firms for its top 50 list based on return on capital and growth over the past 36 months. In commenting on its choice, the magazine credited Jeffrey Bezos' "...unrelenting focus on slashing prices, expanding selection, and making shopping online even easier."[9] In addition, the study's author noted that during the fourth quarter when traditional retailers suffered a 1.7 percent loss in sales, Amazon.com's revenues increased by 18 percent.

Amazon.com was also rated by *Business Week* as 43rd in its "100 Best Global Brands" study. According to the chief marketing officer at Landor Associates, a brand consulting firm, "It's not about splaying their log everywhere. They [Amazon.com] are all about ease of use."[10]

Amazon.com, the number-one retailer on the Web, has 81 million active customers who, as of the first half of 2008, each spent over $184 per year at the site (versus $150 in 2006). And according to Forrester Research, 52 percent of consumers who shop online conduct their product research at Amazon.com's web site.[11] In the first six months of 2009, Amazon.com reported sales growth of 16 percent; this was during a time period when most retailers reported declines in sales.[12]

Amazon.com's web site had the third-highest conversion rate among web-based retailers, with at least 500,000 unique visitors in

December 2008. And 23.7 percent of Amazon.com's web site visitors purchased an item during December 2008.[13] In comparison, the industry average is about a 2 percent conversion rate. Clearly, if roughly 25 percent or so of in-store shoppers made a purchase, retailing would be flourishing in the current economy!

L.L.Bean

L.L.Bean's web site had the second-highest conversion rate (25.7 percent) among web-based retailers, with at least 500,000 unique visitors in December 2008.[14] In addition, its main store in Freeport, Maine, is a true tourist destination that attracts 3 million visitors a year.

L.L.Bean's revenues for fiscal year 2009 were $1.5 billion from its catalog and web-based sales (as well as its 14 stores and 15 outlet locations). According to one retail consultant, less than 7 percent of L.L.Bean's sales apparel come from Internet and catalog orders.[15] This means that L.L.Bean is missing out on major opportunities due to its small store base. As part of its growth strategy, L.L.Bean plans to open in shopping centers with accessible parking. This will enable shoppers to conveniently take large goods like kayaks home without lugging them through crowded mall locations.

Costco

The most accurate way to analyze Costco's financial performance is to compare it with Sam's Club (where the data are available). In instances where Sam's Club data are unavailable, the comparison will be made with Wal-Mart. Costco has a 49.3 percent market share of the U.S. warehouse club industry sales versus 42.4 percent for Sam's Club and 8.3 percent for BJ's. According to one estimate, Costco generates $124 million in sales per store, almost 75 percent higher than the average Sam's Club.[16] With 512 warehouse clubs, Costco easily outsells Sam's Club's 591 locations.[17]

Costco has sales per square foot of $920 versus Sam's Club's $568. In terms of efficiency measures, Costco's overhead is 9.8 percent of revenue versus 17 percent at Wal-Mart, and Costco's operating profit per employee is $13,647 versus $11,039 at Wal-Mart.[18] In its 2008 fiscal year, Costco's same-store sales growth was 8 percent, a truly enviable number. Costco also exceeds Sam's Club in terms of their respective consumer demographics. Costco's shoppers have a median income of $72,000, while the equivalent figure is closer to $50,000 for Sam's Club.[19] In 2009, Costco was ranked number 22 on *Fortune*'s list of the world's most admired companies.[20]

Costco's success extends to its apparel, electronics, and household items. In its fiscal year 2007, it sold $1.9 billion in televisions, $867 million in wine, and 2.4 million pairs of eyeglasses. This is aside from its $550 million in seafood, $173 million of rotisserie chickens, and 69.3 million hot dog and soda combinations at its in-store food service stands.[21]

Nordstrom

In 2009, Nordstrom was ranked number 22 on *Fortune*'s list of the "World's Most Admired Companies."[22] Table A.2 compares the five-year cumulative return of Nordstrom's common stock with that of the Standard & Poor's Retail Index and the Standard & Poor's 500 Index for years 2004 through 2009. As can be seen in Table A.2, for years 2005 through 2007, Nordstrom outperformed both of these indices by a considerable margin. From 2004 through 2007, Nordstrom's common stock increased by 72 percent, versus a 1 percent decline for the Standard & Poor's Retail Index and a 19 percent increase for the Standard & Poor's 500 Index. Unfortunately, most of the gains in Nordstrom's stock and the other two indices were erased as of 2008. In 2009, Nordstrom common stock value rebounded to a 58 percent growth versus 2004.

TABLE A.2   Comparison of Five-Year Cumulative Return of Nordstrom Common Stock Performance with the S&P Retail Index and S&P 500 (Based on Year-End Trading Price)

	2004	2005	2006	2007	2008	2009
Nordstrom stock (1)	100	179	243	172	56	158
S&P Retail Index (2)	100	108	123	99	61	93
S&P 500	100	110	124	119	71	92

(1) The cumulative total return of Nordstrom Inc. common stock assumes $100 invested on January 29, 2005, in Nordstrom common stock and reinvestment of all dividends.

(2) The Standard & Poor's Retail Index is made up of 30 companies, including Nordstrom, that represent an industry group of the Standard & Poor's 500 Index.

Source: Nordstrom Inc. 10-K for the Fiscal Year Ended January 30, 2010, p. 14.

Publix

Publix was America's ninth-largest privately held company in 2009.[23] It was also the seventh-largest supermarket chain in sales.[24] Table A.3 compares the five-year cumulative return of retailer stocks for Publix with a peer group of other food retailers and the S&P 500 index. As this table indicates, between 2004 and 2009, the year-end trading price of Publix shares increased more than 52 percent versus an increase of 20 percent in peer food retailer stocks and an increase of 3.3 percent in the Standard & Poor's 500 index.

In 2008, Publix was chosen by wRatings Corporation as first place winner (for the second year in a row) on its "Most Competitive Retailers" list. The other top-five companies on the list were Coach, Family Dollar, Claire's Stores, and Staples. The rankings were based on a firm's capability to produce an economic profit, as well as to achieve high scores in studies of consumer preference. The report states that Publix's exceptional customer service is a byproduct of its being employee-owned.[25]

TABLE A.3 Comparison of Five-Year Cumulative Return of Publix Common Stock Performance with Food Retailer Stocks and the S&P 500 (Based on Year-End Trading Price)

	2004	2005	2006	2007	2008	2009
Publix (1)	100.00	133.34	171.20	185.16	162.95	152.30
Peer Group (2)	100.00	103.93	136.43	156.81	119.74	120.28
S&P 500	100.00	105.07	121.66	129.23	78.13	103.30

(1) Publix's company stock is not traded on any public exchange. Virtually all transactions of the company's common stock have been among the company, its employees, former employees, their families, and the benefit plans established for the company's employees.

(2) Companies in the Peer Group are A&P, Ahold, Albertson's (included for 2004 and 2005 but is no longer publicly traded), Delhaize Group, Kroger, Safeway, Supervalu, Weis Markets, and Winn-Dixie (included through December 2005 as the company filed for bankruptcy protection). Winn-Dixie's new common stock is not included for 2006 but is included for 2007 through 2009.

Source: Publix 10-K for the Fiscal Year Ending December 26, 2009, p. 8.

Stew Leonard's

According to one estimate, Stew Leonard's has average sales of $80 million per store per year. Stew Leonard's sales per square foot has been estimated as high as $3,750.[26] And Stew Leonard's weekly sales per store is an "eye-popping" $1.7 million versus a Food Marketing Institute industry median of $361,564. Stew Leonard's return on sales has also been estimated to be 2.5 percent versus 1 percent for the industry as a whole.[27] It is especially noteworthy that Stew Leonard's is able to achieve this financial success with four stores and total annual sales of about $376 million.

Trader Joe's

Trader Joe's was purchased by the Albrecht family in the late 1970s. Because Trader Joe's, like Aldi, is privately held, the financial data is estimated. *Supermarket News*, a trade magazine, estimates that Trader Joe's had about $8 billion in total sales in 2009.[28]

Another report states that Trader Joe's has had 24 years of consistent growth and profit and is one of the few major food-based retailers with no long-term debt.[29] Trader Joe's has funded its expansion to about 344 stores strictly from the cash flow generated by its existing store base. Other industry observers have commented that Trader Joe's sales have grown an average of 23 percent a year since 1990.[30]

In the past ten years, Trader Joe's profits increased 10 times as its number of stores increased five fold.[31] Some analysts argue that Trader Joe's could end up being a 1,000- to 2,000-store chain.[32] Another source estimates Trader Joe's average sales per square foot to be $1,750.[33] With no service departments (even its fruits, vegetables, meats, and fish products are prepacked), small stores, low-rent locations, astronomic sales per square foot, and with 70 percent to 85 percent of sales in high-profit-margin private labels, Trader Joe's profits have been characterized by one analyst as "nothing short of spectacular."[34]

Wegmans

Wegmans is a 73-store supermarket chain with stores in five states: New York, Pennsylvania, New Jersey, Maryland, and Virginia. Each of Wegmans' stores average about $46 million in annual sales, according to *Supermarket News*. In comparison, Wal-Mart averages $23.5 million in grocery sales at each of its 1,243 stores, and Kroger averages $14 million at each of its 3,685 stores.[35] And although other stores have contracted in light of Wal-Mart's competitive entry into their markets, Wegmans has expanded. This is no small feat!

Wegmans' operating margins are about 7.5 percent—double what the big four grocers earn and even higher than Whole Foods.[36] Its sales per square foot are also 50 percent higher than the industry average.[37] Wegmans was named the nation's top supermarket by *Food Nation* in 2007.

Whole Foods

Whole Foods Market is the nation's fastest-growing grocery chain and the largest seller of organic/natural foods. Let's look at Whole Foods' recent financial data:

- Whole Foods had $833 in sales per square foot in its 2008 fiscal year.
- Whole Foods' operating profits as a percent of sales in fiscal year 2008 was 3.0 percent, significantly higher than the supermarket average.
- Whole Foods' sales growth is nearly 20 percent annually between 2001 and 2008, more than twice the rate of its closest competitor.[38] Organic food sales have grown 15 percent to 21 percent each year for the past decade with the exception of 2009, versus 2 percent to 4 percent for total food sales (see Table A.4).

TABLE A.4   Whole Foods' Revenue Growth

Fiscal Year	Total Revenues ($ Billion)	Annual Revenue Growth (%)
2001	$2.27	23.6
2002	2.69	18.5
2003	3.15	17.1
2004	3.86	22.5
2005	4.70	21.8
2006	5.61	19.4
2007	6.59	17.5
2008	7.95	20.6
2009	8.03	1.0

Source: Whole Foods 10-Ks, various years.

Whole Foods also has an enviable record in terms of overall social responsibility and as an employer. The firm was voted among the 100 Best Corporate Citizens for 2006 by *Business Ethics* magazine. This award is based on a firm's capability to provide good jobs for employees, environmental sustainability, healthy community relations, and great products for customers.[39] Whole Foods also placed 12th overall on a recent *Wall Street Journal* ranking of firms in terms of best corporate reputations and received the best score of any company studied for social responsibility.[40]

Composite Data on Best-Practice Retailers

This section analyzes the benchmark retailers based on three important dimensions: financial performance, customer service, and employee satisfaction. The financial performance data reports on sales per square foot and the strategic profit model (that looks at the relationship among net profit margin, asset turnover, and financial leverage). The customer service section relies on survey data from such sources as The National Retail Foundation (NRF)/American Express 2008 Consumer Service Survey, *Consumer Reports*, and the American Customer Satisfaction Index (ACSI). The employee satisfaction data are derived from "*Fortune*'s 100 Best Companies to Work For" annual study. The retailers' performance on each of these separate measures provides further affirmation for their choice as benchmark retailers.

Financial Performance Data of Best-Practice Retailers

This section compares the financial performance of these best-practice leaders to a group of traditional retailers. Table A.5 shows that the range in sales per square foot for the best-practice food-based retailers is between $517 and $3,750 (versus the average U.S. supermarket having sales of $500 per square feet). Note that both Trader Joe's and Stew Leonard's have sales per square foot in excess of $1,500. Costco's sales per square foot (not counting membership fees) is $929.

Table A.6 shows sales per employee for the benchmarked and competing retailers. This is an especially important figure because employee salaries constitute one of the largest expenses for most retailers. Note the exceptionally high sales per employee for Aldi ($1,347,657) and Trader Joe's ($1,111,111), despite their low prices. Amazon.com's sales per employee is also an astounding $1,008,600.

TABLE A.5 Sales per Square Foot of Selected Food Chains and Average Number of SKUs Per Unit

Retail Chain	Sales per Square Foot of Selling Space
Aldi (2009 data)	$ 620 est.
Costco (2009 global data)	$ 929 (1)
Publix (2009)	$ 517
Stew Leonard's (2008)	$1,534-$3,750 est.
Trader Joe's (2009)	$1,750
Wegmans (2008)	$ 750
Whole Foods (2009 global data)	$ 761
Average supermarket	$ 500

(1) Revenues exclude membership fees.

Sources: "Supermarket Facts," *Food Marketing Institute*: 2008; and author's estimates and calculations.

TABLE A.6 Sales per Employee for Selected and Best-Practice Retailers

Food Chains	Sales per Employee
Kroger	$ 233,128 (2009)
Safeway	$ 219,627 (2010)
H.E. Butt Grocery Co. (private)	$ 214,279 (2009)
A&P (Tenglemann)	$ 198,254 (2009)
Winn-Dixie	$ 147,340 (2009)
Best-Practice Food Chains	
Aldi	$1,347,657 (2006)
Publix	$ 171,265 (2009)
Stew Leonard's	$ 184,585 (2009)
Trader Joe's	$1,111,111 (2008)
Wegmans	$ 130,731 (2009)
Whole Foods	$ 152,982 (2009)

TABLE A.6 Sales per Employee for Selected and Best-Practice Retailers (continued)

Food Chains	Sales per Employee
Best-Practice General Retailers	
Costco	$ 502,971 (2009)
Nordstrom	$ 172,041 (2009)
Amazon.com	$1,008,600 (2010)
L.L.Bean	$ 371,069 (2008)
Selected General Retailers	
Wal-Mart	$ 192,857 (2010)
Sam's Club	$ 688,916 (2010)
BJs	$ 455,790 (2009)
Saks Inc.	$ 233,053 (2009)

Sources: Business & Company Resource Center; and author's calculations.

Table A.7 contrasts the overall financial performance of the selected and best-practice chains using the strategic profit model. This model separates financial performance into three components: net profit margin (net profit/net sales), asset turnover (net sales/assets), and financial leverage (net profit/equity). Net profit margin depicts net profit as a percent of sales revenues, asset turnover shows sales per dollar of assets, and financial leverage depicts the extent to which assets are financed. Net profit margin is a commonly used measure of profitability, asset turnover shows a firm's efficiency, and financial leverage is a measure of a firm's relative debt load.

Of the major retailers in Table A.7 where data are available, Nordstrom has the highest net profit margin and net profit on equity returns. The net sales to total assets deals primarily with each retailer's capability to have high inventory turnover levels. High inventory turnover enables a retailer to have fresh merchandise, as well as to use trade credit as a means of financing inventory. Of the best-practice retailers, Costco has net sales/assets of 3.18. This is higher than all of the selected retailers where data are available (except Kroger). Costco's net sales/assets is so high due to its very high inventory turnover rates. The assets/equity ratio describes the extent to which each retailer has debt. A ratio of 1 means that the retailer has no debt, as a firm's assets and equity are equal. Note that, on average, the best-practice retailers (where information is available) have considerably less debt than the other selected retailers (with the exception of Nordstrom with $4.19 in assets per dollar of equity).

TABLE A.7 The Strategic Profit Model Applied to Selected and Best-Practice Retail Food Chains (2009)

	$\dfrac{\text{Net Profit}}{\text{Net Sales}}$ X	$\dfrac{\text{Net Sales}}{\text{Assets}}$ X	$\dfrac{\text{Assets}}{\text{Equity}}$ =	$\dfrac{\text{Net Profit}}{\text{Equity}}$
Selected Retail Food Chains				
Kroger (2010 data)	0.10 %	3.32	4.71	1.43 %
Safeway	2.69 %	2.73	3.03	22.19 %
Wal-Mart (2010 data), T	3.67 %	2.37	2.41	21.10 %
Best-Practice Food Chains				
Aldi	NA	NA	NA	NA
Publix	4.78 %	2.70	1.43	18.43 %
Stew Leonard's	NA	NA	NA	NA
Trader Joe's	NA	NA	NA	NA
Wegmans	NA	NA	NA	NA
Whole Foods	1.83 %	2.12	2.33	9.00 %
Other Best-Practice Retailers				
Amazon.com	3.68 %	1.77	2.63	17.16 %
L.L.Bean	NA	NA	NA	NA
Costco	1.55 %	3.18	2.19	10.84 %
Nordstrom	5.34	1.26	4.19	28.05 %

T = Total stores domestic and foreign

NA = Not Available

Note: There may be rounding errors.

Sources: Company 10-Ks; and author's computations.

Customer Service Scores of Best-Practice Retailers

In addition to superior financial performance results, the best-practice retailers have exceptionally high customer service scores. The National Retail Foundation (NRF)/American Express 2008 Consumer Service Survey that was conducted from September 2 to September 9, 2008, asked 8,167 consumers the following open-ended question: "Thinking of all the different retail formats (store, catalog, Internet, or home shopping), which retailer delivers the best customer service?" To make the comparison among retailers fair, rankings were based on each retailer's revenues. This balanced out high rankings due to a retailer's size or geographic coverage. Of the best-practice general merchandise retailers featured in this book, three were in the top ten NRF/American Express rankings: L.L.Bean (ranked 1), Amazon.com (ranked 4), and Nordstrom (ranked 10).[41]

Table A.8 shows customer satisfaction scores of selected food retailers that have been compiled by *Consumer Reports*, ACSI, and the *Business Week* Customer Service Champs listings. In this study, *Consumer Reports* analyzed consumer perceptions of grocery stores (including supermarkets, supercenters, warehouse clubs, and limited assortment stores). The ratings are based on 32,599 responses of their experiences at one or two stores (related to service, prices, cleanliness, and quality of perishables) between April 2007 and April 2008. A score of 100 on this measure means that all respondents were completely satisfied; 80 means they were very satisfied; and 60 shows that consumers were fairly well satisfied. Differences of less than 6 points are not significant. Especially interesting is that Costco (a warehouse club with an austere warehouse-type atmosphere, bulk-wrapped foods, huge stores, and few service personnel except in some specialty departments like jewelry) was ranked seventh highest of the 59 stores studied, with a score of 81.[42]

The top three stores in *Consumer Reports'* supermarket study are Wegmans, Trader Joe's, and Publix. Aldi, an extreme-value food store, received a score of 79; this is equivalent to a customer service ranking of 14 of the 59 supermarkets studied. (Stew Leonard's was not included due to the small number of stores.) Also noteworthy are the especially low scores for Food Lion (69—ranked 53 of 54 supermarkets), Winn-Dixie (69—ranked 55 of 59 supermarkets), Wal-Mart's supercenters (69—ranked 56 of 59 supermarkets), A&P (68—ranked 58 of 59 supermarkets), and Waldbaum's (64—ranked 59 of 59 supermarkets).

TABLE A.8   Customer Service Scores for Selected Retailers

	Consumer Reports **Rating**	**ACSI Rating**	*Business Week* **Customer Service Elite**
Selected Retail Food Chains			
Ahold USA (Royal Ahold)			
Stop & Shop	71		
Tops	70		
H.E. Butt	77		
Delhaize America			
Hannaford	77		
Food Lion	69		
Kroger	74	78	
Safeway	73	72	
Supervalu		77	
Jewel/Osco	73		
Albertson's	73		
Sam's Club		79	
Tenglemann			
(A&P)	68		
Wal-Mart Stores	69	71	
Winn-Dixie	69	74	

TABLE A.8   Customer Service Scores for Selected Retailers (continued)

	Consumer Reports Rating	ACSI Rating	Business Week Customer Service Elite
Best-Practice Food Chains			
Aldi	79		
Publix	84	86	Ranked 5 of 25
Stew Leonard's	NA		
Trader Joe's	86		
Wegmans	87		Ranked 12 of 25
Whole Foods	81	76	
Best-Practice Specialty Retailer			
Amazon.com		86	Ranked 11 of 25
Costco	81	81	
Nordstrom		83	Ranked 6 of 25
L.L.Bean			Ranked 1 of 25

Sources: "Ratings Supermarkets," Consumer Reports (May 2009), p. 22; www.theacsi.org, as of June 6, 2010; and "L.L.Bean Tops Bloomberg Business Week's Fourth Annual Ranking of Customer Service Champs," Business Wire (February 18, 2010).

A second major analysis of customer satisfaction is the ACSI rating (covering 10 economic sectors, 53 industries, and 200 companies) compiled by the American Society for Quality, the Ross School of the University of Michigan, and CFI Group. ACSI ratings are based on questionnaires completed by 80,000 consumers that cover customer expectations, overall quality, and perceived value. In general, the vast majority of ACSI ratings range from the low 50s to the high 80s. Paralleling *Consumer Reports'* evaluations, Publix and Costco received high scores (of 86 and 81, respectively), whereas low scores were received by Wal-Mart (68) and Winn-Dixie (73). Whole Foods' score was 76. Amazon.com's score on the American Customer Satisfaction Index (ACSI) of 86 is tied for second place among E-tailers (with Newegg). Amazon.com is tied with Publix as one of the highest-scoring companies in the survey (with the exception of Netflix's score of 87). Nordstrom's score of 83 topped ACSI's department and discount store category.[43] Both Publix and Nordstrom have had leading customer satisfaction scores in their category since 1994 when the ACSI rating first started.[44]

The *Business Week* Customer Service Elite study is based on multiple measures of customer service: perceived friendliness and the competency of a company's workers, as well as what customers think of its processes, such as return policies and reservation procedures. *Business Week's* analysis is based on a survey of 5,000 of its readers asking each to nominate three companies they felt were best at providing customer service and three that were poorest. J.D. Powers then ranked all of the brands using scores from its database and additional surveys. Of the 25 brands studied, five of the benchmarked retailers made the list. In its 2010 study, L.L.Bean was ranked 1; Publix, 5; Nordstrom, 6; Amazon, 11; and Wegmans, 12.[45]

Consumer Reports has also conducted studies on subscriber experiences in warehouse clubs and department stores, online clothing retailers, and electronics web and brick-and-mortar stores. Of the 11 warehouse club and retailers studied, Costco was the highest-ranking retailer, easily outscoring traditional department stores such as J.C. Penney, Sears, and Macy's, as well as mass merchandisers Wal-Mart and Kmart. Although many observers would have felt that Costco's high ratings would be limited to its home-related goods, Costco's consumers were significantly more satisfied with the product quality of watches and jewelry, personal care items, hardware, home décor, kitchenware, electronic equipment, and sporting goods and toys than at most of the other ten stores rated by consumers.[46]

In a *Consumer Reports* study of 39 online clothing retailers, L.L.Bean received the highest ranking (with a reader score of 92). Nordstrom was ranked fourth with a score of 90, and Amazon.com was ranked ninth with a score of 88. According to *Consumer Reports*, L.L.Bean (and other high scorers such as Zappos and Lands' End) tended to provide superior clothing quality, more accurate descriptions and sizing information, an informative web site (including virtual models that let consumers "try-on" merchandise, sizing guides, 360-degree and zoom views, as well as buyer reviews), and an easy way to both order and return items. Respondents also stated that value at L.L.Bean was excellent for almost two-thirds of their purchases.[47] Similarly, in its report of *Consumer Reports*–rated electronics web stores and walk-in stores, of 14 online stores, Amazon.com ranked third and Costco.com ranked fourth. Costco also ranked fourth of 27 walk-in stores.

Keynote Competitive Research evaluated customer service of two types of web merchants: those specializing in consumer electronics and those featuring books, music, movies, and games. Each study examined customers' online experience, as well as a site's responsiveness (such as how fast pages are loaded) and reliability (such as low downtime). On the basis of this research, Amazon.com was ranked as the top web site for both consumer electronics and books, music, movies, and games. Amazon.com's site was also the top-ranking site on a consistent basis in terms of price satisfaction, search satisfaction, product research satisfaction, and customer support.[48]

Similarly, Amazon.com and Netflix were tied for the highest score among web merchants on a customer satisfaction poll conducted by Foresee Results in 2008.[49] The same study ranked L.L.Bean as 6 and Nordstrom as 18 among a total of 40 top-ranking firms.[50]

All of the best-practice retailers except Stew Leonard's were cited by *Consumer Reports*, ACSI, or *Business Week* for superior customer service. Publix was cited by all three analyses for superior customer service, whereas Trader Joe's was cited by both *Consumer Reports* and *Business Week*. Costco received high scores by both *Consumer Reports* and ACSI, and Amazon.com and Nordstrom received high rankings by both ACSI and *Business Week*.

Employee Satisfaction Measures of Best-Practice Retailers

Table A.9 outlines the findings of "*Fortune*'s 100 Best Companies to Work For" from the magazine's most recent annual study. In the magazine's analysis, two-thirds of a firm's ranking comes from employee responses to 57 questions. All companies are evaluated on the basis of their credibility (communication to employees), respect (opportunities and benefits), fairness (compensation and diversity), and price/camaraderie (philanthropy and celebrations). The remaining third of a firm's ranking comes from employees' demographic makeup and benefits. Five of our benchmark retailers were included in *Fortune*'s 2010 listing of 100 firms: Wegmans (ranked 3 of 100), Whole Foods (ranked 18 of 100), Nordstrom (ranked 53 of 100), Stew Leonard's (ranked 64 of 100), and Publix (ranked 86 of 100). Many of these retailers have been on *Fortune*'s list for many consecutive years. Whole Foods, Wegmans, Publix, and Nordstrom have been on the *Fortune* magazine's "100 Best Places to Work For" list every year since the list began in 1998. Stew Leonard's has been on the list every year from 2002 through 2010.

TABLE A.9   100 Best Companies to Work For 2010

Retail Chain	Ranking
Wegmans	Ranked 3 of top 100 firms
Whole Foods	Ranked 18 of top 100 firms
Nordstrom	Ranked 53 of top 100 firms
Stew Leonard's	Ranked 64 of top 100 firms
Publix	Ranked 86 of top 100 firms

Source: Milton Moskowitz, Robert Levering, and Christopher Thaczyk, "*Fortune*'s 2010: 100 Best Companies to Work For," *Fortune* (February 8, 2010), pp. 75–88.

Chapter 5, "Differentiation Strategies II: Enhancing the Service Experience," explored the relationship between employee and customer satisfaction. This concept suggests that employee satisfaction

and loyalty translates into high levels of customer service and customer loyalty. According to Kusum Ailawadi, a professor of business
administration at Dartmouth's Tuck School of Business, "There are
strong links between employee and customer satisfaction and customer loyalty and profitability." He adds that good wages and benefits
are key factors in building employee loyalty. It is employees, not management, who interact with customers. And if employees feel good
about the company, they will make customers feel good."[51]

The value profit chain concept is based both on the service profit
chain (that has found direct relationships between profit and customer loyalty, employee loyalty and customer loyalty, and employee
satisfaction and customer satisfaction) and on total quality concepts
(which encourage companies to continually measure and benchmark
employee satisfaction, customer satisfaction, and business performance).[52]

Takeaway Points

- Each of the benchmarked retailers had specific strengths with
  regard to financial performance (as measured by sales per
  square foot, sales per employee, and the strategic profit
  model), customer service (as measured by impartial studies by
  NRF/American Express, Consumer Reports, ACSI, and
  Business Week), and employee satisfaction (as measured by
  Fortune magazine). Several of these retailers were repeatedly
  cited by these sources for their excellence.

- In some ways, the benchmarked firms are very different from
  most retailers of their size due to their ownership formats. Only
  four of the ten retailers (Amazon.com, Costco, Nordstrom, and
  Whole Foods) are public companies; the balance are privately
  held. One interesting question is whether this is a coincidence
  or whether private ownership has distinct advantages, such as
  freedom from concern for meeting analysts' quarterly sales and
  profit expectations. Thus, privately held firms are in no hurry to
  grow too fast to suit analysts' or shareholders' expectations. One
  could argue that private ownership fosters a true long-term orientation, whereas public ownership focuses too much attention

to maximizing short-run quarterly sales and profit performance (which may be at the expense of long-term profitability). Privately held companies also have advantages in terms of less filing requirements, less disclosure, and faster decision making.

- The grocery retailers used as benchmarks operate very different types of retail formats. Cannondale Associates has segmented grocery stores into four types: routine replenishment, big shops, experience makers, and quick shops.[53] In routine replenishment stores, shoppers make frequent trips and use shopper card programs. These stores excel through appealing to shoppers based on high shopper frequency and their wide and consistent selections. Wegmans and Publix are examples of routine replenishment stores that feature a wide array of store services, and wide, consistent selections. In contrast, at big shops like Costco, consumers are exposed to bulk-packaged products. Stew Leonard's, Trader Joe's, Wegmans, and Whole Foods can be classified as experience makers with unique items, signage that informs shoppers and also tells a story about each product, as well as high levels of customer service. Due to its limited selection, Aldi can be considered a quick shop.

Endnotes

1. Anna Bernasek, "The World's Most Admired Companies 2010," *Fortune* (March 22, 2010), pp. 121–126.

2. "The List of Industry Stars," *Fortune* (March 22, 2010), pp. 129–133.

3. Murray Forseter, "The Differentiated Retailer," *Chain Store Age* (June 2006), Vol. 82, Issue 6.

4. Jan-Benedict E.M. Steenkamp and Nirmalya Kumar, "Don't Be Undersold," *Harvard Business Review* (December 2009), pp. 90–95.

5. Cecile Rohwedder and David Kesmodel, "Aldi Looks to U.S. for Growth," *Wall Street Journal* (January 13, 2009), p. B1; and Mark Ritson, "Aldi Feeds Off Lean Times," *Marketing* (August 27, 2008), p. 20.

6. Mark Ritson, "Aldi Feeds Off Lean Times," *Marketing* (August 27, 2008), p. 20.

7. Jan-Benedict E.M. Steenkamp and Nirmalya Kumar, "Don't Be Undersold," *Harvard Business Review* (December 2009), pp. 90–95.

8. "Aldi's the Chain That Really Does It for Me, Leahy Tells Astonished Audience," *The Grocer* (March 31, 2007), p. 6.

9. Dean Foust, "The Business Week 50," *Business Week* (April 6, 2009), p. 55.

10. Spencer E. Ante, "At Amazon, Marketing Is for Dummies," *Business Week* (September 28, 2009), p. 53.

11. Joe Nocera, "Put Buyers First? What a Concept," *New York Times* (January 5, 2008), p. C1; and Brad Stone, "Amazon Offers Other Sites Use of Its Payment Service," *New York Times* (July 30, 2008), p. C5.

12. Spencer E. Ante, "At Amazon, Marketing Is for Dummies," *Business Week* (September 28, 2009), p. 53.

13. "Chart of the Week: December 2008 Conversion Rates," www.practicalecommerce.com/articles, as of April 6, 2009.

14. "Chart of the Week: December 2008 Conversion Rates," www.practicalecommerce.com/articles, as of April 6, 2009.

15. Jenn Abelson, "Six Years Later, L.L.Bean Gets Back in Gear for Expansion," *Boston.com* (September 1, 2006).

16. Katia Watson, *Industry Outlook: Warehouse Clubs* (Columbus, OH: Retail Forward, November 2006), pp. 1–34.

17. *Costco Wholesale Corporation 10-K for the Fiscal Year Ending August 31, 2008*; and *Wal-Mart Stores Inc. 10-K for the Fiscal Year Ending January 31, 2008*.

18. Esther Cervantes, "The Costco Alternative?" *Dollars and Sense* (January/February 2006).

19. Kris Hudson, "Warehouses Go Luxe; Costco, Sam's Club Stock Wine Coolers, Grand Pianos to Tempt Holiday Shoppers," *Wall Street Journal* (November 11, 2005), p. B1.

20. Geogg Colvin, "The World's Most Admired Companies 2009," *Fortune* (March 16, 2008), pp. 75–78.

21. Andy Hanacek, "Costco Wholesale: On the Mark," *The National Provisioner* (April 2008), pp. 1, 18.

22. Geogg Colvin, "The World's Most Admired Companies 2009," *Fortune* (March 16, 2008), pp. 75–78.

23. "America's Largest Private Companies," *Forbes* (October 28, 2009).

24. "America's 50 Largest Supermarket Chains," http://supermarketnews.com/profiles/top75/2010/, as of April 30, 2010.

25. "Publix Claims No. 1 Spot in Most Competitive Retailers Survey," *Chain Store Age* (September 2008), p. 22.

26. "Stew Leonard's," www.freeenterpriceland.com/BOOK?STEWLEONARD.html, as of April 4, 2007.

27. Ivor Morgan and Jay Rao, "Making Routine Customer Experiences Fun," *MIT Sloan Management Review*, Vol. 45 (Fall 2003), pp. 93–95.

28. Beth Kowitt, "Inside Trader Joe's," *Fortune* (September 6, 2010), p. 88.

29. "Trader Joe's Retail Explosion," *Display & Design Ideas* (April 1, 2005).

30. Irwin Speizer, "The Grocery Chain That Shouldn't Be," *Fast Company* (February 2004), p. 31.

31. Len Lewis, *The Trader Joe's Adventure* (Dearborn Trade Publishing, 2005), p. 20.

32. Len Lewis, *The Trader Joe's Adventure* (Dearborn Trade Publishing, 2005), p. 13.

33. Beth Kowitt, "Inside Trader Joe's," *Fortune* (September 6, 2010), p. 88.

34. "Trader Joe's Is Not Your 'Average Joe,'" *All Business*, www.allbusiness.com, as of April 2, 2007.

35. Elayne Robertson Demby, "Two Stores Refuse to Race to the Bottom," *Workforce Management* (February 2004), pp. 57–59.

36. Matthew Boyle, "The Wegmans Way," *Fortune* (January 24, 2005), pp. 62 ff.

37. Matthew Boyle, "The Wegmans Way," *Fortune* (January 24, 2005), pp. 62 ff.

38. "It Feels Natural: As Consumer Trends Lean Toward Healthy Eating, Natural Products Retailing Becomes Bigger Business," *Private Label Buyer* (July 2005).

39. "Companies That Excel," *Natural Foods Merchandiser* (December 2006), p. 14.

40. "How Boss's Deeds Buff a Firm's Reputation," *Wall Street Journal* (January 31, 2007).

41. "J.C. Penney Company, Inc. Customers Vote JC Penney Tops in Customer Service," *Science Letter* (February 9, 2009).

42. "Rating Supermarkets," *Consumer Reports* (May 2009), p. 22.

43. www.acsi.org, as of June 6, 2010.

44. "Netflix, Amazon, Publix Top in Customer Satisfaction," *Chain Store Age* (March 2010), p. 16.

45. "Standouts in Customer Service" *Business Week*. http://bwnt.businessweek.com/interactive_reports/customer_service_2010/, as of April 14, 2010.

46. "America's Top Stores," *Consumer Reports* (July 2010), p. 20.

47. "Buying Clothes Online," *Consumer Reports* (December 2008), pp. 22–23.

48. "Amazon.com Ranked Best Consumer Electronics Shopping Experience," www.ecoustics.com, posted October 24, 2007; retrieved April 6, 2009.

49. Peter Kafka, "Amazon Wins an Award It Didn't Give Itself: Tops in Customer Satisfaction," *All Things Digital* (December 30, 2008).

50. Peter Kafka, "Amazon Wins an Award It Didn't Give Itself: Tops in Customer Satisfaction," *All Things Digital* (December 30, 2008).

51. Elayne Robertson Demby, "Two Stores Refuse to Race to the Bottom," *Workforce Management* (February 2004), pp. 57–59.

52. James L. Heskett, Thomas W. Earl Sasser, Jr., and Leonard A. Schlesinger, *The Service-Profit Chain to Work* (New York: The Free Press, 1997).

53. Stephen Dowdell, "Cannondale Associates Propose That Food Merchants Rewrite Their Fates by Thinking Less Like Retailers, and More Like Shoppers," *Progressive Grocer* (April 15, 2006).

INDEX

FT Press
FINANCIAL TIMES

In an increasingly competitive world, it is quality
of thinking that gives an edge—an idea that opens new
doors, a technique that solves a problem, or an insight
that simply helps make sense of it all.

We work with leading authors in the various arenas
of business and finance to bring cutting-edge thinking
and best-learning practices to a global market.

It is our goal to create world-class print publications
and electronic products that give readers
knowledge and understanding that can then be
applied, whether studying or at work.

To find out more about our business
products, you can visit us at www.ftpress.com.